T0330158

Transportation and Economic Development Challenges

NECTAR SERIES ON TRANSPORTATION AND COMMUNICATIONS NETWORKS RESEARCH

Series Editor: Aura Reggiani, *Professor of Economic Policy, University of Bologna, Italy*

NECTAR (Network on European Communications and Transport Activities Research) is an international scientific, interdisciplinary association with a network culture. Its primary objective is to foster research collaboration and the exchange of information between experts in the fields of transport, communication and mobility.

NECTAR members study the behaviour of individuals, groups and governments within a spatial framework. They bring a wide variety of perspectives to analyse the challenges facing transport and communication, and the impact these challenges have on society at all levels of spatial aggregation.

This series acts as a companion to, and an expansion of, activities of NECTAR. The volumes in the series are broad in their scope with the intention of disseminating some of the work of the association. The contributions come from all parts of the world and the range of topics covered is extensive, reflecting the breadth and continuously changing nature of issues that confront researchers and practitioners involved in spatial and transport analysis.

Titles in the series include:

Transportation and Economic Development Challenges

Edited by

Kenneth Button

George Mason University, USA

Aura Reggiani

University of Bologna, Italy

NECTAR SERIES ON TRANSPORTATION AND
COMMUNICATIONS NETWORKS RESEARCH

Edward Elgar

Cheltenham, UK • Northampton, MA, USA

© Kenneth Button and Aura Reggiani 2011

All rights reserved. No part of this publication may be reproduced, stored in a retrieval system or transmitted in any form or by any means, electronic, mechanical or photocopying, recording, or otherwise without the prior permission of the publisher.

Published by
Edward Elgar Publishing Limited
The Lypiatts
15 Lansdown Road
Cheltenham
Glos GL50 2JA
UK

Edward Elgar Publishing, Inc.
William Pratt House
9 Dewey Court
Northampton
Massachusetts 01060
USA

A catalogue record for this book
is available from the British Library

Library of Congress Control Number: 2010939209

ISBN 978 1 84980 167 6

Typeset by Servis Filmsetting Ltd, Stockport, Cheshire
Printed and bound by MPG Books Group, UK

Contents

Contributors

Nihan Akyelken, Transport Studies Unit, University of Oxford

Vicki Been, Furman Center for Real Estate and Urban Policy, New York University

Kenneth Button, School of Public Policy, George Mason University

Roger Cheng, Dept of Civil and Environmental Engineering, Institute of Transportation Studies, University of California, Davis

Anne Dunning, Department of Planning and Landscape Architecture, Clemson University

Regine Gerike, Technische Universität München, mobil.TUM

Jürgen Gerlach, University of Wuppertal

Moshe Givoni, Transport Studies Unit, University of Oxford

Andrew R. Goetz, Department of Geography and Intermodal Transportation Institute, University of Denver

Erica Jones, Dept of Civil and Environmental Engineering, Institute of Transportation Studies, University of California, Davis

Hyunwoo Lim, Department of Geography, University of Maryland

Josiah Madar, Furman Center for Real Estate and Urban Policy, New York University

Simon McDonnell, Furman Center for Real Estate and Urban Policy, New York University

Jason S. Myers, Department of Planning and Landscape Architecture, Clemson University

Deb Niemeier, Department of Civil and Environmental Engineering, Institute of Transportation Studies, University of California, Davis

Tom Pauwels, Department of Transport and Regional Economics, University of Antwerp

Andreas Rau, Technische Universität München, mobil.TUM

Aura Reggiani, Department of Economic Science, University of Bologna

Piet Rietveld, Department of Spatial Economics, Free University Amsterdam

Narushige Shiode, School of City and Regional Planning, Cardiff University

Eddy Van de Voorde, Department of Transport and Regional Economics, University of Antwerp

Thierry Vanelslander, Department of Transport and Regional Economics, University of Antwerp

Ann Verhetsel, Department of Transport and Regional Economics, University of Antwerp

Preface

This collection of papers stems from a meeting of NECTAR (Network on European Communications and Transport Activities Research) held in Arlington, Virginia in the summer of 2009. As its name suggests, NECTAR is primarily a European-based academic activity, and this was its first transatlantic conference. It is an association with a network culture that has been developed in the framework of a European Science Foundation Network initiated in the late 1980s with the objective of fostering collaboration and exchange of information between experts in the field of transport, communication and mobility. As such, NECTAR is a multidisciplinary, social science oriented activity that brings together a wide range of perspectives on transportation and communication issues and their impacts on society.

NECTAR has numerous thematic seminars and workshops and every two years organizes a major conference. While previous conferences have been in European venues, the 2009 meeting was hosted by George Mason University in Virginia. This collection of papers represents revised contributions to that meeting which focus on the broad theme of transportation and development.

We would like to thank the contributors for the time and effort that has gone into preparing the chapters that make up this volume and hope that readers will find them insightful. Additionally, we would like to acknowledge support for the NECTAR conference from the US Department of Transportation's Research and Innovative Technology Administration through the University Transportation Centers Program, the Free University of Amsterdam, and the University of Las Palmas.

1. Introduction

Kenneth Button and Aura Reggiani

1.1 INTRODUCTION

Modern, positive economics is generally traced back to Adam Smith's *Wealth of Nations* and, with perhaps less agreement, the normative side to his *Theory of Moral Sentiments*. These books provide a consistent and structured way of looking at both matters of overall economic efficiency and questions concerning the distribution of the gains from this efficiency. In combination, they emphasize that economic efficiency does not automatically correlate with social welfare, although the links are generally strong. The importance of this when considering transportation policies is apparent in many areas, not least of which is the challenge of how to weigh up broader issues of access and mobility with the narrow considerations of increasing more conventionally defined income levels. The focus of the contributions to this edited volume, however, is on the more limited notions of economic development.

Economic development is one of the primary objectives of most democratic governments; dictatorships and despots often have somewhat different goals. But economic development by these governments, whether they are national, state, or local, is not, as we have highlighted, normally seen as simply a matter of maximizing some standard economic index such as gross domestic product (GDP). Certainly there are strong links between trends in GDP and social welfare, if nothing else a fast growing GDP allows governments more flexibility and opportunities in meeting their wider policy agendas. Governments, for example, have clearly been shown to be as much, if not more, concerned over the long term in the distribution of the benefits of economic growth across their populations, even if this has some adverse effects on GDP growth. In a democracy, this is perhaps understandable when there is a need to retain the support of the majority of the population, or at least the median voter, but the longer-term sustainability of more centrally controlled political systems also requires the cultivation of the support of large groups within the populace even if they do not constitute the majority.

In terms of transportation, this has historically meant that road, rail, and other networks have not necessarily linked areas so as to maximize the narrow economic efficient use of resources but have often involved larger objectives of spatial integration and military security. Equally, access to transportation infrastructure is seldom prioritized in terms of maximizing openness to those who would generate the most economic gain from its use, but rather considerations of such things as social equity often dominate. One reason for the direct public involvement in the provision of many major pieces of transportation infrastructure is to increase mobility and enhance social and political cohesion. Nevertheless, the majority of transportation infrastructure involves some degree of public interest in enhancing the economic performance of a country or a region.[1] The public involvement is generally seen as necessitated both by institutional requirements, for example the acquisition of appropriate land to construct the infrastructure, and as an agent to ensure that the economies of optimal connectivity are exploited. The need for a more complete understanding of the role of connectivity and its complex relationship with economic development is, however, required.[2]

In a sense, the underlying issue revolves around how one defines 'development'. Material possessions are relatively easy to quantify and are a standard gauge, although even here there are problems in expressing them in terms of any common unit; certainly using monetary measures such as GDP are far from adequate. The World Bank and United Nations often use measures such as life expectancy, and more recently this has been extended to embrace wider quality of life attributes. While unquestionably having merit, these measures again are influenced by judgments. Development is also sometimes seen as reflected in educational attainments, such as levels of literacy or years of secondary education, on the premise that they reflect the pool of intellectual capital in a society or region. Again deciding on appropriate cut-off points, and the problems of separating out quality from quantity attributes, move the measure away from anything strictly scientific. Perhaps the most tractable approach to defining development is to accept that strict definitions are always likely to be nebulous and to just accept the broad view of such things as expressed in the United States by Justice Potter Stewart, 'I shall not today attempt further to define the kinds of material I understand to be embraced within that shorthand description ["hard-core pornography"]; and perhaps I could never succeed in intelligibly doing so. But I know it when I see it . . .'.

The aim of this Introduction is not to just offer abstracts of the papers in the book but rather to put them into a much broader context, and to spend some time looking at some of the difficulties that exist in trying to relate transportation provision to levels of economic development. While some of the contributions are mentioned, we try to avoid the contrived nature of many collections and do not try to artificially inject all. The challenges involved in defining transportation strategies that positively stimulate economic growth remain large despite the energies some of the greatest minds have exercised on the topic. This is not very encouraging from an intellectual perspective, and certainly not very helpful in terms of good policy formulation. We begin by looking at what we currently know about the forces influencing economic development.

1.2 WHAT DO WE KNOW ABOUT ECONOMIC DEVELOPMENT?

Given the importance in policy formulation of understanding the underlying forces that shape economic development, very little is known about why some countries or regions develop faster than or differently to others. In the distant past when it has been estimated that economies grew at about 0.5 percent per decade, the issue was perhaps more pressing, but given the very limited expectations and aspirations of the populace at the time, much less explored. The change in attitude came in the late eighteenth century with Smith's work that explicitly considered economic development, and in a rather basic way through his trade and transport analysis, the role of spatial interactions in bringing this about.[3]

The modern formalized theories of economic development, while expressed in a general form by Adam Smith, are usually seen as stemming from the neo-classical model developed by Solow (1956) and Swan (1956) with the focus on changes in the factor endowment of a country or region. In these models, the long-run rate of growth is exogenously determined. In other words, it is determined outside of the model resulting in the common prediction that an economy will always converge towards a steady-state rate of growth and that this rate depends on the rate of technological progress and the rate of factor accumulation. A country with a higher saving rate, for example, will experience faster growth.

Critics of this growth theory cite a number of major limitations of the neo-classical model:

● It relies heavily upon notions of technological change to supply growth in per capita income, but has no mechanism for explaining the sources for such change.
● It offers only a very rudimentary framework for assessing the effects of government policy, and while government actions may not be able to raise long-run growth rates, government interventions do

affect behavior and this, in aggregate, affects the growth path (be it positively or negatively) in at least the short term.

- The model has limited capabilities for analyzing trade between regions or countries and the links between such trade and economic growth; a major weakness as globalization forces have expanded.
- A key assumption of the neo-classical economic growth model is that capital is subject to diminishing returns, but there are many industries that enjoy various forms of scale economies at least for significant variations in output.

Refinements to the neo-classical model came as some of these assumptions were gradually relaxed. Kaldor and Mirrlees (1962), for example, posited the existence of a 'technical progress' function with per capita income treated as an increasing function of per capita investment. Thus 'learning' was regarded as a function of the rate of increase in investment and not exogenous. Arrow (1962) took a more nuanced view that the level of the 'learning' coefficient is not associated with the rate of growth in investment but rather with the absolute level of knowledge already accumulated, a stock rather than a flow concept.

The 1980s saw an up-surge of interest in economic development theory partly because major structural shifts were occurring in the service sector and information based industries. Essentially, changes were taking place at both the technical and institutional levels that were seen as potentially affecting economic growth. According to the 'New' or endogenous growth theory that began to emerge at that time, economic growth can be understood as a process of learning-by-doing, within a firm, within an industry, and within a given spatial jurisdiction such as a region or metropolis. While there were the earlier attempts to indigenize technical progress, much of the credit for the modern formulation of endogenous growth theory is attributed to the likes of Romer and Lucas (Romer, 1994).

The practical challenge in policy making has been in deciding whether the largely supply driven, neo-classical or the endogenous theories have greater validity. Empirically testing the validity of the alternative theories, in the absence of easily quantifiable counterfactuals, has frequently involved looking at secondary evidence, and in particular at evidence shedding light on whether there is convergence in the economic growth paths of regions or, at the macro-level, nations.

The empirical question that is explored becomes one of whether there is convergence in regional economic development rates in, generally, per capita income, as is an outcome of the neo-classical model, but only possible with endogenous growth under rather particular circumstances. The body of empirical analysis that has emerged has been assisted by the availability of improved data sets as well as new modeling frameworks, enhanced econometric techniques, and better understandings of how to measure convergence. In particular, there has been the development of the concept of β-convergence measures (Barro and Sala-i-Martin, 1992) that have allowed a more rigorous analysis of economic convergence than the more traditional s-convergence measure that only normally looks at the variances in regional incomes. The estimation of possible β-convergence involves a mean-reversion calculation with β-convergence occurring if there is a negative relationship between the growth rate of income per capita and the level of initial income. More recent work has made use of β-convergence measures, and embrace a number of sub-national studies, and has tended to find little general support for overall convergence. Those using conditional convergence indicators that allow for homogeneity between, for example, the local economies within a country but also diversity between countries, suggest potential differences in steady-state growth rates for the more local areas, offering little support for the exogenous growth idea.[4]

What does this all mean in broad public policy terms? If there are indeed endogenous growth affects, this would seem to provide decision-makers with some opportunity to intervene to stimulate economic development and to combat spatially divergent growth paths. This contrasts to the Solow model where only a change in the savings rate could generate long-run growth in per capita income. Although when in disequilibrium, the neo-classical model does allow for fairly limited public policy interventions that would *de facto* lubricate the system and facilitate a more rapid move to a steady-state growth path this would not produce movement along it or shift it. In the context of migration, for example, this may involve improved information and enhanced transportation services to allow existing resources to move and be used more effectively along Adam Smith's lines of argument of greater divisions of labor.

If there is endogeneity in the growth process then the policy options are somewhat wider. Since knowledge is important, then diffusion of ideas and broader national policies for R&D can be deployed to bring lagging regions up to the production frontier enjoyed by the leading regions. To stimulate a nation's growth, Romer, for example, in the case of the US, argues for a reduction in the federal deficit to reduce interest rates that would in turn increase the amount of human capital devoted to R&D, by raising the discounted value of any given stream of future revenues associated with a new design. The Romer framework would also suggest subsidies for R&D because of the currently uncompensated external benefits that it generates; in contrast, the Lucas models suggest that those subsidies aimed at economic development need largely to go to the education and training of workers.

There is also a case for freer trade in that it allows for the more rapid diffusion of knowledge and thus breaks down the monopoly of those regions and countries that current enjoy its 'ownership'.[5] More generally, it releases knowledge workers to invent new designs rather than for those in the lagging regions having to expend energies on catching up and effectively continually having to reinvent the wheel. If one accepts Florida's (2005) line of argument that the creative classes are attracted and retained by the larger environment in which they live and work, then investment in various forms of local social and economic infrastructure become important.

1.3   THE ROLE OF TRANSPORTATION

From a policy perspective, if there were indeed endogenous growth affects this would seem to provide decision-makers with some opportunity to intervene to stimulate growth and to combat spatially divergent growth paths. This contrasts with the neo-classical Solow type of model where only a change in the savings rate could generate long-run growth in per capita. Although when in disequilibrium, the neo-classical model does allow for fairly limited public policy interventions that would *de facto* lubricate the system and facilitate a more rapid move to a steady-state growth path but not movement along it. In the context of migration, for example, this may involved improved information and enhanced transportation services to allow existing resources to migrate and be used more effectively along Adam Smith's lines of argument.

If there is endogeneity in the growth process then the policy options are somewhat wider. Since knowledge is important, then diffusion of ideas and broader national policies for R&D can be deployed to bring lagging regions up to the production frontier enjoyed by the leading regions. The role of air travel in this context has been explored and higher growth areas for high-technology developments are mainly at large hub airports that allow for extensive personal interactions between those in the component industries. Equally, at a more micro level, the role of transportation in shaping urban form and scale has been extensively studied, with no clear consensus on the direction of the forces at work.[6]

One of the major difficulties, is that networks, and interactions between various substitute and complementary networks (e.g. transportation, telecommunications, social, and intergenerational networks), are complicated and their consequential effects on economic development are hard to disentangle. The problem has become more pronounced in practical and institutional terms, as transportation and other networks have both played a major role in facilitating the globalization of trade that has taken place in recent years, and have themselves been shaped by it. Although short-term disruptions to the transportation system have occurred, for example during the SARS epidemic and after the attacks on the United States in 2001, the efforts to rapidly restore transportation services indicate their social, economic, and political importance.

1.4   THE MICROECONOMIC ANALYSIS

While we have largely focused on the broader issues linking transportation and economic development, there are also very practical matters to consider at the more micro level pertaining to decisions regarding individual projects and policies.[7] The options at this level often revolve around which transportation option from a range available best fulfill predetermined strategic goals. That transportation will achieve some level of economic development is effectively taken as axiomatic, and the question becomes one of selection rather than deciding to put resources into transportation per se. In this situation, there are three broad types of assessment tool available, all with their respective pros and cons.

Subjective quantitative assessment involving surveys to elicit the views of experts on how affected parties, often stakeholders in addition to stockholders, are likely to respond to any change in transportation provision. From this information judgments can be made about the economic development effects of alternative policies. The difficulty is to decide who to question, how to question them, and how much weight to put on each of their replies. The potential for capture by vested interests is large, especially if a significant portion of the costs are to be borne by third parties outside of the area of interest or responsibility. But even if the ability to remove this bias exists, the complex interactions between the various actors, and the ways that they assume others will behave, makes it difficult to frame useful questions. Delphi techniques involving iterations of the responses through several rounds allowing participants to modify their answers, offer a partial but incomplete way of circumventing this problem. The development of experimental economics over the past 20 years or more offers a more rigorous methodology but it has yet to be widely applied.

Econometric studies using statistical analysis looking at the impacts of transportation infrastructure on local economic development are fairly limited. They often focus on some particular aspect of the link between the transportation change and economic development, for example local job creation or enhancement of the tax base. The aim of the approach is often to apportion things like job changes and income effects in a region between various influencing factors including transportation costs and capacity. It does, however, require considerable data, and specifying the appropriate model can be challenging. The ugly head of causality also resurfaces – does improved transportation quality increase the productivity of a region, or do productive regions have more resources to invest in better transportation? While there are techniques that allow econometric analysis to move towards answering this question, such as Granger causality tests, the methods are not ideal and data is generally not readily available.

A common approach often used by consultants to quantify the regional and local economic implications of transportation investment is to use exogenously determined multipliers. A facility goes through a number of stages from its planning to becoming a fully operational piece of infrastructure, and each generates its own particular type of income and employment multiplier effects. We critique these multipliers in the context of a physical investment but they largely hold for any form of policy change.

Primary effects
The primary multiplier stems from the income associated with the multiplicand inherent in construction of the transportation facility and the rounds of expenditure that emanate as part of that money is recycled through the local economy. Its size is often tempered, if there is a need for significant inflows of labor, raw materials, and equipment to plan and construct the facility. Hence, there is a tendency for primary multipliers to decline with the geographical area being considered and with the resources available locally to construct the infrastructure.

Secondary effects
Once a piece of transportation infrastructure is operational, it pumps money into the local economy through the staff that it employs for maintenance and, where applied, net fees collected from users. This income, in turn has multiplier effects on the regional economy. Some forms of transportation infrastructure, such as airports and seaports, can be major employers but there can be a bimodal distribution in the labor force. While transportation facilities do employ many highly skilled and generally highly paid workers, many jobs are unskilled or semi-skilled and thus generate limited income to re-circulate in the local economy.

Tertiary effects
The tertiary multiplier concerns the amount of economic activity drawn to the region by the existence of the enhanced transportation facilities, and with the subsequent ripple effects that results as this pumps income

into the area. These effects can be substantial. For example Memphis Shelby Airport, the major United States airline hub for FedEx, is surrounded by warehouse and distribution facilities that handle products as varied as just-in-time surgery and orthopedic devices, home decor products, and DVDs. At much smaller facilities, the presence of air services is important to companies not necessarily to move their cargo but often in terms of allowing their employees and customers easy access to facilities and markets. High-technology industry makes extensive use of air transportation, as do tourists.

Perpetuity effects
The perpetuity effect is often associated with the development chunks of transportation infrastructure that shift the regional production function upwards by changing the structure of the economy. For example, many islands in the Caribbean and the Mediterranean have seen their economies moving from fishing and agriculture to tourism with the construction of an airport. Additionally, high-technology corridors have emerged on former farmland or where there was more traditional industry. Within many cities, the arrival of metro systems and freeways has stimulated the development of high-technology and bio-technology centers on their outskirts, that have on occasions led to the emergence of an edge city.

It is easy, however, to overestimate local economic development using multipliers. The concept was initially derived as part of closed economy, demand-side macroeconomics in the 1940s when factor supply constraints were not an issue. Many local areas, however, are not initially well endowed with factors and the need to import can limit the size of multiplier effects. It may also not just be a shortage of transportation capacity that is holding local development back but inadequacies in other types of infrastructure, limitations of the local labor force, institutional land-use planning constraints, etc. may be more important. Most empirical work also tends to just transfer macro-parameters that may not be relevant for the region under consideration.

Multipliers analysis often only considers the gross impacts of transportation changes. The initial injection of resources is, however, often from outside the region, for example, and there are opportunity costs associated with resources drawn-in during successive multiplier rounds. In other words there is an opportunity cost involved for the entire economy – essentially a 'crowding-out effect'. In the case, for example, of a road aimed at opening up a tourist area, this may stimulate more tourism in aggregate, but some of the visitors will be attracted away from alternative destinations. As with any activity that allows trade, transportation investments have both a development generation and a development diversion effect.

Finally, multipliers and their disaggregated counterparts, input–output analyses, must be taken in context, and in particular it should be remembered that they were developed to look at the effects of changes in inputs on outputs, and not as tools for assessing the importance of a capital stock. In other words, they are designed for flow analysis and the implications of, say, adding capacity on income or employment. While there may be reasons for using them for looking at changes over time, they were not originally conceived as tools for examining the implications of a stock of inputs on the economic performance of a region. In particular, they assume constant scale effects and a common technology across systems when comparisons are made.

1.5   THE NUMBERS GAME

To assess the impact of any transportation policy on economic development requires reasonable forecasts of the transportation implications themselves – traffic flows, congestion levels, numbers of tons moved, etc. – before any relationship with local income or employment can be established. The empirical evidence, however, is that predicting the internal transportation effects of new infrastructure or a change in regulatory regime is remarkably difficult. This is partly due to inadequate knowledge of causal linkages, but also often reflects a lack of appropriate dynamic data.

Transportation forecasting, as we now understand it, is relatively new, going back to the urban master plans for United States metropolitan areas developed in the 1960s. The early forecasts were largely driven by the prevailing philosophy of the time that urban revitalization would require road capacity to cope with growing automobile traffic and freight deliveries. At the inter-urban level freeways were seen as important to allow trade between cities and for strategic reasons. But the performance of the models used transpired to be uniformly poor. A study in the late 1980s of 41 road schemes in the United Kingdom concluded from a comparison of actual and projected flows that only in 22 cases were the actual flows within 20 percent of the original forecast. Of the remainder, flows ranged from 50 percent below to 105 percent above the original estimate. The forecasts for the M25 London orbital road, for instance, were that on 21 of the 26 three-lane sections the traffic flow would be between 50,000 and 79,000 vehicles a day in the fifteenth year whereas the flow within a very short time was between 81,400 and 129,000.

The later focus on enhancing local public modes of transportation, and in particular transit systems, did not show any demonstrable improvement in forecasts. The traditional method for transit demand forecasting is to use a conventional gravity model. An oft cited example relates to the *ex ante* Bar Area Rapid Transit (BART) impact study that relied on aggregate gravity model and forecast a 15 percent modal share for BART after its opening. What is of particular note about this, is that the economist, McFadden (2001) applied a disaggregate random utility model to generate an alternative forecast of a 6.3 percent mode shift; the actuality was 6.2 percent. Perhaps more disquieting from a policy perspective, is that despite this, BART did not subsequently adopt disaggregate modeling in its policy analysis. McFadden, of course, went on to win the Nobel Prize in economics, which highlights some of the institutional issues involved.

The recent and larger findings in Flyvbjerg et al. (2002, 2006) look more broadly at forecasting issues across a range of countries and modes of transportation and covering projects of traffic flows and costs. The work provides confirmation of the poor performance of forecasting models. There has in particular been a tendency for over-prediction of capacity utilization and under-prediction of the outcome costs of investments – for example for ten rail projects examined from a variety of countries, the passenger forecasts overestimated traffic by 106 percent, whereas for road projects a tendency is found for the forecasts to be wrong by about 20 percent but the errors were spread equally around the ultimate flows. In terms of costs, an examination of 58 rail projects indicates overruns averaging nearly 45 percent, and for 167 road investments, overruns of 20.4 percent; overall for 258 transportation infrastructure projects examined (including rail, fixed-link and roads) costs are found to be generally underestimated and to be systematically misleading.

Why this happens is not a topic dealt with in any detail here, although it is clear from the studies of Flyvbjerg and others, that much of the problem is not technical, but rather lies in the capture of the forecasting processes by politicians and others with vested interests in producing particular predictions. Here we offer some general comments germane to how positive movements could come about. What is clear, however, is if transportation policy is going to be used properly as an input into economic development initiatives, then reasonably accurate forecasts are important.[8] What also seems to be the case is that many of the past errors in forecasting could have been less if state of the art methodologies had been adopted. The continued reliance on essentially engineering models, rather than accepting that travel decisions are made by individuals who exhibit complex socio-economic behavioral patterns is a persistent short-fall in much policy formulation. One example of this given by Dan McFadden (2001) in his Nobel speech is with regard to transit demand forecasting in San Francisco. The conventional aggregate gravity model forecast a 15 percent modal share for BART, McFadden's disaggregate forecast based on a random utility model was 6.3 percent and the actuality was 6.2 percent. Despite this, BART has never adopted disaggregate modeling as a policy tool.

The 'Flyvbjerg Debate', combined with comments of the kind rendered by McFadden, has drawn attention, not only to the poor quality of many forecasts but to the need to explain more systematically why this is so. One obvious explanation is that the forecasting techniques themselves are flawed, either because the underlying models are inappropriate or because there are problems in predicting the exogenous input variables. Another is that the use of forecasts may be distorted for institutional reasons with forecasting processes captured in various ways. Flyvbjerg's analysis, for example, combines behavioral economics and decision-making theory, and focuses on strategic misrepresentation and optimism bias. This approach tends to move the site of the debate away from purely technical matters of deciding on how best to produce numerical forecasts towards developing theories concerning how predictions are used and, *ipso facto*, on how decisions on transportation policies are actually made.

1.6   CONCLUSIONS

Since the late 1980s there has been a renewed interest in the role of transportation provision as a stimulant to economic development.[9] The entangled maze of relationships that exist between transportation and economic development make it problematic to trace out all the causal linkages, much less provide reliable quantification. The empirical analysis is frustrated in particular by the need to define and assess causality and to specify salient elements of connectivity. The theoretical models that often underpin empirical investigations have often been based on excessively simplistic sets of assumptions or on inappropriate assumptions that have little empirical support.

These limitations have gradually become clear with the growth in sophistication in social analysis of all types. Just taking economics as an example, the emergence of the new institutional economics has high-lighted the role of transactions costs in decision making,[10] the growth of experimental economics has allowed for the use of laboratory testing of hypothesis,[11] and behavioral economics has illustrated that human traits such as hysteresis and inertia can affect choices. These, and similar new approaches, are only gradually being introduced into the analysis of transportation and economic development. Work involving the introduction of these and other new generic understandings and methodologies, therefore offers considerable opportunities for research to inject more realism and usefulness into the theoretical analysis of transportation and economic development, and a potentially fruitful sea change in theorizing rather than just the minor tweaking of the theories we have. But producing new, positive theories is not as easy as just tinkering with the details of the old ones.

There are also data and information issues to be considered. The aim of social science is not to produce models and analysis for their own sakes, but rather to provide a better understanding of how society works. For that inductive methodologies are as relevant as the deductive. Inductive analysis tends to be less fashionable in some branches of spatial analysis, possibly because some consider its use of case studies to be somehow less rigorous than the construction of abstract frameworks. Nevertheless, even with that simple concept in economics, the demand curve, there is always that nefarious element 'taste' that largely disguises factors economists cannot explain. Advances in our understanding of taste have come as much from sociology and social anthropology as they have from any other field, and here the methodology is largely inductive in nature. But this requires different forms of data, which are often costly to gather, but can be important if we are to understand links between transportation services and economic development. But even with inductive work there is often a dearth of useful data in many cases, and especially that offering the opportunity to develop good long-term profiles of causal linkages between transportation and economic development.

The papers in this volume obviously do not cover all of the issues that surround the study of transportation and economic development. Indeed, even what we have laid out above, and which lays out the boundaries for the volume, only really briefly covers one side of the challenge, that relating to transportation networks. There is just as much complexity in the many other factors that affect levels of economic development (e.g. in land-use planning, local and global geography, historical legacy, language skills, and forms of government and governance in the region and country). What the papers here do is provide a few insights into some of the topics that are at the forefront of people's thinking and concerns.

NOTES

1. Even Adam Smith (1776) recognized that simple commercial criteria may not be enough to ensure adequate supply of infrastructure and thus saw a role for public provision,

    > The third and last duty of the sovereign or commonwealth is that of erecting and maintaining those public institutions and those public works, which, though they

may be in the highest degree advantageous to a great society, are, however, of such a nature that the profit could never repay the expense to any individual or small number of individuals, and which it therefore cannot be expected that any individual or small number of individuals should erect or maintain.

2. See an application of complex network analysis by Lim and Shiode in this volume.
3. The links between the complexities of connectivity and economic development have subsequently been explored in many contexts, with the work of the geographer, Hägerstrand (1975) on the links between space and time having the largest influence.
4. Some of these issues are implicitly touched upon in Goetz's contribution to this volume.
5. Akyelken's contribution to this volume considers some of the links between transportation, trade and development in more detail
6. The growth of megaregions and the role of planning in this context is considered in the chapter by Myers and Dunning, while McDonnell, Madar and Been look at some of the salient issues on a more micro-scale.
7. This is the sort of topic covered by Pauwels, Van de Voorde, Vanelslander and Verhetsel in a later chapter.
8. This is even more the case if a wide view of social effects is embraced in transportation policy appraisal along the lines suggested by Niemeier, Jones and Cheng in this volume. The recent work by Stern (2007), for example, suggests that appropriate discount rates to be applied in assessment involving global warming effects should be well below the 1 percent that would necessitate much longer forecasting horizons in such things as economic impact studies.
9. Despite its technical flaws, the work of Aschauer (1989) is generally seen as the catalyst for the resurgence of interest in the analysis of links between transportation and economic development. Interestingly, Aschauer is neither a transportation economist nor a regional scientist, and that perhaps indicates the importance of standing back and taking a broader view of things on occasions.
10. A subject important enough to be the topic of the 2009 economics Nobel Prize speech in economics (Williamson, 2010).
11. Another topic for a Nobel Prize winner's lecture (Smith, 2003), but an approach only gradually permeating spatial analysis.

REFERENCES

Arrow, K.J. (1962) The economic implications of learning by doing, *Review of Economic Studies*, 29, 155–73.

Aschauer, D.A. (1989) Is public infrastructure expenditure productive?, *Journal of Monetary Economics*, 23, 177–200.

Barro, R.J and Sala-i-Martin, X. (1992) Convergence, *Journal of Political Economy*, 100, 223–51.

Florida, R. (2005) *The Flight of the Creative Class. The New Global Competition for Talent*. New York, HarperCollins.

Flyvbjerg, B., Holm, M.K.S. and Buhl, S.L. (2002) Underestimating costs in public work projects: error or lie?, *Journal of the American Planning Association*, 68: 279–95.

Flyvbjerg, B., Holm, M.K.S. and Buhl, S.L. (2006) Inaccuracy in traffic forecasts, *Transport Reviews*, 26, 1–24.

Hägerstrand, T. (1975) Space, time and human conditions, in A. Karlqvist, F. Snickars and L. Lundqvist (eds), *Dynamic Allocation of Urban Space*. Lexington, Saxon House.

Kaldor, N. and Mirrlees, J.A. (1962) A new model of economic growth, *Review of Economic Studies*, 29, 174–92.

McFadden, D. (2001) Economic choices, *American Economic Review*, 91, 351–78.

Romer, P.M. (1994) The origins of endogenous growth, *Journal of Economic Perspectives*, 8, 3–22.

Smith, A. (1776) *An Inquiry into the Nature and Causes of the Wealth of Nations*. Oxford, Oxford University Press.

Smith, V. (2003) Constructivist and ecological rationality in economics, *American Economic Review*, 93, 465–509.

Solow, R.M. (1956) A contribution to the theory of economic growth, *Quarterly Journal of Economics*, 70, 65–94.

Stern, N. (2007) *Stern Review: The Economics of Climate Change*. London: Cabinet Office – HM Treasury.

Swan, T.W. (1956) Economic growth and capital accumulation, *Economic Record*, 32, 334–61.

Williamson, O.E. (2010) Transaction cost economies: the natural progression, *American Economic Review*, 100, 673–90.

2. The relationship between megaregions and megapolitans: transportation planning for the two scales

Jason S. Myers and Anne Dunning

2.1 INTRODUCTION

Designations of cities, other localities, states, and countries have long facilitated planning according to politically-determined borders; however, populations and economies naturally undermine this system by evolving according to their own inherent forces and characteristics. The developed world embraced the metropolitan scale several decades ago as a result of the evolution that could not be ignored by the political system, and transportation planning made accommodations. Academic and planning practitioner circles are now recognizing that new scales have emerged and demand attention, notably megaregions and megapolitans.

Although intellectual leaders of planning acknowledge the existence and importance of these scales, no consensus has developed on either how to delineate them or how to serve them. Concepts of how to define a megaregion generally either focus on some density measure, such as population or economic activity, or on some level of cohesion with surrounding areas, such as commute shed overlap. Both approaches create a threshold that delineates a megaregion both from its neighboring megaregions and from surrounding areas not considered to be part of a megaregion. The existence of multiple approaches means maps are divided in different ways, leading to confusion over which megaregion should plan for certain populations or whether a given exurb should be considered in megapolitan planning. While there are difficulties determining which approach is superior, neither approach fully considers the regional functions, economies, and social outcomes that concern planners.

2.2   WHAT IS A MEGAREGION?

The combination of expanding technology with a growing global economy and spreading land development have led to recognition of a new spatial form, the megaregion. While various aspects of the megaregion concept have been a part of regional science since at least the late 1950s, only in the beginning of the twenty-first century did the concept emerge with the form that is in use today. A megaregion is defined as a unit of the global economy that is a collection of metropolitan and micropolitan areas as well as their intervening rural areas. In the context of the United States, metropolitan areas have populations greater than 50,000 people living in contiguous census tracts that meet US Census Bureau thresholds for population density. Micropolitan areas have populations less than 50,000 people and at least one urban cluster greater than 10,000 people. Megaregions can generally be traversed in a day of travel. They contain the majority of the population in the developed world and are expected to attract most population growth in the next half-century (Regional Plan Association, 2006).

Early History

In 1961 Jean Gottmann published a detailed study of the Northeastern United States and introduced the term 'megalopolis'. The study recognized the forms of spatial development in North America were changing. The characteristics that made megalopolis unique were the blurring of exurban areas of the various metropolitan regions in the Northeast (perhaps first described by Spectorsky in 1955) and the magnitude of the human population and economic activity contained within the region. For the next few decades, others investigated and discussed the implications of these changes (Pickard, 1962, 1966; Blumenthal, 1983). Much of the literature heavily discussed urban sprawl (Muller, 1976). Some authors considered planning needs for this large scale of settlement pattern (Friedmann and Miller, 1965), but much of the attention might be better described as geographic inquiries. Others observed changes in spatial form that corresponded to new transportation technology (Garreau, 1991).

New Attention

In the 1990s and early 2000s, lingering fascination with the idea of cities running together combined with growing interest in the global economy. The 2000 census was especially instructive about the former phenomenon (Frey et al., 2004; Lang and Dhavale, 2005). The application of the concept of the metroplex (a name for the combined Dallas and Fort Worth region) to other areas yielded the term 'megapolitan' (Lang and Dhavale, 2005). This term was coined to describe regions where commute sheds significantly overlapped. Interest in global cities and the world's economy was led by sociologists such as Saskia Sassen of the University of Chicago (1991; 2006) and was a separate line of inquiry from geography- and planning-based studies (such as Calthorpe and Fulton, 2001). Whereas the sociological studies focused on evolving economic relationships and their relation to cities, geography and planning studies described a vision of polycentric regional new urbanism and how regional geographies could be described both by a space of flows and a space of places.

Modern Conception of Megaregions

The concepts of global cities and combined metropolitan areas merged in 2004 when the Regional Plan Association and the Lincoln Institute of Land Policy joined forces with a graduate studio course of the University of Pennsylvania School of Design to consider an American counterpart to the European Union policy known as the European Spatial Development Perspective (Lincoln Institute of Land Policy, Regional Plan Association, and the University of Pennsylvania School of Design, 2004). The European Spatial Development Perspective is effectively the supra-national planning policy of the European Union. The document resulting from the studio presented something analogous to a national plan proposed by Theodore Roosevelt in 1908. The studio report primarily discussed five trends:

- 'rapid population growth'
- 'the building-out of suburban America'
- 'uneven and inequitable growth patterns within and between regions'
- 'metropolitan infrastructure that is reaching the limits of its capacity' and
- 'emergence of SuperCities (Emergence of urban networks on a global scale).'

Though all five related to subsequent megaregion planning activities, the fifth concept, about 'super cities', most closely related to megaregions; it was explicitly linked to Gottmann's megalopolis. It was also informed by the global cities research that started more than a decade earlier. In some ways, the studio work pointed to a flaw in the global city model, where one political jurisdiction might not be a unit of global concern, but that a jurisdiction combined with its neighbors might, especially in the politically fragmented settlement in the United States. It appears as if the studio took the Globalization and World Cities Project framework (a network focused on 'the external relations of world cities' – GaWC Research Network, 2009) and organized each 'SuperCity' around the most preeminent nearby city on the global cities scale. The report identified eight SuperCities: the Northeast, the Great Lakes, the Southeast, Texas, Southern California, Northern California, the Northwest, and Florida.

The Penn report introduced the concepts of SuperCity, regional center, regional node, regional network, and region of influence. SuperCity (core) and region of influence (fringe) were most similar to what is now being called a megaregion. Carbonell and Yaro, who helped advise the studio, followed up with an article in the Lincoln Institute's magazine in 2005. The article changed the term SuperCity into 'megalopolitan' but otherwise kept the studio's national planning framework of a possible American Spatial Development Perspective (akin to the European Spatial Development Perspective that inspired the studio work).

The Regional Plan Association published a report that further refined the studio's results and changed 'megalopolitan' to 'mega-region' (Carbonell et al., 2005). Concurrent with these activities, the Regional Plan Association and the Lincoln Institute of Land Policy hosted a meeting to discuss the types of planning activities investigated in the Penn studio (America 2050, 2004). This meeting led to the consortium known as America 2050. In the America 2050 prospectus, 'mega-region' changed a final time into 'megaregion' (Regional Plan Association 2006). Two regions were added to the eight regions delineated as SuperCities in the original studio: the Gulf Coast and the metropolitan core of Arizona. Both were identified by Lang and Dhavale in 2005.

The twenty-first century attention on the topic from the Lincoln Institute and the Region Plan Association stemmed from the two forces identified by Blumenthal. The first was a centrifugal push out of traditional urban centers and the second was a centripetal pull into densely populated areas (out of rural America). These forces have led to traffic congestion and sprawl, as well as uneven economic development of rural areas such as Appalachia or the Great Plains.

The relationship between the global economy and the megaregion is important. In a global hierarchy, megaregions are the units at which global exchange takes place. The megaregion might be described as a global city and its hinterland, but a megaregion might also exist without a global city if the global functions are spread around various parts of the megaregion in a cohesive fashion. For this reason, geographic patterns of population should be augmented with economic linkages. For instance, the Piedmont Atlantic megaregion has often been depicted along the

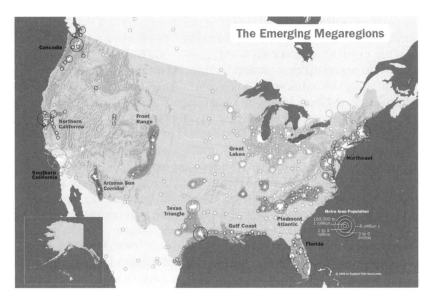

Source: derived from Regional Plan Association (2008).

Figure 2.1   *The 11 emerging megaregions, as defined by the Regional Plan Association*

landlocked Interstate 85 corridor, but a more appropriate designation for this megaregion should include ports such as Savannah, Charleston and Wilmington, which connect this megaregion with global shipping (Ross, 2006).

The Regional Plan Association updated its megaregion designations map in 2008 (Figure 2.1), extending some megaregions and adding an emerging megaregion not described in 2006, the Front Range megaregion, centered on Denver. The Front Range region has no port except for its airports or transcontinental rail and highway. The Arizona corridor is in the same situation, but it is much closer to the largest port in North America, Los Angeles-Long Beach. If a functional definition of megaregions is used, then in some cases, there is poor expression of the agglomeration effects that also lead to megaregions, as seen in the Piedmont Atlantic Megaregion.

America 2050 subsequently coordinated a number of megaregion planning efforts; many of them part of graduate-level planning education. Dewar and Epstein (2007) broadened personal experience planning for the Great Lakes megaregion into questions about the nature of megaregions and planning for megaregions. They concluded geographers and planners have different perspectives on defining megaregions. In short, geographers have attempted to describe what is, while planners have been concerned with what might or should be. Therefore, if it makes sense to plan for an area as a megaregion for its benefit, then (from a planning perspective) it should be done regardless of the current state of the space. Dewar and Epstein also stated that megaregions should be loosely defined, depending on the planning or policy purpose.

Confusion about Megaregions

Because of the concurrent and related nature of the work of Lang and his colleagues (leading to the coining of the term megapolitan) along with the activities that led to America 2050 (and coining of the term megaregion), there appears to be significant confusion about the nature of megaregions and the relationship between the two streams of analysis. After Lang and Nelson's (2007) paper on megapolitans appeared in *Planning* magazine an editorial (Bright, 2007) denying both the existence and the inevitability of 'megas' was published that seemed to confuse megaregions with megapolitans and associated them both with the planner's favorite demon, sprawl. Lang (2007) followed up defending his position and pointing out the differences and relationship between the concepts. He also expressed doubt in the current existence of megaregions. In most cases, the megapolitans described by Lang are components of the megaregions described by the Regional Plan Association and were defined solely by the continuity of development and the overlapping of commute sheds, as opposed to having something to do with a relationship to the global economy. In addition to focus on sprawl, this phenomenon showed itself in the popular media when discussion turned towards epic commutes (Spectorsky, 1955).

This confusion has been repeated elsewhere in the literature. An analysis of economic relationships within and between regions of Western Europe has somewhat conflated the two concepts (Taylor and Pain, 2007). The 'Mega-City Regions' used in this analysis were equivalent to Lang's megapolitans. The combination of the most central of these regions (Paris, Brussels, Köln, Amsterdam, and London) might be more analogous to the Northeast megaregion or the Texas Triangle.

2.3   DEFINING MEGAREGIONS

To help resolve the confusion, as well as to provide guidance to transportation planners regarding megaregions and megapolitan geography, it is important to consider the underlying phenomena that lead to various spatial definitions. This entails looking at outside structure that describes ways in which boundaries may be drawn around a region and inside structure that describes some of the relationships which define a region in terms of internal cohesion.

Outside Structure

According to the Regional Plan Association (2006), five forms of relationships define megaregions: environmental systems and topography, infrastructure systems, economic linkages, settlement patterns and land use, and shared culture and history.

In many ways, these interrelated relationships can define any scale of settlement not defined by political boundaries. They are interrelated because environmental systems and topography greatly influenced early infrastructure systems such as transportation linkages, and these linkages in turn created the economic systems that followed. Land use and urban design developed out of all of these relationships.

The evolution of American hinterland
In a manner of thinking, the American megaregion identifies one layer of the hinterland structure that can categorize the entire nation, with New York and Washington respectively leading economic and political activities. The megaregion is a layer on the development continuum that has the global economy on one end and the neighborhood on the other. In this nested structure an important concept is the hinterland. A hinterland is the sum of the areas that are subordinate predominately to one particular unit of space or economy.

The infrastructure and economic relationships that have developed hinterlands have been described in detail, as have been the changes that have occurred to these relationships during the latter part of the industrial revolution. Between the American colonial period and the early nineteenth century water transportation was the most reliable form of long-distance transport for both goods and people. It was a great concern of the American founding fathers that effective transportation across the Appalachian Mountains be provided to link the port cities on the Atlantic with the growing frontier around the Great Lakes and the Ohio River valley. The alternative water routes fed to British or Spanish controlled ports. The Gallatin Plan of 1808 was created to overcome the mountain barriers with a combination of water navigation improvements and mountain roads (Fishman, 2007).

After the construction of the Erie Canal, which linked New York City to the Great Lakes in 1825, a portion of the Plan was in place, and New York's hinterland grew to include the entire Great Lakes basin, helping to solidify its role as the center of the United States' economy. Portages and canals linking the Great Lakes and the Mississippi basin in places like Chicago, Green Bay and Toledo further expanded New York's hinterland. In this time, a city's wealth stemmed largely from the amount of rural production that could be concentrated in its markets. The rural production took the form of agriculture, forest, and mine products; the city with the largest geographic hinterland was in the best position to accumulate capital.

The development of the Illinois and Michigan Canal between the Great Lakes and the Mississippi River system, followed by railroad construction in Chicago, helped to create a special relationship between New York and Chicago. The effective result was that Chicago gained the majority of the Great Plains as its hinterland and New York gained Chicago as part of its hinterland (Cronon, 1991). Previous to the rapid rise of Chicago in the mid nineteenth century, cities like Cincinnati, Saint Louis and New Orleans, all situated directly on the great rivers, handled a large amount of the rural trade of the West. With the help of capital from New York, Chicago extended railroads west that intercepted large swaths of Saint Louis' hinterland.

The changes brought by the railroads and the industries of the late nineteenth and early twentieth centuries altered the economic landscape of the nation. Chicago's adaptations to problems of congestion and inefficient markets, coupled with railroad and telegraph technology, created a national economy in a way that had not been achieved previously. These developments, often in information and management systems, first increased the value of the Chicago location and therefore the city's wealth, but later the same developments allowed the system of rural hinterlands and urban markets to begin to break down. For instance, the development of the Union Stockyards in Chicago and the refrigerated railcar changed the meat industry and made it national, instead of local, in scope. The innovations of the central packing plant and cold shipping could not be contained within Chicago and eventually allowed the industry to move west, closer to the rangelands, into cities like Omaha and Kansas City. The meat industry has since geographically decentralized further.

These rural hinterlands were, in the resource-based economy of their days, analogous to the citizens of the many metropolitan and micropolitan areas that make up a megaregion in today's information economy. A century or more ago, a seaport was necessary to tie the hinterland to the global, or national, economy. Today, telecommunications and airports have joined with seaports in providing this economic link. Because the concept of the megaregion has emerged largely from an interest in global cities, and the interactions between large civilizations around the globe, the megaregion is the first order of civilization that participates in the global economy, just as eastern United States seaports were the first order of civilizations of America that participated in global trade in the nineteenth century.

Culture
Cultural geography has been closely related to the planning concepts of megaregions; maps of American cultural areas match remarkably well with current megaregion maps (Zelinsky, 1992). Perhaps regional cultural similarities have been products of shared economic histories and therefore effects of the same cause that creates megaregions. One of the factors that might contribute to megaregions being useful units of analysis is the extent to which people identify with 'their' megaregion (Dewar and Epstein, 2007) implying that cultural identity and shared heritage can be a useful factor in delineating megaregions.

Natural geography
Natural geography and geology have influenced spatial form and economic relationships. Natural processes have largely dictated agricultural and mining systems, water transportation routes, and the siting of ports. Mountain ranges, watercourses and wetlands have contained communities and separated them from each other. Watersheds dictated the shape of rural hinterlands before the development of railroads (Vance, 1990b). Climate and the natural environment influenced where Europeans settled in America (Jakle and Wheeler, 1969); they also influenced settlement by directing migration around major barriers and along accessible corridors. Natural systems of many types initially influenced all five of the megaregion-defining criteria and the systems' imprints have remained on the landscape. In addition, natural geography has continued to influence perceptions of regional identities.

Inside Structure

Internal spatial form is a somewhat separate way to characterize megaregions. Put simply megaregions have been defined based on the nearness of various metropolises. By running together, places that were once deemed separate become parts of a new spatial unit as it has become difficult to tell where one part ends and another begins.

Agglomeration/decentralization
Hinterlands, as we have seen, have become more a function of agglomeration of labor and talent rather than rural/urban supply networks. As a

result, the central place has become defined by accessibility to people more than the relationship between central markets in cities and rural hinterlands. The demand for places with high talent accessibility grew with these economic changes. The skyscraper was an early sign of this phenomenon beginning to show (Gottmann, 1966). Skyscrapers were built in locations accessible to major transit systems, such as the elevated loop in Chicago or the subway network in lower Manhattan.

It could be that the slowness with which European cities adopted new transportation technologies is partially a reason for their general lack of skyscraper development (Vuchic, 2007). In the United States, streetcar, subway and elevated transit companies all rushed to build lines to the most desirable real estate, creating a spiral of accessibility where desirable locations became more valuable due to transit, creating the economic conditions for skyscrapers. In many European cities, transportation companies rarely received the same leeway. The result seems to have been that European transit grew more slowly and the resulting network was less centralized. The economic conditions for skyscrapers never materialized. This history might have resulted in transit that is more ubiquitous and useful for a wider cross section of trip purposes in Europe today. Washington, DC is a notable case in the United States where the same conditions are evident, a transit system without a clearly defined center and a lack of skyscrapers, but in the Washington case, the lack of skyscrapers might have been the cause for a transit system constructed to serve the realities of the existing urban fabric. In contrast, the Washington Metro's contemporary, the Metropolitan Atlanta Rapid Transit Authority (MARTA), has a strong central orientation on the Five Points station, which is the traditional city center of Atlanta.

One of the primary characteristics identified in megaregion literature has been urban decentralization. The phenomenon was featured strongly in the book *Megalopolis* (Gottmann, 1961), but it was not the first to call attention to it. The word exurb was invented in 1955 by Spectorsky in reference to high-level information workers of New York who had moved their households a considerable distance away from their offices, taking advantage of their automobiles and extensive commuter rail lines.

Decentralization in some forms is even older. Vance (1990a) wrote how cross-town streetcar routes in the early twentieth century helped to spread focal points of development and began to break down the dominance of central market and shopping districts. Before this time, early commuter rail systems created a beaded pattern of residential development, but it was supplanted by a more evenly-developed but polycentric morphology at junctions of streetcar lines. Shopping for everyday goods shifted to these streetcar locations while downtown served special trips only. This situation is analogous to the current American form with malls for the uncommon trips and suburban strips (neighborhood commercial districts) for the common trips. Streetcars tended to focus on the central shopping district which at that time started to be differentiated in American downtowns from the office districts.

After the Second World War, decentralization accelerated and took on new forms. Much ink has been devoted to describing the changes in spatial form in America. Various researchers described the changes and pressures in various terms. Pickard (1962, 1966) forecasted urban regions remarkably similar to the megaregions described much more recently. Friedmann and Miller (1965) as well as Blumenthal (1983) described competing forces in American spatial development: a centripetal pull from rural areas into more developed regions and a centrifugal push of decentralization out of the urban core. These forces in some ways underlie the outside and inside aspects of megaregions. Muller (1976) investigated the implications of continued suburbanization. The realization that suburbs had become more than residential hinterlands to downtowns led to coining the terms edge city (Garreau, 1991) and edgeless city (Lang, 2003), respectively meaning the high-density activity centers built at the intersections of major highways and the centerless commercial equivalent to exurban housing. These trends have reflected components of both the centripetal and centrifugal forces.

Communications technology and technological innovation have been driving forces for megaregions. They have helped shape the global economy and they have also influenced the internal forms of regions. Digital communications have allowed a certain amount of decentralization but not remotely to the extent that was theorized decades ago (Bolan and Peng, 2004). Instead, improved communications have increased the need for face-to-face interaction, even when it is not needed on an everyday basis to accomplish simple transactions. Just as Sassen (2007) theorized that greater communication on a global scale increases the demand for highly specialized local services, extensive communication networks seem to support greater demand for specialized face-to-face interactions.

The nature of the knowledge- and innovation-based global economy can be related to the centripetal pull discussed by Friedman and Miller and Blumenthal. Moss and Townsend (2000) found that while the internet has been an important part of the modern American metropolis, it does not appear to have had any geographic leveling effects. Similarly, innovation seems to have been concentrated in geographically narrow spaces, though it is not understood why (Lim, 2003). Both of these findings support a presumption that without intervention, regions lagging in the global economy are going to have a difficult time catching up; however, Taylor and Pain (2007) have shown that regional agglomeration might have economic benefits in some cases, such as the development of new information technology concentrations, for instance in the San Francisco Bay area.

Functional/economic relationships
While decentralization and the running together of metropolitan areas dominate the internal aspects of megaregions, functional and economic internal aspects also deserve attention. Regional agglomerations have afforded benefits to both producers and consumers by increasing the size of given markets. For example, the transition to hub-and-spoke airline networks from the previous point-to-point networks concentrated accessibility at a few locations where travel demand has been the greatest. Hub-and-spoke freight systems have now also evolved to function on a similar scale.

The development of e-commerce has taken advantage of similar agglomeration economies through what has been called the 'long-tail' phenomenon (Anderson, 2004). Demand in small niche markets can only be effectively served when the markets grow large enough to get the niche past a break-even threshold. The phenomenon likely works at the megaregional scale as well and might have been at least partially responsible for the centripetal pull noted by Freidmann and Miller (1965), as more densely populated areas allow greater diversity of goods and services. Jane Jacobs (1961) described similar effects on a neighborhood scale.

Knowledge and creative industries have generally taken advantage of similar effects in the search for workforce talent, though the effect existed in the previous industrial economy as well (Feser and Hewings, 2007). Agglomeration of metropolitan areas fostered the economic development of portions of these economic regions (Taylor and Pain, 2007). Sassen has theorized that firms with larger global reach require more specialized services at their headquarters. This need has driven the distinction of global cities.

Sassen discusses how the global economy and megaregions relate. At a basic level, the global economy interacts at the megaregion scale; however, not all megaregions could replace global cities. Agglomeration economies must exist to function as global cities. Places like New York, Chicago, Silicon Valley, and Los Angeles have had this agglomeration, but not all other premier cities in American megaregions have. Sassen (2007) proposed megaregions could on-shore many of the low-cost business functions that have been recently off-shored to low-cost countries, which could possibly benefit underperforming portions of American megaregions. Connectivity between these on-shore locations and headquarters must be strong to overcome the cost and beachhead advantages that overseas locations have.

The combination of the idea that on-shoring might be possible with the tension between physical agglomeration and functional definitions of megaregions suggests physical space is not as important as travel time and cost. For instance, it is about 2.75 hours by train, highway is slower, between New York City and Washington, DC, which is the same surface travel time as from New York City to the state capital in Albany; highway or rail. Travel time, monetary cost, departure flexibility, and capacity all contribute to travel cost. An analogous trip in the Piedmont Atlantic megaregion between the port city of Savannah and Atlanta is 3.75 hours by highway, and flights are expensive and infrequent. High costs of time or money have made economic integration between this governmental/financial center and this port more difficult.

2.4   TOWARDS A REFINED DEFINITION OF MEGAREGIONS

We now look at a layered, functional, and transportation-focused definition of regional geography. The objective is to provide guidance for transportation planners to evaluate service and infrastructure changes based on economic and social purposes. The definition is layered because it includes various scales of geography and transportation that build on each other. It is functional because instead of defining regions by the degree of some characteristic, it leads to definitions based on the inclusion of necessary or important functions within a region. It uses transportation systems to illustrate layers and function both because many spatial relationships closely relate to transportation and because this point of view helps to meet the objective of providing transportation planning guidance.

Layered Megaregions

Recognizing the fuzzy and sometimes conflicting ideas of the exact scales of megaregions, a detailed description of megaregion geography is necessary and should explicitly consider both megaregions (Regional Plan Association, 2006) and megapolitans (Lang and Dhavale, 2005). Megaregions are defined by links between themselves and the larger global economy while megapolitan areas have emerged from spatial agglomeration of proximate metropolitan and micropolitan regions that have run together. Megapolitans are therefore a primary component of most megaregions. For instance, the Northeast megaregion (Figure 2.2) is made up of three distinct megapolitans, which themselves formed from

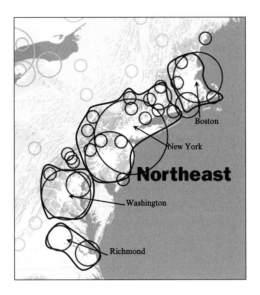

Source: derived from Regional Plan Association (2008).

Figure 2.2 *The Northeast megaregion; irregular shapes denote megapolitans*

metropolitan and micropolitan regions: New England, Mid Atlantic, and Chesapeake (Lang and Nelson, 2007), to which we add Southeast Virginia. Similar phenomena can be demonstrated in other American megaregions, as seen in Figure 2.3.

The Paris, Brussels, Köln, Amsterdam, London (PBKAL) megaregion is made up of numerous megapolitans (Figure 2.4), including the areas of influence around the large cities of London and Paris, as well as the clusters of smaller metropolitan regions such as the Randstad, made up of Amsterdam, Rotterdam, The Hague and Utrecht in the Netherlands, the Flemish Diamond of Belgium, and the Rhine-Ruhr area around Köln and Düsseldorf in Germany.

Megaregions can include megapolitans; however, these are not solely the combination of megapolitan areas. They include rural areas as well as metropolitan and micropolitan areas that are not a part of a larger megapolitan region. Areas outside of megapolitans often look like an intercity version of the early commuter rail suburbs that formed a 'string of beads' within walking distance of commuter rail lines (Vance, 1990a). In this form, beads of independent metropolitan and micropolitan areas are 'strung' along a rail and/or highway corridor. The California Central

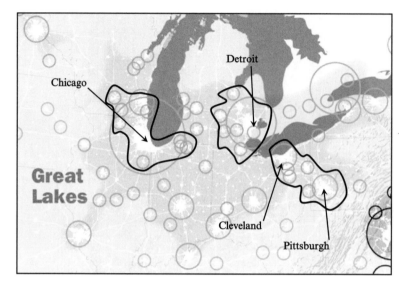

Note: The figure does not delineate all clusters that could be indentified on the megapolitan scale.

Source: derived from Regional Plan Association (2008).

Figure 2.3   The Great Lakes megaregion

Valley (Figure 2.5) and the Detroit-to-Chicago (Interstate 94) corridor are both examples of this type of development form.

Megaregions can also include rural hinterlands. Some of these rural areas fall between the various mega-, metro-, and micropolitan areas that make up the economic core of a megaregion, but they also exist around the outside of the megaregion. These areas should be considered part of a megaregion when they meet one of two criteria.

- First, they are recreational areas that are primarily used by residents of the megaregion for day and weekend trips (as opposed to long-distance and long-term vacations). In this function, the areas are likely to be home to vacation homes and well-visited parks.
- The second rural criterion is based on production value functioning in the megaregion's economic system. Rural areas should be considered to be part of a megaregion when their primary agricultural products could or do supply the urban core of the megaregion. This type of relatively high-value agriculture is often associated with farmers' markets but sometimes is related to a local food-based

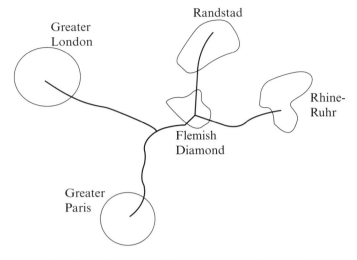

*Figure 2.4   The Paris, Brussels, Köln, Amsterdam, London (PBKAL)
megaregion showing transportation connectivity*

industry. Its counterpart is the production of commodity products for which it is foreseeable that they be shipped anywhere in the world for consumption (Gottmann, 1961).

There is no solid boundary line where either of these criteria is true on one side but not the other, but rather they are examples of gradient criteria for defining megaregions.

Functional Definitions

Megaregions are defined such that they contain all of the functions that allow a region to operate. For instance, except for land-locked regions like the Front Range, all megaregions likely contain seaports, even when metropolitan densities do not reach all the way to the ports. The Piedmont Atlantic megaregion in the Southeast (Figure 2.6) exemplifies this idea as discussed previously. The densest core of the megaregion has roughly followed Interstate 85 through the geological Piedmont region, away from the Atlantic coast, but port cities such as Savannah, Charleston, and Wilmington have existed largely to serve the shipping needs of the citizens and industries further inland. Despite distance and lack of population density between the coast and the major metropolitan areas, the ports are less than a day's travel from the population and economic activity cores; without the ports, the cores would not economically function as they do.

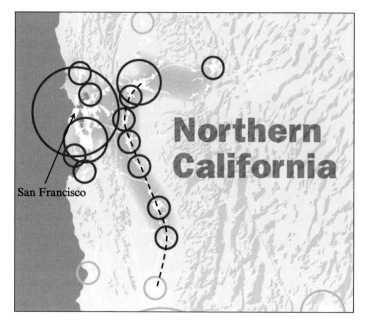

San Francisco

Northern California

Source: derived from Regional Plan Association (2008).

*Figure 2.5   The 'string of beads' megaregional form in the California
              Central Valley*

Other functional aspects of megaregions include governmental centers, recreational lands, major airports, and major surface transportation links.

Megaregional Scale

Finally, megaregions have imprecise boundaries that shift over time, and their borders depend on the purposes and considerations of the person drawing the map (Dewar and Epstein, 2007). Metropolitan areas on the fringe of potential megaregion boundaries will fit in or out of the border depending on current needs. The Great Lakes megaregion, for instance, could be drawn to stretch as far west as Minneapolis, Omaha, or Kansas City and as far east as Pittsburgh, Rochester, and Toronto. The diameter of this region could therefore be almost 1000 miles across because the case could always be made that the next city beyond the last boundary should be included. This problem becomes especially acute when a planner's perspective on megaregions is taken; meaning that a future-oriented view of what could or should be trumps the present view of what exists.

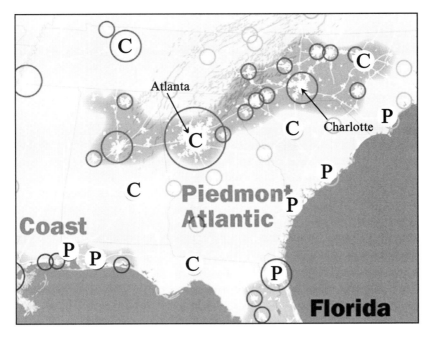

Source: derived from Regional Plan Association (2008).

Figure 2.6   The Piedmont Atlantic megaregion showing ports (P) and state capitals (C)

For this reason, it might be appropriate to refrain from defining the boundaries of a megaregion and instead to focus on planning for activities on a megaregional scale. This scale is somewhat fluid but seems to be defined by a competitive distance for high-speed rail or the limits of a productive one-day round trip in a car. One advantage of this approach is that areas that are not in any way megaregions, such as the northern Great Plains, might still find it appropriate to plan on a megaregional scale, because the scale of a megaregion can be overlaid on areas that are not megaregions by accepted criteria. In other words, where stakeholders find reason to work together, the collaboration should be encouraged and supported with planning tools.

Transportation Planning for Megaregions

The 2001 US National Household Travel Survey revealed that Americans traveled about 4.0 trillion miles (6.4 trillion km) in 2001 for daily trips and about 1.4 trillion miles (2.25 trillion km) for long-distance trips. These categories are not mutually exclusive; long-distance travel consists of trips that at some point reach a point greater than 50 miles (80 km) from home. In fact, 12.7 percent of long-distance trips were for commuting purposes, but the numbers demonstrate the magnitude of intercity travel. Of the 1.4 trillion miles (2.25 trillion km) of long-distance travel, the majority of the distance was traversed in private vehicles (as opposed to air travel), pointing to a need for surface transportation planning to address intercity travel (US Bureau of Transportation Statistics, 2003).

Much of this intercity transportation, especially transportation over private vehicle, rail and bus modes, is likely to be happening within megaregions. According to America 2050, more than 70 percent of the population and economic growth anticipated by 2050 is expected to be in megaregions. Some definitions of megaregions include a component of transportation scale. For instance, some state that megaregions can generally be traversed in a day's drive (Metcalf and Terplan, 2007).

A number of megaregion plans have been put together in the past few years, many of them by graduate students as part of educational experiences (Dewar and Epstein, 2007). While these developments have been interesting and valuable, they do not appear to have deeply penetrated planning practice yet. In addition, while virtually all megaregion planning discussions have identified transportation as an important piece of the megaregion puzzle, little research in the transportation field has been done on the topic. Because of the distances involved, most of the long-distance travel identified by the 2001 National Household Travel Survey likely left the confines of metropolitan planning area boundaries. In many places, this type of travel has likely crossed state lines as well. For these reasons, planning for megaregion transportation has challenged the current metropolitan- and state-based planning model.

Scales of transportation

To begin transportation planning for megaregions, or at megaregional scales, it is important to consider what types of transportation exist. Different researchers have described the issue of transportation scales in different ways. The I-95 Corridor Coalition has delineated four different scales of transportation (Ankner and Meyer, 2009):

- transportation within metropolitan areas
- within megaregions
- between nearby megaregions
- national and global flows of goods and people.

Others have expanded on the issue of scale within metropolitan areas. Guthrie (2007) described three different scales of passenger transportation, urban, metropolitan, and megaregion. Other research has also looked into the planning conflicts between local and regional transportation. This research also questions how megaregional scale transportation, such as high-speed rail, can fit into large regions, such as the California Bay Area, the Randstad, or the Bologna, Italy, region (Lowe, 2008).

Combing these discussions with the study of megaregion geography, six overlapping scales of transportation must be considered:

- urban/local
- metropolitan
- megapolitan
- megaregion
- between adjacent megaregions
- national and global linkages.

These designations describe a continuum rather than discrete categories. The following discussion distinguishes scale in terms of freight transportation.

- The most *local* of freight transportation are services like local deliveries provided by local business (such as pizza or flowers) or the local postal delivery.
- Much more freight transportation demand is describable at the *metropolitan* level. Retail inventory replenishment through metropolitan area warehouses is one example and the delivery of freight through services like Federal Express or United Parcel Service from their metropolitan distribution points is another. In many places, just-in-time supply chains operate at the metropolitan scale, but they also show up at the megapolitan scale. The boundary between metropolitan and megapolitan is especially difficult to distinguish in large metropolitan areas and areas where many metropolitan areas are nearby.
- *Megapolitan* freight transportation might be best described by the length of truck trip. Megapolitan freight is when a driver is able to make a few round trips in one day. Shipping container drayage is one megapolitan freight transportation service when a driver is only able to make two to three round trips a day.
- *Megaregional* freight transportation on the other hand is likely to include only one round trip or one-way trip per day for a trucker. For time-sensitive freight, most megaregional freight goes by truck,

as terminal time for rail container shipping makes rail shipping too time consuming.

- For transportation between megaregions and on a national scale, rail shipment becomes relatively more attractive. *National and global freight* shipping usually involves railroads and port facilities, including both airports and seaports.

Passenger transportation is somewhat easier to characterize using the continuum.

- *Local* transportation is short and everyday, such as shorter commutes and grocery shopping. On common carriers, these trips are likely to be urban transit.
- *Metropolitan* passenger transportation includes most commutes and more special trips, such as shopping at a regional mall. A common carrier example is commuter rail such as S-bahn systems in Germany and the RER in the Paris metropolitan region.
- *Megapolitan*-scale passenger transportation includes very long commutes, short business trips, and visits to people or events involving a more significant time investment. Long commuter rail, short intercity rail, and short intercity bus trips are examples. Rail systems such as the Amtrak Capitol Corridor in California, Regional-Express lines in Germany, and the Transilien system centered on Paris are examples of megapolitan-scale common carrier transportation.
- *Megaregional* scale transportation is the smallest scale at which some travelers begin to use commercial air travel, but most trips are still in automobiles. These trips involve a significant portion of a day's drive, but are unlikely to take more than one day. Where quality intercity passenger rail exists, this mode is appropriate for this type of travel. Passenger transportation between nearby megaregions is even more likely to be through air travel or a lengthy drive; a 'road trip'.
- *National or global* transportation is virtually all through air travel.

2.5   CONCLUSION

One of the most important geographic units of today's world is the megaregion, because it is the unit that functions in the global economy. A megaregion will by definition contain the functions that allow a place to participate in the global economy, including ports, airports, research and higher education institutions, government centers, commercial and financial strongholds, places for recreation and cultural destinations.

Transportation within megaregions is tasked with connecting these various functions together so they can work together. Instead of focusing energy on defining boundaries of a particular type of region, it is more valuable to think about the various scales of transportation that help to define the geographic scale. Some parts of the transportation system, such as major hub airports and shipping terminals are tasked with connecting a megaregion to the outside world. Improving megaregional-scale transportation requires improving linkages to the outside world as well as improving the ability to move people, goods, and services from place to place within the megaregion.

Another geographic unit is the megapolitan, which is a geographic region with strong internal cohesion, usually marked by significant overlapping commuting flows or semi-contiguous urbanization. Efforts to improve transportation within megapolitans seek to increase the agglomeration scales of being in a megapolitan and must acknowledge the implications of the new polycentric geography. Transit systems should move beyond a focus on the core of each metropolitan region to connect the entire region together in the way that most highway systems do. Improving transportation at the megapolitan scale effectively increases the talent pool available to employers. It also increases the number of universities it is possible for a person to attend without relocating. Transportation between megapolitans is effectively the same thing as transportation within megaregions.

Transportation planners should look at these emerging geographies through the lenses of the transportation systems that function best at each scale. At both scales, the goal is to increase accessibility and reduce transaction costs. At the megaregional scale, it is to connect various functions together. At the megapolitan scale, it is to increase agglomeration economies.

While some idea of boundaries might be helpful when planning transportation for both scales, well-delineated boundaries are not the most important input to the transportation planning process. Existing and potential trip purposes along with existing and potential land uses are the foundation. Indentifying how a particular type of transportation contributes to social and economic outcomes and improves a region's ability to function in the global economy is the next foundational step that must come before traditional transportation planning techniques such as alternatives analysis and travel demand forecasting.

ACKNOWLEDGMENTS

This work was funded in part from the Federal Highway Administration, US Department of Transportation. The views and opinions of the authors expressed herein do not necessarily state or reflect those of the Department.

REFERENCES

America 2050 (2004) *Minutes from the Meeting: Toward an American Spatial Perspective.* Hosted by Rockefeller Brothers Fund, Pocantico Conference Center, Tarrytown, www.america2050.org/pdf/ASDPminutes04.pdf (accessed 15 January 2010).
Anderson, C. (2004) The long tail, *Wired*, October, 170–77.
Ankner, W.D. and Meyer, M.D. (2009) Investing in megaregion transportation systems: institutional challenges and opportunities, in C.L. Ross (ed.), *Megaregions: Planning for Global Competitiveness.* Washington, DC, Island Press.
Blumenthal, H. (1983) Metropolis extended, *Journal of the American Planning Association*, 52, 346–48.
Bolan, R. and Peng, X. (2004) *Spatial Patterns of Information Workers in Six United States Metropolitan Areas.* Minneapolis University of Minnesota, Humphrey Institute of Public Affairs.
Bright, E. (2007) Viewpoint, *Planning*, 73, 46.
Bureau of Transportation Statistics (2003) *Highlights of the 2001 National Household Travel Survey.* Washington, DC, US Department of Transportation, Report: BTS03-05.
Calthorpe, P. and Fulton, W. (2001) *The Regional City.* Washington, Island Press.
Carbonell, A. and Yaro, R.D. (2005) American spatial development and the new megalopolis, *Land Lines*, 17, 1–4.
Carbonell, A., Pisano, M. and Yaro, R.D. (2005) *Global Gateway Regions.* New York, Regional Plan Association.
Cronon, W. (1991) *Nature's Metropolis: Chicago and the Great West.* New York, W.W. Norton & Company.
Dewar, M. and Epstein, D. (2007) Planning for 'megaregions' in the United States, *Journal of Planning Literature*, 22, 108–24.
Feser, E. and Hewings, G. (2007) US regional economic fragmentation and integration: selected empirical evidence and implications, in P. Todorovich (ed.), *The Healdsburg Research Seminar on Megaregions.* New York, Lincoln Institute of Land Policy and Regional Plan Association.
Fishman, R. (2007) *National Planning for America.* New York, Regional Plan Association.
Frey, W., Wilson, J., Berube, A. and Singer, A. (2004) *Tracking Metropolitan America into the 21st Century: A Field Guide to the New Metropolitan and Micropolitan Definitions.* Washington, DC, Brookings Institution.
Friedmann, J. and Miller, J. (1965) The urban field, *Journal of the American Institute of Planners*, 31, 312–19.
Garreau, J. (1991) *Edge City: Life on the New Frontier.* New York, Doubleday.

GaWC Research Network (2009) About us, www.lboro.ac.uk/gawc/group.html (accessed 18 February 2009).

Gottmann, J. (1961) *Megalopolis: The Urbanized Northeastern Seaboard of the United States*. New York, The Twentieth Century Fund.

Gottmann, J. (1966) Why the skyscraper? *Geographical Review*, 56, 190–212.

Guthrie, D.P. (2007) *Understanding Urban, Metropolitan and Megaregion Development to Improve Transportation Governance*, Virginia Polytechnic Institute and State University.

Jacobs, J. (1961) *The Death and Life of Great American Cities*. New York, Random House.

Jakle, J.A. and Wheeler, J.O (1969) The changing residential structure of the Dutch population in Kalamazoo, Michigan, *Annals of the Association of American Geographer*, 59, 441–60.

Lang, R.E. (2003) *Edgeless Cities: Exploring the Elusive Metropolis*. Washington, DC, Brookings Institution Press.

Lang, R.E. (2007) Defending megapolitans (letter to editor), *Planning*, 73, 52–3.

Lang, R.E. and Dhavale, D. (2005) Megapolitan areas: exploring a new trans-metropolitan geography. Metropolitan Institute Census Report Series. Alexandria, Metropolitan Institute at Virginia Techology.

Lang, R.E. and Nelson, A.C. (2007) Boomburb politics and the rise of private government, *Housing Policy Debate*, 18(3), 627–36.

Lim, U. (2003) The spatial distribution of innovative activity in US metropolitan areas: evidence from patent data, *The Journal of Regional Analysis and Policy*, 33, 97–126.

Lincoln Institute of Land Policy, Regional Plan Association, and the University of Pennsylvania School of Design (2004) *Toward an American Spatial Development Perspective: A Policy Roundtable on the Federal Role in Metropolitan Development*. New York, Regional Plan Association.

Lowe, C. (2008) Transit planning in polycentric regions: the challenge of scale, presentation at the Association of Collegiate Schools of Planning – Association of European Schools of Planning Fourth Joint Congress, Chicago, IL, paper #731.

Metcalf, G. and Terplan, E. (2007) History of the megaregion concept, sidebar from The Northern California megaregion, *Urbanist*, 466. San Francisco Planning and Urban Research, San Francisco.

Moss, M.L. and Townsend, A.M. (2000) The internet backbone and the American metropolis, *The Information Society*, 16, 35–48.

Muller, P. (1976) *The Outer City: Geographical Consequences of the Urbanization of the Suburbs*. Washington, DC, Association of American Geographers Resource Paper.

Pickard, J.P. (1962) Urban regions of the United States, *Urban Land*, 21, 3–10.

Pickard, J.P. (1966) US urban regions: growth and migration patterns, *Urban Land*, 25, 3–10.

Regional Plan Association (2006) *America 2050: A Prospectus*, New York: Regional Plan Association.

Regional Plan Association (2008) The Emerging Megaregions, www.america2050.org//sync/elements/america2050map.png (accessed 15 January 2010).

Ross, C.L. (2006) Piedmont Atlantic megaregion, presentation at the second annual policy roundtable on megaregional development, February, 2006, Atlanta, Center for Quality Growth and Regional Development, Georgia Institute of Technology.

Sassen, S. (1991) *The Global City: New York, London, Tokyo.* Princeton, Princeton University Press.

Sassen, S. (2006) *Cities in a World Economy,* 3rd ed. Thousand Oaks, Pine Forge Press.

Sassen, S. (2007) Megaregions: benefits beyond sharing trains and parking lots?, in K.S. Goldfeld (ed.), *The Economic Geography of Megaregions*, Princeton, Princeton University.

Spectorsky, A.C. (1955) *The Exurbanites*. Philadelphia, J. B. Lippincott.

Taylor, P.J. and Pain, K. (2007) Polycentric mega-city regions: exploratory research from western Europe, in P. Todorovich (ed.), *The Healdsburg Research Seminar on Megaregions*. New York, Lincoln Institute of Land Policy and Regional Plan Association.

Vance, J.E. Jr (1990a) *The Continuing City: Urban Morphology in Western Civilization.* Baltimore, Johns Hopkins University Press.

Vance, J.E. Jr (1990b) *Capturing the Horizon: The Historical Geography of Transportation since the Sixteenth Century.* Baltimore, Johns Hopkins University Press.

Vuchic, V.R. (2007) *Urban Transit: Systems and Technology*. Hoboken, John Wiley & Sons, Inc.

Zelinsky, W. (1992) *The Cultural Geography of the United States: A Revised Edition*. Englewood Cliffs, Prentice Hall.

3. The global economic crisis, investment in transport infrastructure, and economic development

Andrew R. Goetz

3.1 INTRODUCTION

On September 18, 2008, the Secretary of the US Treasury Henry Paulson and Federal Reserve Chairman Ben Bernanke held a meeting with leaders from the US Congress, informing them that without direct government intervention to save troubled financial institutions, the United States economy was in grave danger of a complete meltdown within a few days. The roots of this economic crisis lay in the subprime mortgage market, in which billions of dollars in toxic assets were packaged, re-packaged, and sold in ever-larger bundles to financial institutions which then ultimately became stuck with huge financial liabilities. After an initial bailout package was voted down, the US Congress soon thereafter approved a $700 billion federal bailout, authorizing the US Treasury Secretary to buy troubled assets from and provide capital injections to the major United States banks.

These actions helped to avoid a complete economic meltdown, but the scale of the problem nevertheless led to a global economic crisis, plunging the United States and many other countries around the world into a severe economic recession. The United States stock market plummeted from a high of over 14,000 in the Dow-Jones Industrial Average in October 2007 to a low of 7000 in December 2008. The United States gross domestic product declined at an annual rate of 6 percent during the last quarter of 2008 and the first quarter of 2009. The United States unemployment rate grew to over 10 percent by October 2009. Across the world, too, economic conditions worsened considerably. The annualized rate of decline in GDP based on the first quarter of 2009 was 14.4 percent in Germany, 15.2 percent in Japan, 7.4 percent in the UK, 9.8 percent in the Euro area, and 21.5 percent in Mexico (Baily and Elliott, 2009).

Facing such grim economic prospects, world leaders began to consider additional measures that could be taken to provide a stimulus to their ailing economies. In the United States, the crisis occurred during the 2008 presidential campaign, which saw Barack Obama elected as president in November 2008, replacing George W. Bush. Even though the crisis occurred while Bush was president, it would be up to Obama to lead efforts to address the fallout from the crisis.

During the immediate period after his election, the new Obama administration and Congressional leaders began to debate the merits of an economic stimulus package. From both politicians and the media, many comparisons were made between the current crisis and the Great Depression of the 1930s. President Obama himself invoked the spirit of Franklin D. Roosevelt and his New Deal policies, by suggesting that government would need to become more involved in helping to stimulate the economy. Many people expressed concern and outrage that the United States government provided $700 billion to bail out banks on Wall Street, but nothing was provided for struggling people and businesses on 'Main Street'.

Discussions about stimulus plans included consideration of investments in transportation and other critical infrastructure systems. Like many of FDR's New Deal employment programs, one of the main thrusts of a stimulus package was to invest in public works projects that would provide immediate employment, as well as short-term and long-term economic benefits. It was felt that transportation investment fit this prescription particularly well, especially in light of the backlog of projects in many states that had been delayed due to lack of funding.

Indeed, much of the discussion in transportation policy over the previous ten years had been focused on how to address a looming transportation infrastructure crisis. Due in part to massive increases in the volume of international trade, as well as continued population growth, congestion on the nation's highways, railways, sea ports, and airports grew worse each year, imposing costs that sapped economic productivity. Furthermore, many of the highways and bridges originally constructed during the early phases of the Interstate Highway System in the 1950s and 1960s needed to be upgraded or replaced because of their deteriorating condition. This reality was dramatically revealed by the I-35W bridge collapse in Minneapolis, Minnesota on August 1, 2007 in which 13 people died. After the onset of the economic crisis, Congressional and private sector leaders who had been voicing their concerns over the lack of investment in transportation infrastructure suddenly found a very receptive ear in the new Obama administration as a consensus began to emerge regarding the need for an economic stimulus package that featured 'shovel-ready' transportation projects.

There were others, however, who questioned the need for a government-sponsored stimulus, and raised doubts specifically about the efficacy of transportation investments in spurring economic growth. Citing especially the case of massive public works investment in Japan during the so-called 'lost decade' of the 1990s, critics claimed that many transportation projects turned out to be 'white elephants' that did not generate the expected economic benefits. From 1991 to 2008, Japan spent $6.3 trillion on construction-related public investment, including such projects as the $70 million Hamada Marine bridge that connected the city of Hamada to a small, sparsely-populated island (Fackler, 2009). Given Japan's lackluster economic performance during this period, critics warned of this lesson for other countries contemplating a similar strategy.

The divergence in viewpoint concerning the impacts of transport infrastructure investment on economic growth naturally invites the need for a deeper level of analysis. Accordingly, this paper revisits the conceptual, theoretical and empirical literature concerning the economic impacts of transport infrastructure investment. Following a similar methodology employed by Bhatta and Drennan (2003), an analysis of empirical studies over the past 20 years should reveal evidence to support or reject the hypothesis that investment in transport infrastructure results in long-term economic benefits. Also, one year after the implementation of the $787 billion American Recovery and Reinvestment Act (ARRA), early results from the transportation portion of this economic stimulus package will be discussed.

3.2   THEORETICAL AND CONCEPTUAL BACKGROUND

The relationship between transportation and economic growth has a long history and is well documented in academic publications. The exact nature of this relationship, however, is not altogether clear, especially when one examines the empirical literature.

Theoretically, transport infrastructure is expected to have both direct and indirect impacts on economic activity. Direct impacts come in the form of increased employment in transportation construction activity, travel time and cost savings that accrue to businesses and travelers, and reduction in the number of accidents from improvements in transportation infrastructure, among others. Indirect impacts are the secondary effects that result from improved transportation infrastructure, including: increased trade activity; new businesses, residences, and other development activity; and multiplier effects from expanded economic activity.

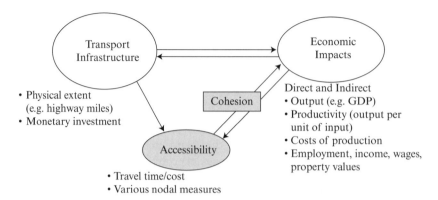

Figure 3.1   Linkages between transport and economic growth

The connection between transport and economic growth also has intermediate linkages in the form of accessibility and cohesion (Figure 3.1). Improvements in transport infrastructure should increase levels of accessibility between places, thus facilitating an increase in spatial inter-action and economic activity. As cities, regions, and states are brought closer together as a result of improved transport, these places should also become more cohesive across political, social, and cultural dimensions. The increased cohesiveness may also lead to a greater economic impact.

Commonly Used Measures

The relationship between transportation and economic growth has been assessed using a variety of metrics. Transport infrastructure is usually measured by either the physical extent of the system (e.g. highway miles or kilometers) or by the monetary investment in the system. Additional measures include those related to the concept of accessibility, such as travel time or travel cost as well as various indexes that measure the accessibility of one place (node) to all others within a given region (network). Economic growth has been measured by increases in economic output (e.g. gross domestic product), increases in productivity (output per unit of input), reductions in costs of production, and increases in employment, wages, income, property values, or land use intensity.

Complicating assessments of the transport–economic growth relation-ship are the two critical dimensions of geographic scale and historical timeframe of analysis. Empirical results can vary significantly based on the geographic scale (e.g. international, national, regional, metropolitan, city, or neighborhood) as well as the specific geographic context (e.g.

United States or Europe or Japan, rural or urban, and developed or developing country). Some studies assess the effects of national or regional transportation infrastructure broadly on economic growth while others may focus on the impacts of individual projects for specific places and/or firms (Apogee Research and Greenhorne & O'Mara, 1998). Likewise, the timeframe selected can influence results greatly, such as comparing periods of overall economic growth or periods of economic decline. Other things equal, it would not be unreasonable to assume that a stronger transport–economy relationship would be found in time periods when economic growth overall was much stronger.

One other complication is the bi-directionality between transport and economic growth. Whereas most studies assume the direction of causality is from transport infrastructure to economic growth, it is also apparent that economic growth itself creates more demand for transport infrastructure. Indeed, the arguments for making investments in transport infrastructure are bolstered by the demonstration of needs based on current and projected volumes of transport demand which result from increased population and economic activity.

Theoretical Foundations

There are several clusters of literature that have provided the theoretical support for the transport infrastructure–economic growth connection, as follows.

Microeconomic analysis

In the realm of microeconomic analysis, the focus is on the improved productivity of individual firms and/or consumers (Rietveld and Bruinsma, 1998; Lakshmanan, 2010). According to microeconomic theory, as the supply of transport infrastructure is expanded, the generalized cost per trip is reduced, and the number of trips increases. User benefits result from both cost reductions and the accommodation of an increased number of trips. The analytical method that has been used most often to measure these effects is cost–benefit analysis (CBA). Most planning studies that contemplate whether to build transport infrastructure attempt to account for all the direct and indirect costs and benefits of a project, and then determine if the project can be justified based on whether the benefits exceed the costs.

Macroeconomic analysis

The macroeconomic modeling approach theorizes that improvements in transport infrastructure reduce costs of production inputs (e.g. labor, materials, land) and expand overall economic output. The production function approach is most often used to measure these effects. This approach attempts to measure the aggregate output of the economy as a function of private factors of production (e.g. labor, capital, energy, materials) and public capital (e.g. transport, water, sewer, electricity infrastructure). Once relevant data are obtained and analyzed, it is possible to estimate the effect that any form of public capital investment has on economic output. A typical measure is the output elasticity that represents the percentage change in output for a 1 percent change in public capital (e.g. transport infrastructure) investment (Mikelbank and Jackson, 2000). A positive output elasticity suggests that public capital is contributing to economic output.

A related concept is the so-called 'crowding-in effect'. When public capital investment leads to increases in private capital, the crowding-in effect occurs. This can happen, for example, when infrastructure investments create a competitive advantage for a city or a region, thus attracting additional firms and private capital to the area. Likewise, if public capital investment reduces private capital, a crowding-out effect can occur whereby public investment forestalls private investment. The raising of public capital through tax increases or through the sale of bonds may result in a negative impact on private investment or consumption, thereby depressing economic growth (Rietveld and Bruinsma, 1998).

Transport and international/interregional trade and spatial interaction
This branch of literature stems from classical trade theory (Ricardo, Hecksher/Ohlin), and emphasizes the gains from trade that accrue as transport infrastructure development makes interaction possible between nations or regions. The role of transport in this regard was highlighted by Ullman (1956) who defines the three fundamental bases of spatial interaction: complementarity (supply–demand relations), intervening opportunities (competition effects), and transferability (e.g. transportation, communication infrastructure). In other words, trade between nations or regions will occur depending on whether there is a supply–demand basis for trade as a result of absolute or comparative advantage in factor endowments. The existence and volume of trade will also depend on the proximity and accessibility of other nations and regions that can act as competitors. Finally, trade can be expanded dramatically if new and improved transport links allow easier transferability. These dynamics apply not only to trade of physical commodities, but to any form of spatial interaction, for example passenger movements, telephone calls, internet connectivity.

Extensions from classical trade theory also suggest that as transport links are developed between nations, regions, or cities, changes in the size and structure of these economies will occur. In a simple abstract example of two regions that have no spatial interaction, each region must provide all of its needs itself, that is, a state of autarky would exist. This situation would require each region to allocate resources in such a way that necessary requirements in all economic sectors (agriculture, manufacturing, services, etc.) would be provided internally. But if a transport link is established between these regions, if a complementarity relationship exists, and if no intervening opportunities are present, interregional trade should increase. As trade begins and expands, each regional economy will begin to specialize in those economic sectors for which they possess absolute or comparative advantages. Because of different factor endowments (e.g. land, resources, capital) Region A may begin to devote more resources to manufacturing while Region B may be better suited to specializing in agriculture. Each regional economy will adjust to the evolving trade relationship, and expand production in certain economic sectors that may yield productivity increases due to economies of scale and other specialization effects. Furthermore, the overall size of the regional economies will increase because of the pooling of resources between the two regions and the more efficient use of those resources (Krugman, 1991; Taaffe et al., 1996).

Transport and industrial location: agglomeration, spillovers, core/periphery
Transport costs have traditionally been a major factor in industrial location. Classical industrial location theory (Weber, 1929; Hoover, 1948; Isard, 1956; Smith, 1981) postulates that industries will locate in places where transport costs of assembling raw materials and distributing finished products are minimized. Thus, proximity to materials and markets has historically been the driving factor behind industrial location. As transport improvements are made and transport costs decline, locational flexibility increases and additional factors such as availability and cost of labor, access to capital, site location costs, agglomeration economies, technological spillover effects, and firm preferences based on climate or other locational amenities have become more important in industrial location (Glaeser and Kohlhase, 2004). But even as transport improvements in speed and efficiency have changed the location decision process, transport still remains an important location factor.

In studies of firm location behavior, access to convenient and reliable transport is often one of the most highly cited location factors (Markusen et al., 1986; Chapman and Walker, 1991; van Dijk and Pellenbarg, 2000; Elgar and Miller, 2010). Industrial firms need to be close to highways, seaports, rail lines, and/or airports to be able to access needed materials and distribute products to customers. Frequent and convenient access to air transport is an especially important factor in the location of high-tech firms. Retail firms seek locations that maximize accessibility to their target markets, usually in high traffic volume corridors and major highway intersections. Office firms cite accessibility to clients and employees as key factors in their location decisions.

In many contemporary economic geography studies, especially those associated with the 'New Economic Geography' (Porter, 1990; Fujita et al., 1999), the role of transport in facilitating agglomeration economies, technological spillovers, and core/periphery dynamics helps to explain spatial patterns of economic activity. Transport infrastructure helps to provide a competitive advantage for certain regions that can become specialized industrial districts, characterized by a high density of complementary firms that benefit from agglomeration economies and technological spillovers. Industrial regions, such as the American Manufacturing Belt or Silicon Valley, emerged over time as highly competitive core centers for specialized production that propelled economic development. In these and other cases, transport infrastructure, and the accessibility it provided, played a leading role in the development of industrial clusters.

Transport and urban land use/values
At the scale of the individual urban area, there is a large body of literature that explains and illustrates how transport has helped to shape urban land use and land values (Alonso, 1964; Muth, 1969; Mills, 1972; Giuliano, 2004; Muller, 2004). With origins in the work of von Thunen on agricultural land use, urban land use theory relied on a monocentric model of the city that featured more intensive land use and land values near the central business district and a tapering of land use intensity with distance away from the center. The central business district has historically been the point of maximum accessibility, resulting in the most intensive land use and highest land values in the city. Other high land use/land value locations tend to be found at important transport intersections, such as along major road or rail arterials, and at highway interchanges. Furthermore, as transport improvements are made within the urban area, sites that previously had limited accessibility become ripe for new development, and the urban area expands outward to encompass these sites. It then becomes possible to trace historical periods of urban expansion related to eras of urban transport innovation from the small walking/horsecar city (up to the 1880s), the electric streetcar city (1890–1920s), the recreational automobile city (1920s–1940s), and the expansive automobile/highway city (1950s to today).

Historical models of transport network development and spatial economic theory

The extension of historical models to the national and international scale has emphasized the role that transport has played in shaping the settlement and development of whole regions (Hirschman, 1958; Taaffe et al., 1963; Borchert, 1967; Vance, 1986; Cronon, 1991). Some of these models illustrate how urban centers emerge and develop in new frontier areas as a consequence of transport network evolution. One of the key phases in national economic development is the opening of a 'penetration' higher-speed transport line linking two or more regions. A classic example is the Erie Canal completed in 1825 in upstate New York that represented the first major link between the United States Eastern Seaboard and the Midwest, conferring significant economic benefits for both regions and especially for New York City. Another example is how the city of Chicago benefited from its location as the hub of an extensive rail network that provided unparalleled access to materials and markets throughout the United States Midwest and Great Plains regions. Many other cities and regions throughout the world owe their existence to advantageous locations for transport and trade, and important decisions made to develop transport infrastructure.

The work of regional growth theorists (Perroux, 1955; Myrdall, 1957) introduced concepts such as growth poles, 'spread and backwash' spillovers, and bypass effects. By concentrating infrastructure development in key centers that could act as growth poles, it was believed that economic development could be generated through appropriate policies. In these scenarios, it is anticipated that economic growth from a growth pole would spill over into surrounding areas as part of positive economic 'spread' effects. In some instances, however, negative 'backwash' effects could occur in which human and capital resources from a surrounding region are attracted to a growth center, thus draining the outer areas of these resources. Thus, transport investments designed to stimulate economic growth in economically lagging regions could either stimulate or stunt regional growth, depending on these two potential outcomes. Economic impacts from transport infrastructure improvements can be very geographically specific with a strong distance decay effect. For example, new transport routes can breathe new economic life into a community, while the bypassed towns and cities can suffer deprivation that can lead to economic decline and a struggle for survival (Goetz and Bandyopadhyay, 2007).

3.3   REVIEW OF THE EMPIRICAL LITERATURE

The preceding overview of the theoretical literature relevant to the connection between transport and economic development provides a basis to consider the empirical literature conducted on this topic. First, the literature prior to 2000, is summarized, including the results of Bhatta and Drennan (2003) that focus on the period from 1989 to 1999. Following a similar approach, I analyze empirical studies from 1999 to 2009.

Summary of Pre-2000 Period

Early empirical studies of the role that transport plays in economic development focused on the impacts of large-scale programs, such as the United States Interstate Highway System (Adkins, 1959; Garrison et al., 1959; Mohring, 1961) or the Appalachian Development Highway System (Gauthier, 1973). Using variations of simple cost–benefit analyses, most of the studies from this period found that there were significant positive economic impacts from the highways, especially because they represented a major improvement in speed, time saved, and accessibility. There were also studies that evaluated the impact that urban transit lines had on land use and land values, although the results in these studies were more mixed (Allen and Boyce, 1974; Knight and Trygg, 1977; Lerman et al., 1978; Dvett et al., 1979).

Another branch of empirical research relied on the macroeconomic modeling approach using a production function framework to estimate the contribution of public capital, especially transportation infrastructure, towards economic growth and productivity. Mera (1973) was one of the first to show that investments in transport and communications had a substantial positive impact on output in the case of Japan from 1954 to 1963. Specifically, Mera used a production function to calculate output elasticities of 0.35 for manufacturing and 0.40 for the service sector, meaning that a 1 percent increase in infrastructure investment would yield a 0.35 percent increase in manufacturing output and a 0.40 percent increase in service sector output. Other subsequent studies (Blum, 1982; Ratner, 1983; Wigran, 1984; Eberts, 1986; Costa et al., 1987; Elhance and Lakshmanan, 1988) followed a similar approach and found more modest impacts but none of these studies generated much interest among mainstream macroeconomic analysts (Mikelbank and Jackson, 2000; Lakshmanan, 2010).

The level of interest dramatically increased with the publication of a study by Aschauer (1989). Using an aggregate Cobb-Douglas production function to analyze United States economic output from 1949 to 1985,

Aschauer came up with output elasticities of 0.39 for nonmilitary public capital and 0.24 for core public capital (i.e. highways, airports, utilities, mass transit and water and sewer systems), showing that public capital investment had a large positive impact on private sector output in the United States economy overall (Lakshmanan, 2010). Subsequent studies by Aschauer (1990) and Munnell (1990) found similar large positive economic effects from infrastructure investment for the United States during this time period. Furthermore, the practical implication of these studies was that a slowdown in United States economic growth since 1973 could be traced to lack of investment in public capital, especially infrastructure.

The Aschauer and Munnell studies were subject to numerous methodological and conceptual critiques, and a flurry of research ensued on this topic during the 1990s. Charges of spurious relations, lack of time-lag consideration, and uncertain direction of causality, among others, were made (Eberts, 1990; Eisner, 1991; Hulten and Schwab, 1991, 1993; Tatom, 1993; Gramlich, 1994). On the basis of these critiques and more sophisticated analyses, subsequent production function studies tended to find smaller or negligible positive impacts from public capital investment.

Bhatta and Drennan (2003) conducted a review of empirical literature on the economic benefits of public investment in transportation during the 1989–1999 period. Of the 40 studies they analyzed, 15 used a production function approach to calculate output elasticities with results ranging from +0.04 to +0.39, which represents positive impacts on economic output from transport infrastructure investment, but a relatively wide range of magnitude. Another nine studies calculated changes in costs of production due to transport infrastructure investment, with results ranging from −0.05 to −0.21, which supports the hypothesis that investment in transport infrastructure should reduce costs of production for firms. Changes in employment, income, wages, or property values were the focus of 14 studies, of which nine found a significant positive relation between public transport capital and economic benefit, three found no significant relation, and two found a negative relation. Another two studies calculated rates of return on public capital with results ranging from 4.9 to 7.2 percent for public capital compared to 8.65 percent for private capital. Bhatta and Drennan sought to test the hypothesis that 'public sector investments in transportation infrastructure result in long-term economic benefits on the production, or supply side, such as increased output, increased productivity, reduced costs of production, or increased income'. Their conclusion was that a preponderence of the studies reviewed could not reject the hypothesis.

Empirical Studies: 1999–2009

Following the approach of Bhatta and Drennan, I conducted a search using the ISI Web of Science to find 55 studies from 1999 to 2009 that provided empirical results concerning the relation between economic growth and transport infrastructure investment (Table 3.1). The studies covered a range of geographic contexts, from developed to developing countries at national, regional, and local scales over different time periods. Of the 55 studies, 43 found that investment in transport infrastructure had a positive impact on one or more measures of economic growth, while the other 13 studies found no impact or negative effects.

The findings revealed a wide variation in level of impacts, especially the numerical productivity elasticities attributed to transport and/or public capital. For example, a study by Demetriades and Mamuneas (2000) found an output elasticity of 1.03 for public capital in the United States for the period 1972–1991, while Pereira (2001) revealed an output elasticity of 0.257 for public capital in the United States for the period from the early 1960s to the late 1980s (Lakshmanan, 2010). Canning and Bennathan (2007) found a rate of return of 0.07 to paved roads in the United States in 1985 while Hulten (2007) found that the output elasticity for highways in the United States for 1970–1986 was not significantly different from zero.

Analyses comparing results across countries reveal even wider disparities. Middle-income developing countries (e.g. China, India) tended to exhibit greater positive impact change than developed countries. Canning and Bennathan (2007) found high rates of return to paved roads for South Korea (15.76), Colombia (9.47), Bolivia (7.96), the Philippines (7.19), and Chile (5.24), while the lowest rates of return were found for Australia (-0.01), Austria (0.00), Norway (0.02), Ireland (0.06) and Sweden (0.06). Many of the middle-income developing countries had significant infrastructure shortages which were stunting economic growth, thus new transport investment yielded a strong return. The marginal impact of new transport investment in already well-developed countries had much less of an effect.

An increasing number of historical studies on a longer-term, larger scale reveal a strong positive connection between transport and economic growth. Decker and Flynn (2007) found that railroads increased agricultural land values by 20 percent in the trans-Mississippi United States West during the 1800s, while Lakshmanan and Anderson (2007) cited the strong influence of the railroad in integrating the United States Northeast to the Midwest to form the United States Manufacturing Belt by the beginning of the twentieth century. Field (2006) discovered that United States manufacturing growth from 1919 to 1941 was significantly influenced

Table 3.1 Impacts of transportation infrastructure on economic development, summary of studies, 1999–2009

Author and Year	Transport Measure	Development Measure	Units of Observation	Results
Khadaroo & Seetanah 2009	transport investment	foreign direct investment (FDI)	33 African countries	(+) transportation contributed to relative attractiveness for FDI
Lopez, Monzon, & Ortega 2009	transport investment	accessibility improvements	Spain and border countries	(+) spillover benefits in France and Portugal from Spanish road and rail investments
Yamaguchi 2007	airport infrastructure	accessibility, GDP growth	47 Japanese prefectures	(+) significant productivity gains from improvement in air transport accessibility especially in agglomerated regions such as Tokyo due to deregulation and infrastructure improvements
Albala-Bertrand & Mamatzakis 2007	transport, electricity, and telecommunications infrastructure	productivity, cost savings	Chile, 1960–2000	(+) transport infrastructure investment contributed to cost savings in 1990s
Olsson 2009	road improvements	direct and indirect economic impacts	Philippines	(+) extensive direct effects and substantial indirect effects
de Bok 2009	accessibility, agglomeration	choice behavior of firms	South Holland province, Netherlands	(+) Significant influence

53

Table 3.1 (continued)

Author and Year	Transport Measure	Development Measure	Units of Observation	Results
Zou et al. 2008	roadway investment	economic growth, poverty alleviation	China, 1978–2002	(+) especially in poor rural areas
Ewing 2008	highway investment	growth and development	US metro areas	(-) Small net effects, close to zero-sum, (+) suburbs, (-) central cities
Siegesmund et al. 2008	maritime investment	economic output	Texas & US economy	(+) equilibrium model yields significant benefits
Gunasekera et al. 2008	highway investment	firm output, household income	Sri Lanka	(+) firm output >70 percent, output higher, more capital-intensive, and higher household income closer to highways
Kenny 2008	construction investment	economic output	developing countries	(-) corruption in construction
Keating 2008	investment	economic growth	Australia	(-) infrastructure crisis is overblown

Study	Variable	Outcome	Sample	Findings
Peterson & Jessup 2008	cumulative investment	employment, wages, establishments	counties in Washington state, US	(-) investment did little to alter already existing economic trends
Wu et al. 2008	Construction investment	GNP, employment	China	(+)
Hulten 2007	investment	productivity, output	US, India, Spain	dependent on level of economic development, (-) more developed countries had shift in location of development, (+) less developed countries had improvement in productivity efficiency and expansion in net output
Canning & Bennathan 2007	investment	aggregate output, rates of return	123 countries	(+) higher in middle-income countries, (-) rates of return on paved roads are on par with or lower than other forms of capital in most countries
Kopp 2007	investment	productivity	13 W European countries	(+) variance explains small part of productivity
Andersson & Andersson 2008	investment	productivity	historical	(+)
Sloboda & Yao 2008	public spending	commodity flows	48 US states, 1989–2002	(-) crowding out

Table 3.1 (continued)

Author and Year	Transport Measure	Development Measure	Units of Observation	Results
Gkritza et al. 2008	investment in specific projects	cost savings, productivity	Indiana, US	(+) adding lanes and new interchanges have significant impact
Khadaroo & Seetanah 2008	public capital	output	Mauritius, 1950–2000	(+) transport and non-transport public capital crowd-in private capital
Glass 2008	public expenditure	output, investment	US, 1959–2003	(+)
Lopez, Gutierrez, & Gomez 2008	investment	cohesion, accessibility	Spain, 1992–2004	(+) cohesion improvements for roads, regional disparities for rail
Graham 2007	investment	density of economic activity, productivity	UK	(+) agglomeration benefits from transport infrastructure
Ozbay et al. 2007	investment	output	counties in NY metro area, 1990–2000	(+) time lag effect between investment and output, spillover effects decrease with distance
Ihara & Machikita 2007	investment	economic growth	Japan	(-) political competition leads to overprovision of infrastructure and negative influence on rural development

Study	Infrastructure	Outcome	Region/Period	Findings
Lall 2007	transport and communication	regional growth	India	(+) signifcant determinants of regional growth, positive externalities from network expenditures made by neighboring states
Holl 2007	motorway investment	accessibility	Spanish municipalities, 1980–2000	(+) accessibility improves, especially for more peripheral regions
Decker & Flynn 2007	railroad expansion	land values	US trans-Mississippi west, 1800s	(+) railroads increased agricultural land values by 20 percent
Moreno & Lopez 2007	local and transport infrastructure	economic returns	Spain	(-) returns to local infrastructure greater than transport, negative spillovers across regions in transport capital investment
Berechman et al. 2006	investment	economic growth	US states, counties, municipalities	(+) strong spillover effects with respect to space and time, larger impacts at larger scales, benefits decline with length of lag time
Fedderke et al. 2006	investment	economic growth	South Africa, 1875–2001	(+) investment in infrastructure leads economic growth, growth impact is robust
Field 2006	investment in public infrastructure	manufacturing growth	US, 1919–1941	(+) manufacturing growth influenced by transport and public utility investment
Thomas 2006	Channel Tunnel project	economic growth	cross-channel Euroregion	(-) area on either side of Channel tunnel (Kent, Pas-de-Calais) benefited least

Table 3.1 (continued)

Author and Year	Transport Measure	Development Measure	Units of Observation	Results
Baird 2005	public capital, highway investment	output, productivity		(-) public capital output elasticities declining over time, (-) highways have negative economic spillover effects, (-) transport infrastructure subject to congestion that reduces productivity, (+) highways enhance productivity for manufacturing firms
Alam et al. 2005	investment	economic growth		(+) importance of time lag between investment and economic return
Pereira & Andraz 2005	investment	output, rate of return	Portugal	(+) public investment crowds-in private investment, 15.9 percent rate of return
Marr & Sutton 2004	roadway expansion	accessibility, economic activity	Purpecha region of Mexico	(+) more accessible towns have increased volume of goods produced and agglomeration economies
Gospodini 2005	urban transport infrastructure	urban development	12 European cities	(+) urban transport infrastructure may have a catalytic effect on development, redevelopment, and regeneration
Kancs 2005	rail and road investment	economic activity	Latvia	(+) rail more effective than road projects in promoting regional economic activity

Mikelbank 2005	transport investment	housing prices	Cuyahoga county, Ohio, US, 1995–2000	(−) impacts of transport investments on housing prices can be positive or negative
Alam et al. 2004	transport investment	economic efficiency, rate of return	Bangladesh	(+) higher rate of return from transport investment in less-efficient regions
Kawakami & Doi 2004	port capital	GDP, private capital, transport costs	Japan, 1966–1997	(+) significant impact
Yoshida & Fujimoto 2004	airport investment	economic efficiency	Japan	(−) smaller, regional airports are less efficient, especially those built in 1990s
Cantos et al. 2005	transport investment	spillover effects, regional growth	Spain	(+) strong spillover effects
Holl 2004	motorway investment	agglomeration economies, firm birth	Portugal, 1986–1997	(+) motorways increase attractiveness of locations close to new infrastructure, more diverse local economy leads to firm births
Deichmann et al. 2004	transport investment	economic structure, productivity	Southern Mexico	(+) stronger economic structure and productivity effects
Shirley & Winston 2004	highway investment	economic returns		(−) returns from highway investment <5 percent and falling due to inefficient policies
Hodge et al. 2003	highway investment	business formation	North country, New York, US	(+)

Table 3.1 (continued)

Author and Year	Transport Measure	Development Measure	Units of Observation	Results
Bollinger & Ihlanfeldt 2003	highway investment	employment	Atlanta, Georgia, US	(+) highway improvements increase a census tract's share of employment
Kim 2002	transport capital stock	economic growth, transport costs	Korea, 1975–1992	(+) higher levels of transport capital stock leads to higher economic growth and lower transport costs, underprovision of transport reduced by 4.6 percent
Demurger 2001	transport investment	economic growth	Chinese provinces, 1985–1998	(+) transport is key differentiating factor in explaining regional growth disparities
Chandra & Thompson 2000	highway investment	transport costs, economic activity	US counties	(+) reduced transport costs, some industries grow and some decline due to relocation, positive impacts in county where highway is located, no or negative impacts on surrounding counties
Henderson 1999	transport investment	rural development		(+) transport infrastructure facilitates hinterland development
Groote et al. 1999	transport investment	output	Netherlands, 1853–1913	(+) transport infrastructure 'caused' Dutch economic growth

by transport and public utility investment. In an historical study of the Netherlands, Groote et al. (1999) found that transport infrastructure 'caused' Dutch economic growth from 1853–1913, while Summerhill (2001, 2005) identified enhanced productivity and increased specialization from railroad development in Brazil and Argentina in the late 1800s and early 1900s.

The results overall underscored the importance of geographic and historic context in understanding and interpreting the relation between transport and economic growth. Most of the studies found a positive relation, but because there is such a wide range in results, it is vital that contextual factors be fully understood in any evaluation. One of the key factors is the catalyzing effect of 'breakthrough' transport technology investment on economic growth, especially in countries well positioned for an economic take-off. Transport infrastructure is a necessary ingredient in the recipe, but that by itself will not result in a significant impact. Likewise, where the transport technology is not of 'breakthrough' caliber, or where transport infrastructure is already well developed, economic returns will be minimal or non-existent.

Among the studies that concluded there is no positive economic impact from transport infrastructure investment, the main arguments could be summarized as:

1. Public investment is inherently wasteful; all investment should be private.
2. Public investment could be more productive if government was more efficient (e.g. ineffective policies, byzantine funding structures, bloated costs, corruption).
3. Other needs (education, health care, social services) are more important.
4. There are negative spillovers on adjacent regions (zero-sum effect).
5. Transportation investment (especially highways) has negative impacts on the environment (energy consumption, sprawl, open space and habitat encroachment).

Considering more specifically the case of Japan from the 1990s, some empirical studies showed that many 1990s projects were unnecessary and wasteful (Yoshida and Fujimoto, 2004; Ihara and Machikita, 2007), while others found positive benefits from Japanese infrastructure investment (Kawakami and Doi, 2004; Yamaguchi, 2007). In comparing Japan and the United States, other commentators noted that Japanese government investment has historically been much higher than many other countries, including the United States, and that the United States has a much greater backlog of needed transportation infrastructure (National Surface Transportation Policy and Revenue Study Commission, 2007).

3.4 AMERICAN RECOVERY AND REINVESTMENT ACT OF 2009 (ARRA)

The debate about transport infrastructure investment became a pressing policy issue for a number of countries in the wake of the onset of the global economic crisis. Some countries, including the United States, decided to invest in transport infrastructure projects as part of an economic stimulus package to reduce unemployment and generate increased economic activity.

On February 17, 2009, soon after his inauguration, President Barack Obama signed the American Recovery and Reinvestment Act (ARRA) into law in Denver, Colorado. The ARRA included $787 billion in tax cuts, expansion in unemployment benefits, and investments in education, health care, and infrastructure. Included in the infrastructure category was $48.1 billion for transportation, including:

- $27.5 billion for highways and bridges
- $8.4 billion for transit
- $8.0 billion for high speed rail
- $1.3 billion for Amtrak
- $1.5 billion for National Surface Transportation Discretionary Grants.

As of January 29, 2010, over 12,000 transportation projects totaling $33.9 billion have been obligated (United States Department of Transportation, 2010). Many of these projects have been for highways, bridges, and public transit systems, and had been previously identified by state departments of transportation and regional transit agencies as 'shovel-ready' projects that had already gone through environmental review. The states with the largest funding amounts for transportation projects include California (1041 projects at $3.58 billion), Texas (491 projects; $2.26 billion), New York (493 projects; $2.25 billion), Florida (612 projects; $1.62 billion), Illinois (804 projects; $1.41 billion), and Pennsylvania (351 projects; $1.39 billion).

While it is still too early to determine the full economic impact of investments in these transportation projects, the U.S. House of Representatives Transportation and Infrastructure Committee estimates that over 280,000 jobs have been created or sustained as a result of projects funded by the ARRA (Smart Growth America, 2010). By contrast, the Associated Press analyzed stimulus spending and found that local unemployment rates were unchanged by investments in highway and bridge projects. They concluded that 'a surge in spending on roads and bridges has only barely helped the beleaguered construction industry' (Apuzzo and Blackledge, 2010). In response, US Department of Transportation Secretary Ray LaHood argued that the relevant comparison should be in transportation construction employment, not all construction employment. LaHood (2010) and the American Association of State Highway and Transportation Officials (2010) noted that spending on highway and street construction was up by 5.7 percent in one year and other public transportation construction was up 18.8 percent, while spending for construction was down by 13 percent over the last year. And, they argued that this additional spending was having a positive effect on local economies that have been hard hit by the economic crisis.

3.5 SUMMARY

Governments of countries gripped in the throes of economic crisis have considered various strategies to help stimulate economic growth and reduce unemployment. One area that has received much attention historically in such circumstances, as well as in contemporary times, is investment in public infrastructure, particularly transportation. Diverse viewpoints expressed during recent debates in the United States over the efficacy of investment in transportation infrastructure as part of an economic stimulus package underscore the need for a deeper level of analysis.

On the basis of reviewing the historical and recent literature concerning the economic impacts of transport infrastructure investment, it was found that there is relatively strong theoretical and empirical support for positive economic benefits from transport infrastructure investment. The theoretical foundations in the literature from microeconomic analysis, macroeconomic analysis, trade, industrial location, urban land use, and historical models all contribute to a deeper understanding of the variety of ways in which transport positively affects economic growth. A review of the recent empirical literature shows that a sizeable majority of studies from 1999–2009 found that investment in transport infrastructure had a positive impact on one or more measures of economic growth. A minority of studies found neglible or negative economic impacts from transport infrastructure investment, arguing that private capital investment would yield greater returns than public capital, among other explanations.

Findings also revealed a wide variation in level of impacts, especially the numerical productivity elasticities attributed to transport and/or public capital. There is a considerable amount of variation in results depending on geographic area of analysis, whereby already developed countries tend to have lower impact estimates in comparsion to middle-income developing countries. There is also considerable variation depending on the time periods under analysis.

Some of the conclusions drawn from this research are that transport infrastructure alone will not guarantee economic success, but that the positive stories of the effects of transport investment are more common than the negative ones. This is particularly true when looking at case-by-case examples, especially those that are historically-based. Historical periods of economic take-off in many cases can be linked to investments in advanced transport systems that significantly improved regional accessibility, thus producing a quantum leap forward in economic growth and productivity. The spin-off or multiplier effects from these improvements rippled through the regional and national economies, creating a basis for long-term sustainable growth.

The lessons from this research for contemporary debates over the economic values of transport infrastructure investment are that the benefits tend to be more long-term in nature, and that they depend on the specific context within which the investments are being made. If transport investments are being made in developed countries with already well-developed transport systems (for example, Japan in the 1990s) then the expected economic impacts should not be overwhelming. If, however, investments are made in middle-income developing countries on the verge of economic take-off with real transport infrastructure needs (for example, China in the 2000s) then the impacts may be quite significant.

In the case of the 2009 economic stimulus package for the US in the wake of the global financial crisis, it is still too early to gauge the full economic impacts of the transport infrastructure investment. While the number of transport construction jobs created or saved has been small relative to the national unemployment rate, the transport funding has had a positive impact on specific cities and regions. Furthermore, given the backlog of transport infrastructure needs within the US, especially the replacement of 1950s Interstate Highway System bridges such as the I-35W bridge in Minneapolis, it would seem that transport infrastructure investments in the US today should yield long-term economic benefits.

REFERENCES

Adkins, W. (1959) Land value impacts of expressways in Dallas, Houston, and San Antonio, Texas, *Highway Research Bulletin*, 227, 50–65.
Alam, J.B., Sikder, S.H. and Goulias, K.G. (2004) Role of transportation in regional economic efficiency in Bangladesh – data envelopment analysis, *Transportation Research Record*, 1864, 112–20.

Alam, J.B, Sikder, S.H. and Goulias, K.G. (2005) Assessing the time lag between transportation investment and economic development by the data envelopment approach, *Transportation Research Record*, 1932, 79–88.

Albala-Bertrand, J.M. and Mamatzakis, E.C. (2007) The impact of disaggregated infrastructure capital on the productivity growth of the Chilean economy, *Manchester School*, 75, 258–73.

Allen, W. and Boyce, D. (1974) Impact of a high speed rapid transit facility on residential property values, *High Speed Ground Transportation Journal*, 8, 53–60.

Alonso, W. (1964) *Location and Land Use*. Cambridge, MA, Harvard University Press.

American Association of State Highway and Transportation Officials (2010) *Reaction to AP Analysis on Economic Recovery Spending*. http://news.transport ation.org/press_release.aspx?Action=ViewNews&NewsID=281/ (accessed 24 February 2010).

Andersson, D.E. and Andersson, A.E. (2008) Infrastructural change and secular economic development, *Technological Forecasting and Social Change*, 75, 799–816.

Apogee Research, Inc and Greenhorne & O'Mara (1998) *Research on the Relationship between Economic Development and Transportation Investment*. National Cooperative Highway Research Program Report 418, Transportation Research Board. Washington, DC, National Academy Press.

Apuzzo, M. and Blackledge, B.J. (2010) *Stimulus Watch: Unemployment Unchanged by Projects*. Associated Press, 11 January 2010. http://abcnews. go.com/Business/wirestory?id=9527995&page=1/ (accessed 24 February 2010).

Aschauer, D.A. (1989) Is public expenditure productive?, *Journal of Monetary Economics*, 23, 177–200.

Aschauer, D.A. (1990) Is government spending stimulative?, *Contemporary Policy Issues*, 8, 30–46.

Baily, M.N. and Elliott, D.J. (2009) *The US Financial and Economic Crisis: Where Does It Stand and Where Do We Go From Here?*, Washington, DC, The Brookings Institution.

Baird, B.A. (2005) Public infrastructure and economic productivity: a transportation-focused review, *Transportation Research Record*, 1932, 54–60.

Berechman, J., Ozmen, D. and Ozbay, K. (2006) Empirical analysis of transportation investment and economic development at state, county and municipality levels, *Transportation*, 33, 537–51.

Bhatta, S.D. and Drennan, M.P. (2003) The economic benefits of public investment in transportation – a review of recent literature, *Journal of Planning and Education and Research*, 22, 288–96.

Blum, U. (1982) Effects of transport investments on regional growth: a theoretical and empirical investigation, *Papers of the Regional Science Association*, 49, 169–84.

Bollinger, C.R. and Ihlanfeldt, K. (2003) The intraurban spatial distribution of employment: which government interventions make a diference?, *Journal of Urban Economics*, 53(3), 396–412.

Borchert, J.R. (1967) American metropolitan evolution, *Geographical Review*, 57, 301–32.

Canning, D. and Bennathan, E. (2007) The rate of return to transportation infrastructure, in *Transport Infrastructure Investment and Economic Productivity: Report of the One Hundred and Thirty Second Round Table on Transport Economics*. Paris, OECD and ECMT.

Cantos, P., Gumbau-Albert, M. and Maudos, J. (2005) Transport infrastructures, spillover effects and regional growth: evidence of the Spanish case, *Transport Reviews*, 25, 25–50.

Chandra, A. and Thompson, E. (2000) Does public infrastructure affect economic activity? Evidence from the rural interstate highway system, *Regional Science and Urban Economics*, 30, 457–90.

Chapman, K. and Walker, D.F. (1991) *Industrial Location: Principles and Policies*. Oxford, Blackwell.

Costa, J.D.S., Ellison, R.W. and Martin, R.C. (1987) Public capital, regional output and development: some empirical evidence, *Journal of Regional Science*, 27, 419–437.

Cronon, W.G. (1991) *Nature's Metropolis: Chicago and the Great West*. New York, W.W. Norton.

de Bok, M. (2009) Estimation and validation of a microscopic model for spatial economic effects of transport infrastructure, *Transportation Research A*, 43, 44–59.

Decker, C.S. and Flynn, D.T. (2007) The railroad's impact on land values in the upper great plains at the closing of the frontier, *Historical Methods*, 40, 28–38.

Deichmann, U., Fay, M. and Koo, J. (2004) Economic structure, productivity, and infrastructure quality in Southern Mexico, *Annals of Regional Science*, 38, 361–85.

Demetriades, P. and Mamuneas, T.F. (2000) Intertemporal output and employment effects of public infrastructure capital: evidence from 12 OECD countries, *Economic Journal*, 110, 687–712.

Demurger, S. (2001) Infrastructure development and economic growth: an explanation for regional disparities in China?, *Journal of Comparative Economics*, 29, 95–117.

Dvett, M., Dornbusch, D., Fajans, M., Fackle, C., Gussman, V. and Merchant, J. (1979) Land use and urban development impacts of BART (Final Report No. DOT-P-30-79-09, U.S. Department of Transportation and U.S. Department of Housing and Urban Development). San Francisco, Blayney Associates and Dornbusch and Co.

Eberts, R.W. (1986) *Estimating the Contribution of Urban Public Infrastructure to Regional Growth*. Working paper No. 8610, Federal Reserve Bank of Cleveland.

Eberts, R.W. (1990) Public infrastructure and regional economic development, *Economic Review*, 26, 15–27.

Eisner, R. (1991) Infrastructure and regional economic performance: comment, *New England Economic Review*, September/October, 47–58.

Elgar, I. and Miller, E.J. (2010) How do office firms conduct their location search process? An analysis of a survey from the Greater Toronto Area, *International, Regional Science Review*, 33, 60–85.

Elhance, A.P. and Lakshmanan, T.R. (1988) Infrastructure–production system dynamics in national and regional systems: an econometric study of the Indian economy, *Regional Science and Urban Economics*, 18, 513–31.

Ewing, R. (2008) Highway-induced development research results for metropolitan areas, *Transportation Research Record*, 2067, 101–109.

Fackler, M. (2009) Tokyo's wasted trillions buy a costly lesson, *International Herald Tribune*, 6 February.

Fedderke, J.W., Perkins, P. and Luiz, J.M. (2006) Infrastructural investment in long-run economic growth: South Africa 1875–2001, *World Development*, 34, 1037–59.

Field, A.J. (2006) Technological change and US productivity growth in the inter-war years, *Journal of Economic History*, 66, 203–36.

Fujita, M., Krugman, P. and Venables, A. (1999) *The Spatial Economy*. Cambridge, MA, MIT Press.

Garrison, W.L., Berry, B.J.L., Marble, D.F., Nystuen, J.D. and Morrill, R.L. (1959) *Studies of Highway Development and Geographic Change*. US Bureau of Public Roads of the Department of Commerce and the Washington State Highway Commission. Seattle, University of Washington Press.

Gauthier, H.L. (1973) The Appalachian Development Highway System: development for whom?, *Economic Geography*, 49, 103–108.

Giuliano, G. (2004) Land use impacts of transportation investments: highway and transit, in S. Hanson and G. Giuliano (eds), *The Geography of Urban Tranportation*. New York, The Guilford Press.

Gkritza, K., Sinha, K.C., Labi, S. and Mannering, F. (2008) Influence of highway construction projects on economic development: an empirical assessment. *Annals of Regional Science*, 42, 545–63.

Glaeser, E.L. and Kohlhase, J.E. (2004) Cities, regions and the decline of transport costs, *Papers in Regional Science*, 83, 197–228.

Glass, A. (2008) Public expenditure on transport and macroeconomic performance: empirical evidence from the United States, *International Journal of Transport Economics*, 35, 121–43.

Goetz, A.R. and Bandyopadhyay, S. (2007) Regional development impacts of trade corridors: recent experiences from the United States, in D. Gillen, G. Parsons and B. Prentice (eds), *Canada's Asia Pacific Gateway and Corridor Initiative: Policy Trade and Gateway Economics* (Volume 1). Centre for Transportation Studies, University of British Columbia.

Gospodini, A. (2005) Urban development, redevelopment and regeneration encouraged by transport infrastructure projects: the case study of 12 European cities, *European Planning Studies*, 13, 1083–11.

Graham, D.J. (2007) Agglomeration, productivity and transport investment, *Journal of Transport Economics and Policy*, 41, 317–43.

Gramlich, E.M. (1994) Infrastructure investment: a review essay, *Journal of Economic Literature*, 32, 1176–96.

Groote, P., Jacobs, J. and Sturm, J.E. (1999) Output effects of transport infrastructure: the Netherlands, 1853–1913, *Tijdschriuft voor Economische en Sociale Geografie*, 90: 97–109.

Gunasekera, K., Anderson, W. and Lakshmanan, T.R. (2008) Highway-induced development: evidence from Sri Lanka, *World Development*, 36, 2371–89.

Henderson, J.V. (1999) Overcoming the adverse effects of geography: infrastructure, health, and agricultural policies, *International Regional Science Review*, 22, 233–7.

Hirschman, A.O. (1958) *The Strategy of Economic Development*. New Haven: Yale University Press.

Hodge, D.J., Weisbrod, G. and Hart, A. (2003) Do new highways attract businesses? Case study for North County, New York, *Transportation Research Record*, 1839, 150–58.

Holl, A. (2004) Transport infrastructure, agglomeration economies, and firm birth: empirical evidence from Portugal, *Journal of Regional Science*, 44, 693–712.

Holl, A. (2007) Twenty years of accessibility improvements: the case of the Spanish motorway building programme, *Journal of Transport Geography*, 15, 286–97.

Hoover, E. (1948) *The Location of Economic Activity*. New York, McGraw-Hill.

Hulten, C.R. (2007) Transportation infrastructure, productivity and externalities, in *Transport Infrastructure Investment and Economic Productivity*. Report of the 132nd Round Table on Transport Economics. Paris, OECD and ECMT.

Hulten, C.R. and Schwab, R.M. (1991) Public capital formation and the growth of regional manufacturing industries, *National Tax Journal*, 44, 121–134.

Hulten, C.R. and Schwab, R.M. (1993) Infrastructure spending: where do we go from here?, *National Tax Journal*, 46, 261–73.

Ihara, R. and Machikita, T. (2007) Voting for highway construction in economic geography, *Annals of Regional Science*, 41, 951–66.

Isard, W. (1956) *Location and the Space Economy*. Cambridge, MA, MIT Press.

Kancs, D. (2005) Efficiency of European funds in the accession countries: the case of transport infrastructure investments in Latvia, *Transportation Planning and Technology*, 28, 293–313.

Kawakami, T. and Doi, M. (2004) Port capital formation and economic development in Japan: a vector autoregression approach, *Papers in Regional Science*, 83, 723–32.

Keating, M. (2008) Infrastructure: what is needed and how do we pay for it?, *Australian Economic Review*, 41, 231–8.

Kenny, C. (2008) Transport construction, corruption and developing countries, *Transport Reviews*, 29, 21–41.

Khadaroo, J. and Seetanah, B. (2008) Transport and economic performance: the case of Mauritius, *Journal of Transport Economics and Policy*, 42, 255–67.

Khadaroo, J. and Seetanah, B. (2009) The role of transport infrastructure in FDI: evidence from Africa using GMM estimates, *Journal of Transport Economics and Policy*, 43, 365–84.

Kim, E. (2002) Determinants of optimal level of transportation infrastructure, *Journal of Urban Planning and Development – ASCE*, 128, 150–63.

Knight, R.L. and Trygg, L. (1977) *Land Use Impacts of Rapid Transit: Implications of Recent Experiences*. Final Report No. DOT-TPI-10-77-29, US Department of Transportation. San Francisco: DeLeuw Cather and Co.

Kopp, A. (2007) Macroeconomic productivity effects of road investment – a reassessment for Western Europe, in *Transport Infrastructure Investment and Economic Productivity: Report of the One Hundred and Thirty Second Round Table on Transport Economics*. Paris: OECD and ECMT.

Krugman, P. (1991) *Geography and Trade*. Leuven, Belgium, Leuven University Press and Cambridge, MA, The MIT Press.

LaHood, R. (2010) AP misses the transportation stimulus forest for the trees. http://www.whitehouse.gov/blog/2010/01/11/ap-misses-transportation-stimulus-jobs-forest-trees/ (accessed 24 February 2010).

Lakshmanan, T.R. (2010) The broader economic consequences of transport infrastructure investments, *Journal of Transport Geography*, 19, 1–12.

Lakshmanan, T.R. and Anderson, W.P. (2007) Transport's role in regional integration processes, in *Market Access, Trade in Transport Services and Trade Facilitation*, Round Table 134. Paris, OECD-ECMT.

Lall, S.V. (2007) Infrastructure and regional growth, growth dynamics and policy relevance for India. *Annals of Regional Science*, 41, 581–99.

Lerman, S., Damm, D., Lerner-Lamm, E. and Young, J. (1978) *The Effect of the Washington Metro on Urban Property Values*. Final Report CTS-77-18, US

Department of Transportation, Urban Mass Transportation Administration. Cambridge, MA, MIT Center for Transportation Studies.

Lopez, E., Gutierrez, J. and Gomez, G. (2008) Measuring regional cohesion effects of large-scale transport infrastructure investments: an accessibility approach, *European Planning Studies*, 16, 277–301.

Lopez, E., Monzon, A. and Ortega, E. (2009) Assessment of cross-border spillover effects of national transport infrastructure plans: an accessibility approach, *Transport Reviews*, 29, 515–36.

Markusen, A., Hall, P. and Glasmeier, A. (1986) *High Tech America: The What, How, Where, and Why of the Sunrise Industries*. Boston: Allen & Unwin.

Marr, P. and Sutton, C. (2004) Impacts of transportation changes on the woodworking industry of Mexico's Purpecha region, *Geographical Review*, 94, 440–61.

Mera, K. (1973) Regional production functions and social overhead capital: an analysis of the Japanese case, *Regional and Urban Economics*, 3, 157–186.

Mikelbank, B.A. (2005) Be careful what you wish for – the house price impact of investments in transportation infrastructure, *Urban Affairs Review*, 41, 20–46.

Mikelbank, B.A. and Jackson, R.W. (2000) The role of space in public capital research, *International Regional Science Review*, 23, 235–58.

Mills, E.S. (1972) *Studies in the Structure of the Urban Economy*. Baltimore: Johns Hopkins University Press.

Mohring, H. (1961) Land values and the measurement of highway benefits, *Journal of Political Economy*, 79, 236–49.

Moreno, R. and Lopez, E. (2007) Returns to local and transport infrastructure under regional spillovers, *International Regional Science Review*, 30, 47–71.

Muller, P.O. (2004) Transportation and urban form: stages in the spatial evolution of the American metropolis, in S. Hanson and G. Giuliano (eds), *The Geography of Urban Tranportation*. New York, The Guilford Press.

Munnell, A.H. (1990) Why has productivity declined? Productivity and public investment, *New England Economic Review*, January/February, 3–22.

Muth, R. (1969) *Cities and Housing*. Chicago, University of Chicago Press.

Myrdall, G.A. (1957) *Economic Theory and Underdeveloped Regions*. London, Duckworth.

National Surface Transportation Policy and Revenue Study Commission (2007) *Transportation for Tomorrow*. Washington, DC.

Olsson, J. (2009) Improved road accessibility and indirect development effects: evidence from rural Philippines, *Journal of Transport Geography*, 17, 476–83.

Ozbay, K., Ozmen, D. and Berechman, J. (2007) Contribution of transportation investments to county output, *Transport Policy*, 14, 317–29.

Pereira, A.M. (2001) On the effects of public investment on private investment: what crowds in what?, *Public Finance Review*, 29, 3–25.

Pereira, A.M. and Andraz, J.M. (2005) Public investment in transportation infrastructure and economic performance in Portugal, *Review of Development Economics*, 9, 177–96.

Perroux, F. (1955) La notion de pole de croissance, *Economie Appliquee*, 8, 307–14.

Peterson, S. and Jessup, E. (2008) Evaluating the relationship between transportation infrastructure and economic activity: evidence from Washington State, *Journal of the Transportation Research Forum*, 47(2), 21–39.

Porter, M. (1990) *The Competitive Advantage of Nations*. New York, Free Press.

Ratner, J.B. (1983) Government capital and the production function for US private output, *Economic Letters*, 13, 213–17.

Rietveld, P. and Bruinsma, F. (1998) *Is Transport Infrastructure Effective? Transport Infrastructure and Accessibility: Impacts on the Space-Economy.* Berlin, Springer-Verlag.

Shirley, C. and Winston, C. (2004) Firm inventory behavior and the returns from highway infrastructure investments, *Journal of Urban Economics*, 55, 398–415.

Siegesmund, P., Luskin, D., Fujiwara, L. and Tsigas, M. (2008) A Computable General Equilibrium model of the US Economy to evaluate maritime infrastructure investments, *Transportation Research Record*, 2062, 32–8.

Sloboda, B.W. and Yao, V.W. (2008) Interstate spillovers of private capital and public spending, *Annals of Regional Science*, 42, 505–18.

Smart Growth America (2010) http://www.smartgrowthamerica.org/stimulus2009.html/ (accessed 24 February 2010).

Smith, D.M. (1981) *Industrial Location: An Economic Geographical Analysis.* New York, Wiley.

Summerhill, W.R. (2001) *Profit and Productivity on Argentine Railroads, 1857–1913.* Los Angeles, UCLA Department of History.

Summerhill, W.R. (2005) Big social savings in a small laggard economy: railroad-led growth in Brazil, *Journal of Economic History*, 65, 72–102.

Taaffe, E.J., Gauthier, H.L. and O'Kelly, M.E. (1996) *The Geography of Transportation*, 2nd ed., Upper Saddle River, Prentice Hall.

Taaffe, E.J., Morrill, R.L. and Gould, P.R. (1963) Transport expansion in under-developed countries: a comparative analysis, *The Geographical Review*, 53, 503–29.

Tatom, J.A. (1993) The spurious effect of public capital formation on private sector productivity, *Policy Studies Journal*, 21, 391–95.

Thomas, P. (2006) Images and economic development in the cross-channel Euroregion, *Geography*, 91, 13–22.

Ullman, E.L. (1956) The role of transportation and the bases for interaction, in W.L. Thomas (ed.), *Man's Role in Changing the Face of the Earth.* Chicago, University of Chicago Press,

United States Department of Transportation (2010) American Recovery and Reinvestment Act of 2009, http://www.dot.gov/recovery/ (accessed 24 February 2010).

Vance, J.E. Jr. (1986) *Capturing the Horizon: The Historical Geography of Transportation Since the Transport Revolution of the Sixteenth Century.* New York, Harper and Row.

van Dijk, J. and Pellenbarg, P.H. (2000) Firm relocation decisions in the Netherlands: an ordered logit approach, *Papers in Regional Science*, 79, 191–219.

Weber, A. (1929) *Alfred Weber's Theory of the Location of Industries.* Chicago: University of Chicago Press.

Wigran, R. (1984) Productivity and infrastructure: an empirical study of Swedish manufacturing industries and their dependence on regional production milieu, in F. Snickars, B. Johansson and T.R. Lakshmanan (eds), *Economic Faces of the Building Sector.* Stockholm, Swedish Building Institute.

Wu, A., Eisa, M., Fengxia, L. and Liu, X. (2008) *Economic Contribution Rate Analysis of Chinese Transportation Infrastructure Construction: Based on the Input-Output Data Sheet in 2002.* Conference Proceedings Paper, ASCE.

Yamaguchi, K. (2007) Inter-regional air transport accessibility and macro-economic performance in Japan, *Transportation Research E*, 43, 247–58.

Yoshida, Y. and Fujimoto, H. (2004) Japanese-airport benchmarking with the DEA and endogenous-weight TFP methods: testing the criticism of overinvestment in Japanese regional airports, *Transportation Research E*, 40, 533–46.

Zou, W., Zhang, F., Zhuang, Z.Y. and Song, H. (2008) Transport infrastructure, growth, and poverty alleviation: empirical analysis of China, *Annals of Economics and Finance*, 9, 345–71.

4. Distance in the existence of political pathologies: rationalized transport policies and trade

Nihan Akyelken

4.1 INTRODUCTION

The sensitivity of international trade flows to distance is often examined through freight transport costs, although the inclusion of these costs in trade analysis is relatively new. Furthermore, it is seldom sufficiently sophisticated to account for the complexities involved in policy-making either by the authorities that provide transport infrastructure and regulate the system, or trade ministries that have wider responsibilities for such things as currency systems and factor mobility. This becomes more relevant as international agreements on climate change are gaining importance and are affecting transportation, and as individual nations are required to contribute to the meeting of global emissions targets.

Early economic theory explaining international trade largely ignored transport costs, which was in contrast to economic geography models that put emphasis on spatial factors that eventually affect transport costs and, with them, migration and trade-flows. Economic geography has stressed the importance of economic and distance-related factors when explaining trade preferences, and the dispersion of industrial activity by recognizing that transport costs are one of the main determinants of trade and economic growth variations. As concerns about the environment are increasingly shaping national policies, there is a growing perception that more account needs to be taken of the unanticipated longer-term effects of negative environmental externalities on transport services and trade patterns.

Furthermore, transport policies do not necessarily follow a 'rational path'. Political pathologies[1] in policy-making arise as a result of the deviations from socially optimum decisions. In other words, decision-makers do not necessarily take rational decisions, but rationalize their decisions that would compensate their supporters through various means. Because transport is highly politicized due to the existence of its externalities, its nature as being essential for citizens and the fact that it requires long-term commitments (Thatcher, 2007), the consideration of political pathologies, which are ignored in theoretical explanation of trade patterns, become highly relevant.

Here, a conceptual understanding of the consideration of politicized policy-making in trade and spatial economic activity, and more specifically, political pathologies in transport policy-making is proposed. Furthermore, a conceptual solution from an institutional perspective is suggested. The main argument concerns rational-as-rationalized transport policies, particularly in relation to mitigating climate change and how they are neglected in the consideration of trade.

4.2 INTERNATIONAL TRADE AND TRANSPORT COSTS 'IN A BELL JAR'

In the *Wealth of Nations*, Adam Smith introduces the concept of absolute advantage. According to the theory, if country A produces good x at a lower cost than country B does, then country B should import good x from country A, and vice versa. David Ricardo then argued that the concept of absolute advantage does not suffice to explain trade, and he presented the comparative advantage theory. A country is said to have a comparative advantage in the production of a good if it can produce the good at a lower opportunity cost than another country. Ricardo showed that countries should specialize in goods for which they have a comparative advantage in their production. In the 1920s, Hecksher-Ohlin trade models (H-O models) brought new dimensions to international trade by pointing to the number of factors of production. The Ricardian models assume that labor is the only one factor of production; whereas the H-O model points out that there are in fact two factors; capital and labor. The H-O theorem says that a capital-abundant country will export capital-intensive goods and the labor-abundant country will export labor-intensive goods. The theorem ignores transport costs in international trade. It also has not always stood up well to empirical analysis. Leontief, for example, demonstrated that the American economy relied upon skilled labor, not on physical capital, over which it has a comparative advantage.

Finally, the use of gravity models for trade became popular in 1950s. In the simplest form, these show that trade volumes between two countries are directly proportional to the ratio of the product of the sizes of the two countries and the distance between them. Frankel (1997) later developed the model to elucidate the formation of trading blocks. The common feature of the early models was that they largely ignore transport costs. New economic geography models introduced the idea of economies of scale and transport costs to examine the relationship between location and trade. Eaton and Kortum (2001) also brought geographical dimensions to trade models, carrying out an empirical application of the Ricardian model addressing the issues of gains from trade, trade reduction, and the role of trade in spreading technology.

In sum, trade models first focused on factors of endowments and trade tariffs. They then took into account geographical distances. Ricardian and H-O models comply with the former, and the new economic geography models with the latter explanation.

The inclusion of transport costs required a more theoretical tool such as Samuelson's (1952) iceberg formulation of transport costs (ITC function henceforth). Adding spatial factors, new economic geography models made more use of this formulation in explaining trade directions. McCann (2005) summarizes the use of iceberg formulation when looking at the empirical deficiencies of the new economic geography models. According to him, the formulation states that if a good is shipped from an origin to a destination, only a fraction of the goods will reach the destination. In other words, the transport cost function looks at the cost of 'crossing the spatial distance between origin and destination, and considers space as a barrier to economic activities such as trade' (Medda, 2007). This suggests that space is considered only as part of physical capital rather than a living component of economic activity dispersion that involves human interactions. The new economic geography (Krugman, 1991) changes the assumptions of the original Samuelson function by turning the ITC function into a geographical distance-related function. This new model implies that there are now two groups of constraints on long distance freight: trade tariffs and distance-related costs. Illustrating the ITC function for new economic geography models as a continuous function, McCann concludes that the marginal costs of transport increase with distance and the value of the good.

4.3 RATIONALITY-AS-RATIONALIZATION IN TRANSPORT POLICY

As part of a debate on the validity of social science explanations used in public policy, rational choice is used for both refutation and affirmation of theories. Its incorrect use in social sciences and the subsequent effects on scientific evidence based policy-making may be so influential that almost nothing lacks a 'justification': the misuse of the notion of rational choice explanation provides decision-makers with explanations they need to substantiate their decisions.

Given well-founded beliefs and desires, which exist inevitably or not, rational actions require logical consistency between these interrelated concepts. When choosing between alternatives or acts followed by the relevant choices, rationality plays an important role by decimating the choices extraneous to the main motivation. While the significance of rationalist approaches in science brought clear illustrations of the reality as a means to model human beings and social currents, many others involved in the philosophy of social sciences have realized that rationality alone would not bring humanity to an explicable material footing with physical science explanations as there are no laws governing social currents. The validity of this argument still remains open to debate. Nevertheless, the inevitability of key impediments to rationality such as humans' instant inclinations, values, and social surroundings, adversely affect consistency and stability of their actions, simultaneously leading to a lack of scientific explanation of social currents. This value-informed pragmatism gains even more importance at a macro-level: individual rationality is not always a microcosm of the rational bonds at social and political level; therefore things get even more complicated when macro policies are expected to be rational, while the mechanism that is supposed to bring it about is not yet identified.

Given an objective, a motivation and a desired outcome, a policy is supposed to be a means to reach the end prescribed by scientific evidence. The United Nations glossary points out that English language usage treats policies as decisions since they are 'made' and 'implemented' in the same way that decisions are made and implemented.[2] The International Livestock Research Institute (1995) adds that '. . . yet it is possible to have policies that are not or cannot be implemented [and vice versa], so that, conceptually, actions that implement policies [which makes it even more complicated] need not necessarily be part of policy itself.'

Elster's (1994) description of a rational choice would apply to policies as follows: a rational explanation of a policy choice would show that it is the best way of satisfying the full set of the public's needs and wishes, given the best beliefs the public could form about their needs and wishes, relatively to the uniquely determined optimal amount of theoretical and empirical evidence. Rationality requires the objective and the motivation of a policy to be consistent.

Measures supporting the motivation of providing for the well-being of citizens of the welfare state are said to be rational. However, policies are not necessarily rational, because governments do not just solve market failures; they have their own objectives and they reward their supporters and penalize their opponents. Robinson (2005) calls this deviation from the policies dictated by a social planning problem, a political pathology. He further claims that even when one considers an environment with both market failures and political failures, 'it is highly unlikely that the optimum will be a corner solution with zero government intervention'.

A question arises: to what extent are short-term and medium-term transport policies free of ideological bias, *de facto* political power, and long-lasting institutions and are resistant to a tendency for clientelism? And to what extent does this affect the nature of transport costs, which are so far recognized as natural and objective constraints in international trade models?

Pierre Bourdieu's (1977) notion of habitus helps to demonstrate the issue at an individual level and illustrates the relationship between reasons that consist of beliefs and desires and actions by showing that social facts, which include social norms, upbringing, and events in one's surroundings, affect our behaviors through our minds. So, the sequence is this. There exists a social fact. This is acquired by the agent and this, apparently has a good deal of effect on his/her behavior. According to Bourdieu, habitus, 'an acquired system of generative schemes objectively adjusted to the particular conditions in which it is constituted', is embodied in human beings, because it is inside their head, it depends on any sort of social interaction. In the process of producing an action, the habitus is produced by or in line with the objective patterns of social life. It usually functions according to a social field; therefore it can dispose different actions according to the social field and can be transformed by altered expectations. Bourdieu claims that action is caused by society in which the agent makes his/her body a part of it, and after that society and social orders originate from these physical actions.

The same reasoning applies to policy-makers: it is almost inevitable that they are affected by their political goals, ideological bias and populist tendencies. This influence may extend further so that they might get discouraged to ration, and encouraged to rationalize.[3] As Flyvbjerg (2003) states 'Rationality may become rationalization under the influence of power . . . and power blurs the dividing line between rationality and rationalization', and this is often used by policy-makers. He points out that policy-makers do need rationalization to stay in power and they do not really have to be rational by claiming that 'Rationalization presented as rationality is a principal strategy in the exercise of power'.

For instance, in 1980, the goal of Turkish transport policy was summarized as 'to introduce rationality into transportation decision making, to minimize the intermodal imbalances and to develop an integrated system by seeking to use the existing infrastructure most efficiently and to optimize the benefits from future investments' (Szyliowicz, 2004). Turgut Özal, the Turkish prime minister, followed an American oriented path, and this led his government to ignore the intermodal balances and to develop an extensive motorway system. Szyliowicz even quotes him saying that 'railways are for communists, highways for capitalists'. Although economic rationality is not totally ignored in this case given the conditions, this illustrates how the political path of the governments may affect their decision-making.

4.4   THEORY MEETS REALITY

Environmental sustainability, international trade and freight transport are closely connected. Increasing concerns over potential impacts of climate change have led countries to implement policies aimed at reaching specific quantitative targets set at the international level. For instance, the Kyoto Protocol Agreement requires the European Union (EU) to reduce greenhouse gas (GHG) emissions by 8 percent between 2008 and 2012 and under COP-16 the EU has pledged to decrease its emissions by 30 percent by 2020. The Sixth Environmental Action Programme (6th EAP) sets out the EU's priority actions for 2002 to 2012. The actions to tackle climate change in the 6th EAP are aimed at reaching targets set by the Kyoto Protocol and were hammered out as EU and national policies by the member states embracing a variety of measures, including revising the emissions trading system, increasing efforts for reductions outside of the trading system, and providing proposals on CO_2 emissions from vehicles. Transport is a major generator of GHGs and is included in the welfare analysis of climate change, but also has more localized regional and local environmental impacts.

As a broad supporter of international climate change agreements, the EU has taken actions that respond to targets set by the agreement. The EU Greening Transport Package (European Commission, 2008) is one of the recent actions in the area. The main strategies of this package are to ensure that the prices of transport better reflect their real cost to society through the means of charging. If implemented, these policies are likely to have impacts on road freight transport. However, the way they are implemented and the level of customization are left to policy-makers that are subject to political pathologies.

The importance of appropriate pricing/taxation, as suggested by the EU Greening Transport Package to make the best use of transport infrastructure is not new. Because the access to roads is not determined by markets, for an efficient use of them, there is a case for charging to ensure optimal flows (Button and Vega, 2008). There has been a long debate about whether road haulage pays its share of the costs of providing road infrastructure (Powel, 2001). Since the publication of the 1995 Green Paper, *Towards Fair and Efficient Pricing in Transport* (European Commission, 1995), the internalization of external costs of transport has been an important concern on the EU policy agenda (Jorna and Zuiver, 2009). Market failure occurs for a variety of reasons, such as the exercise of market power by monopolists or, and of increasing concern, where social costs differ from private costs due to ill-defined property rights. The strict economic principle requires correction of this type of market failure through the full allocation of property rights, although measures such as road pricing and carbon taxation may offer good second best approaches.

Environmental pricing can pose problems, however, particularly when there are distributional concerns that the countries that adopt lower prices can enjoy competitive advantages in international trade. For instance, countries with mandatory vehicle emission reduction policies may have to compete with exports from countries that are not obliged to implement such policies and thus have lower costs of production through freight transport costs. This may, in turn, have impacts on trade and on the spatial distribution of economic activity. Understanding of such an impact requires a knowing about the process of policy-making under these international agreements and the impact of the process itself. Although the costs of sustainability requirements may seem additional constraints on international trade through freight transport costs, politicizing the decisions through misuse of evidence has even more significant implications. The conceptual reasoning explains how this may occur.

Policy-makers intervene in the market with the aim of closing the gap that *laissez-faire* markets fail to fill. Under the name of the welfare state, governments try to correct these failures through policies, which are a form of government regulation; for example, internalization of external costs in transport paves the way for charging and taxation policies. Because of the very long-term implications of climate change, it is an atypical case. Nordhaus (1991) called it 'the granddaddy of all public goods', and peculiarities of welfare analysis become more apparent. It has distinctive features rendering policy measures more political. Giddens' (2009) paradox states that the issue is a unique feature: the public prefers to do very little since the impact is not yet very visible and will be pronounced only in the long term when, however, it may be too late to take action against it. In addition to the impacts concerned with the long term, the extent and the nature of uncertainties, the global scope of the issue, the uneven distribution of the policies, benefits and costs across space and time, and the need for a collective action and its pervasiveness are other distinctive features of the issue.

The work on the welfare analysis applicable to climate change policies is abundant and diverse. Nordhaus (1991, 1993) took the lead by focusing on climate change policies' uncertain features. Stern (2007) draws attention to the severe impacts of climate change by quantifying it in terms of percentage of GDP. Goulder (1992) looks at the measurement of welfare cost of preceding distortions in the economy through the interactions with other taxes. Overall they all suggest sustainability policies may involve highly politicized elements that are not tangible.

In addition to the peculiarities of the welfare analysis for climate change, transport has even more features rendering it subject to political pathologies. Due to its main role as the facilitator for how we choose to live with each other, transport can become highly politicized. The sole motivation behind government intervention in the transport sector is ostensibly to correct market failures through policy measures, such as the internalization of external costs and regulatory measures. In reality, there are also governments' own incentives to compensate their supporters through clientelistic ties and to penalize their opponents, and this may well end up in the decision-making process, but be hidden in the written rationale of a policy. This way, rationality is veered into rationalization at the point of using power. When emphasizing the importance of regulatory institutions in network industries, Thatcher (2007) points to the strategic interactions involved in network industries. The identification of certain features of network industries sheds light on how transport can become highly politicized.

First, transport infrastructures are generally large-scale capital investments. This causes investors and governments to face the danger of expropriation of returns as the government will tend to yield more returns for social expenditure and the problems of credible commitment as long-term premises lack credibility, respectively. Secondly, Thatcher points out that the necessity of transport for citizens may lead to politically rational decisions. The 'need' for transport services suggests that government has to provide them. Meanwhile, voters seek good services and low prices. This may lead to direct and cross-subsidization of transport by governments. Thirdly, regarding externalities, their positive effects may involve economic growth and increased accessibility and communication, while negative externalities embrace, along with other things, environmental damage and negative distributional impact, that is, emissions and noise from road and rail transport and, in terms of pecuniary externalities, the distributional aspects of charging policies. These market failures may require higher levels of interaction between the economic agents, who are all under the influence of the same national and/or regional policy. The fourth feature is that most transport industries are partly natural monopolies, and that this leads suppliers to have market power. This is the most important feature of the network industries that Thatcher provides as it has a significant impact on the introduction of new technologies. When new technologies are introduced, it is usually recognized as a positive development as it is beneficial both for the government and the public. The problem of standardization arises in having an integrated system of application. However, in so doing, *de facto* monopolies could be created as such a system involves private network, the states, the public and several other economic agencies that have both common and conflicting interests. For instance the EU Directive (2004/EC/52) for interoperability of a road charging implementation system sets common standards for road and toll charging policy among the EU-27 to reduce costs of implementation and transport. However, with the enforcement of the Directive, it could be that the provider of satellite navigation and microwave systems for the German heavy goods vehicle electronic tolling system enjoys a monopoly, to ensure consistency of service. Finally, information asymmetries between governments and suppliers cause transport to be even more susceptible to political pathologies.

Overall, international climate change agreements require nations to implement policies considerably affecting transportation, and the implementation of transport policy measures may not be based on pure welfare analysis, as policy-makers' interests are inevitably cultivated in the decision-making process. There are various regulatory issues involved with transport policy-making and it has distinctive features rendering its welfare analysis more politicized under sustainability requirements.

4.5   LESSONS LEARNED

Going back to the definition of policy, O'Riordan and Jordan (1996) claim that policy is shaped by existing organizational structures, as well as by informal networks of communication, that in turn are the product of values, norms and expectations. The impossibility of turning these into operational study variables that can be tangible so as to avoid such political pathologies requires building a strong institutional base for the democracy where policy decisions are made, and this suggests a conceptual alternative of avoiding the involvement of political pathologies in defining the impact of policies on trade patterns.

When examining the impact of geography on economic development, Easterly and Levine (2003) include policy and institutions as the two separate factors. Rodrik (2003) criticizes this by pointing out that policy is a 'flow variable' and institutions are a 'stock variable'. His conclusion that 'the primacy of institutional quality does not imply policy ineffectiveness' holds strong as well-built institutions are formed through effective policies, and vice versa; therefore it is almost impossible to regard them as two separate factors.

It is very tempting to highlight institutions as 'the rules of the game' (North, 1990) emphasizing that 'institutions rule all other factors in bringing economic development' (Rodrik, 2003). However, one should go even further and look into the correlation between policies and institutions as it may have significant implications for the impact of policies and for the policy-making process. One needs to see how well, if at all, the role played by institutions is correlated with the phase of institution-building in a country with the help of temporary policies and vice versa. This is important as institutions are the only way forward to avoid the impact of rational-as-rationalized policies that may affect the international trade through transport costs and eventually economic development. This key link and how institutions arise suggest some solutions to avoid political pathologies.

Institutions arise according to the way preferences are aggregated, and at the very centre there are two main factors, namely political power, and persisting traditions and social norms, which leads to the question of whose preferences count.

The two aspects of the political power of the state should be distinguished: contract theory of the state and the predatory theory of the state (North, 1981). According to the first theory, the state and associated institutions provide the legal framework that enables private contracts to facilitate economic transactions. According to the predatory theory, the state is an instrument for transferring resources from one group to another (Acemoğlu, 2009). For instance, in a transport infrastructure decision-making situation, the first theory of the state dictates the decisions to reduce the cost of transport and eventually goods and passenger transport. The second theory tells us that in such a situation, the state should take into account the distribution of the investments' benefits, which should be guided by the pre-existing institutions. This shows that the impact of political pathologies is highly correlated by properly defining the tasks of a democratic state, involving both providing welfare for its citizens including sustainability targets set by climate change agreements and providing a competitive environment that reduces the 'friction of distance' in money and in environmental terms.

Secondly, Acemoğlu and Robinson (2006) constructed a model of simultaneous change and persistence in institutions. This consists of landowning elites and workers, and the key economic decision concerns the form of economic institutions regulating the transaction of labor. The main assumption is that equilibrium economic institutions are a result of the exercise of *de jure* and *de facto* political power. A change in political institutions leads to the distribution of *de jure* political power, but the elite can intensify their investments in *de facto* political power, such as lobbying, to compensate for the loss of *de jure* power. This might lead to a different equilibrium in economic institutions, showing that there is always a possibility that traces of past institutions can be preserved, and may affect the way that institutional frameworks are built. The overall argument is that institutions are not exogenous or historically predetermined, but persist for long periods of time. This historically natural tendency of political decisions can be utilized to overcome the adverse effects of political pathologies in transport policy-making. Looking at the EU member states, we see that they do not implement policies shaped by the EU directives as it is. They usually modify them depending on their structure. Therefore, policy innovations might differ from country to country as the formation of institutions follow different paths. This suggests that strong democratic institutional regimes may be less vulnerable to political pathologies.

4.6 CONCLUSION

This chapter has shown how transport costs can be incorporated in trade models by employing Samuelson iceberg transport cost function but that there are complications involved with policy-making. Increasing concerns with climate change have encouraged governments to take measures against global warming including limiting emissions and energy consumption by transport. Under these circumstances, the way the relationship between international trade flows in the absence of adequate consideration of political motivation can be criticized.

We have demonstrated a conceptual lack of understanding of politicized policy-making in trade models and offered a solution from an institutional perspective. There is still a great deal of work remaining to be done to examine how changes in transport policy, and *ipso facto* transport costs, will eventually impact on trade. This is potentially important as transport is likely to be significantly impacted by the increasing awareness of environmental issues and upcoming international climate change agreements. Finally, institutional structures are inevitably important in linking transport, trade, and the environment.

From a policy stand-point, the analysis has been based on the premise that national policies should be carefully designed to be effective in their impact and that would seem to call for a strong institutional base with a clear identification of the impacts of sustainability requirements on freight transport costs avoiding political pathologies.

NOTES

1. This term has been coined by Robinson (2005).
2. http://www.ilri.org/html/trainingMat/policy_X5547e/x5547e05.htm.
3. Strictly, rationalization means giving acceptable reasons for actions, but is sometimes used for giving reasons for inappropriate acts. People tend to find rationalizations for their existence, unacceptable acts, mistakes, etc. However, what we usually see is 'rationalizing the government policies'.

REFERENCES

Acemoğlu, D. (2009) *Lecture Notes for Political Economy of Institutions and Development*. Cambridge, MA, MIT.

Acemoğlu, D. and Robinson, J.A. (2006) Persistence of power, elites and institutions, CEPR Discussion Papers, Centre for Economic Policy Research.

Bourdieu, P. (1977) Cultural reproduction and social reproduction, in J. Karabel and A.H. Halsey (eds), *Power and Ideology in Education*. New York, Oxford University Press.

Button, K. and Vega, H. (2008) Road user charging, in S. Ison and T. Rye (eds), *The Implementation and Effectiveness of Transport Demand Management Measures*. Aldershot, Ashgate Publishing.

Eaton, J. and Kortum, S. (2001) Technology, geography and trade, *Econometrica*, 70, 1741–79.

Easterly, W. and Levine, R. (2003) Tropics, germs, and crops: how endowments influence economic development, *Journal of Monetary Economics*, 50, 3–39.

Elster, J. (1994) The nature and scope of rational-choice explanation, in M. Martin and L. C. McIntyre (eds) *Readings in the Philosophy of Social Science*. Cambridge, MA, MIT Press.

European Commission (1995) *Towards Fair and Efficient Pricing in Transport*. COM (95)691, Brussels.

European Commission (2008) *Communication from the Commission – Greening Transport*. COM (2008)433, Brussels.

Flyvbjerg, B. (2003) *Rationality and Power*. Oxford, Blackwell.

Frankel, J. (1997) *Regional Trading Blocs in the World Economic System*. Washington, DC, Institute for International Economics.

Giddens, A. (2009) *The Politics of Climate Change*. Cambridge, Polity Press.

Goulder, L.A. (1992) Do the costs of a carbon tax vanish when interactions with other taxes are accounted for? NBER Working Paper 4061.

International Livestock Research Institute (1995) *Livestock Policy Analysis*. ILRI Training Manual 2. Nairobi, Kenya, ILRI.

Jorna, R. and Zuiver, H. (eds) (2009) Relevance of EU and national policies on long distance freight transport in Europe and examples of key demonstration projects. Freightvision Deliverables. S. Helmreich, Vienna.

Krugman, P. (1991) *Geography and Trade*. Cambridge, MA, MIT Press.

McCann, P. (2005) Transport costs and new economic geography, *Journal of Economic Geography*, 5, 305–18.

Medda, F. (2007) Free from tyranny: the impact of spatial attributes on the transport cost function, available at http://sadapt.inapg.inra.fr/ersa2007/papers/633.pdf.

Nordhaus, W.D. (1991) A sketch of the economics of the greenhouse effect, *American Economic Review, Papers and Proceedings*, 81, 146–50.

Nordhaus, W.D. (1993) Rolling the 'DICE': an optimal transition path for controlling greenhouse gases, *Resource and Energy Economics*, 15, 27–50.

North, D.C. (1981) *Structure and Change in Economic History*. New York, Norton.

North, D.C. (1990) *Institutions, Institutional Change and Economic Performance*. New York, Cambridge University Press.

O'Riordon, T. and Jordan, A. (1996) Social institutions and climate change, in T. O'Riordan and J. Jäger (eds), *The Politics of Climate Change: A European Perspective*. London, Routledge.

Powel, T. (2001) *The Principles of Transport Economics*. London, PTRC, Training for Transport.

Robinson, J.A. (2005) Politician-proof policy?, *Desarrollo y Sociedad*, 55, 1–56.

Rodrik, D. (2003) Institutions, integration, and geography: in search of the deep determinants of economic growth, in D. Rodrik (ed.), *In Search of Prosperity: Analytic Country Studies on Growth*. Princeton, Princeton University Press.

Samuelson, P. (1952) The transfer problem and transport costs: the terms of trade when impediments are absent, *Economic Journal*, 62, 278–304.

Stern, N. (2007) *Stern Review: The Economics of Climate Change*. London, HM Treasury.

Szyliowicz, J.S. (2004) Turkey's surface transportation policy and sustainable development, *Middle Eastern Studies*, 40, 23–44.

Thatcher, M. (2007) Europe and the reform of national regulatory institutions, in R. Hancke, M. Rhodes and M. Thatcher (eds), *Conflicts and Complementarities: Institutional Change in European Capitalism*. Oxford, Oxford University Press.

5. Access to rail in urban areas: examination of the number of stations

Moshe Givoni and Piet Rietveld

5.1 INTRODUCTION

Policy makers and railway operators share a similar goal, increasing the use of rail, whether to meet policy goals, such as improved accessibility, or to improve the railways' financial viability. Key factors in rail use are the number and location of railway stations and their catchment area, the focus of this chapter. Based on earlier research findings, it is now recognized that to increase rail use and encourage a shift from private road transport to rail transport, attention must be focused not only on improving the rail journey but also on the station environment and, equally important, the journey to and from the station (Givoni and Rietveld, 2007). The findings in past research, in essence, underline the need to consider a rail journey as a 'chain' of journeys from door to door. Rail operators, should, therefore, consider the whole chain as part of the service they provide.

There are two ways to increase the quality of such trip chains: the railway trip itself can be improved, or access to the railway system can be made better. Brons et al. (2009) found that reducing the distance to the station, has the most potential in increasing rail use in this context, and this entails changes in the rail network itself in the form of opening new stations. Other means of improvements in station accessibility, including shortening travel times and increasing service frequency by public transport to and from stations were also found to be statistically significant.

Increasing the number of railway stations within a city will shorten the access journey to the railway station, and it may reduce congestion in crowded railway stations. It also, however, has a number of adverse effects. Building new stations is costly, especially in dense urban areas where land values are high. In addition, more stations will entail longer travel times for passengers passing through, but not using, the new stations. Finally, spreading a given level of demand over a larger number of stations can result in diseconomies as not all stations would be able to offer the same level of service in terms of number of destinations directly served and the frequency of service. Reducing the number of stations has essentially the opposite effect.

From a policy and rail operation perspective, attention must be given to the organization of railway stations serving a particular urban area, accounting for local transport infrastructure and service provision. Given that a rail journey in most cases requires a journey to and from the station by different modes, the main issue from the passengers' perspective is the penalty or benefit, of changing the distance to the railway station by altering the number of stations.

5.2   THE OPTIMAL NUMBER OF TRANSFER POINTS IN A NETWORK

Making a trip generally involves the use of one or more vehicles (train, bus, car) and some walking. The distance to be walked from a point of departure (e.g. home, work or shop) to a vehicle depends on the number of access points available, which differ by mode. Examples of such access points are airports, railway stations, and bus stops. Parking places can be considered as the access points to car travel. Access points to cycling are almost ubiquitous.

Rietveld (2006) estimated that in the Netherlands about three car parking places are available per car, implying about 20 million parking places in total. The number of access points for public transport is much smaller. For example, the number of railway stations in the Netherlands is about 370. This means that for every railway station there are about 50,000 car parking places, underlying the strong competitive position of car versus train. In a similar vein, there are about 25,000 stops for bus, tram and metro in the Netherlands, so for every public transport stop there are about 800 car parking places.

A major factor in the differences in the supply of access and transfer points for different modes concerns the economies of scale in providing them. Public transport access points are normally expensive construction projects because they need to provide shelter and other amenities to passengers, to guarantee a safe transfer and to offer an adequate level of comfort to waiting passengers. In addition to the costs of the construction of transfer points, there are also user costs related to the journey to the access points. To derive the optimal number of stops in a network the following basic model can be used.

Consider a market with a given demand for transport Q and where users of public transport are distributed uniformly along a circular public transport line of length L. Let H be the number of stops on the line. Then the average distance between two stops is L/H. The maximum distance people would have to walk to a station is L/(2*H). Hence, the average distance passengers would have to walk to the nearest stop equals L/(4*H) and the costs involved equal b*Q/H, where b equals VOT*L/(4*v), and VOT and v denote the value of time and the speed of pedestrians, respectively. The fact that the time is inversely proportional to H means that, as the number of transfer points increases, the time needed to get to these points decreases, but at a decreasing rate. The improvement in access times is much bigger at the extreme when H is small.

We now turn to the cost components that are adversely affected by an increase in the number of stops. First, the costs of construction of a stop will be denoted as a_0. Secondly, costs increase with the number of stops as the average speed decreases, and as the stock is used less efficiently. These costs per passenger per station are denoted as a_1. When the public transport vehicle would stop at each transfer point, the extra costs of a stop would be proportional to the number of travelers and the number of stops. Hence we arrive at an extra cost of a_1*H*Q (Van den Heuvel, 1997; van Nes, 2001).

We can conclude that the costs to both supplier and user, as far as they depend on the number of stops, are equal to:

$$C = (a_0 + a_1Q) H + b * Q / H \qquad (5.1)$$

Minimizing the costs leads to the following result for the optimal number of stops:

$$H = [b * Q / (a_0 + a_1Q)]^{0.5} \qquad (5.2)$$

This formula follows from the fact that in the optimum the costs of an extra stop $(a_0 + a_1Q)$ must be equal to the decrease in the access costs $(b*Q/H^2)$. The formula implies that the optimum number of stops increases with the costs of getting to the stop, and decreases with a_1, the costs involved in stopping the vehicle. Another implication of the formula is that the optimum number of stops depends on demand Q. When the number of travelers Q increases, the optimum number of stops will also increase, though at a relatively low rate. This is consistent with the observation that in areas with low population density the number of railway stations per km is lower than in high density areas. Only in the extreme case when a_0 is equal to zero do we find that the optimal number of stops does not depend on travel demand, Q.

Table 5.1   Comparison of the number of access points for various transport modes with an illustration for the Netherlands

Mode; access point	Fixed costs	Stopping costs	Duration of stay at stop	Modal share (%)	Number of nodes in the Netherlands
Bicycle; Bicycle stand	Very low	0	0	25	Infinite
Car; Car parking place	Low (except in urban areas)	0	0	55	about 20,000,000
Bus/tram; Stop	Intermediate	Rather low	Low	3	about 25,000
Train; Railway station	High	High	Low-medium	2	about 370
Air travel; Airport	Very high	Very high	High	<1	6

When we consider this formula from the perspective of a parking place for a car, the fixed costs a_0 are low, and the extra stopping costs $a_1 Q$ do not play a role with this technology, so the optimal value for H will indeed be high. For rail we find that both the fixed and the variable costs related to the number of stops are high (an extra stop means that all passengers in a train incur a time loss), and the time loss per stop is relatively high for rail. This explains the relatively small number of stops in a railway network. For buses intermediate values are found, depending on whether the access stop is a bus stop or a bus terminal/station. Table 5.1 summarizes the discussion.

In dense urban areas some modifications to Table 5.1 are needed. For example, scarcity of parking places at popular destinations lead to long search costs and high parking prices. Furthermore, there is an increasing tendency to reduce the accessibility of attractive urban environments for cars, leading to longer walking distances after parking. Also, the provision of bicycle parking at popular places, like large railway stations, can be costly.

This analysis has a number of limitations. One of them is the assumption that the demand for transport services, Q, is given, and hence does not depend on network structure. When Q depends on the number of stops, the demand side has to be modelled more explicitly, leading to more complex results for the optimal number of stops. In that case it will also be relevant to distinguish two optimality concepts: one in terms of welfare optimization and one in terms of profit optimization. Another limitation is that only walking is considered as an access mode to railway stations, while in the Netherlands, on average, walking accounts for 20 percent, cycling for 38 percent, public transport for 27 percent and car for 14 percent (Givoni and Rietveld, 2007). This has an important implication for the optimal number of railway stops. When the access speed is higher, the factor b in the above model will decrease, so that the optimum number of railway stations will also decrease. Hence, the optimal number of railway stations depends on the structure of the overall transport network, not just on the structure of the railway network itself.

One way of examining the concept, is to see whether reducing the number of nodes (or access points) for one mode of transport can be compensated for by increasing the quality or the number of nodes for another mode. This is examined for railway stations in the Amsterdam area. Rail transport is a relevant mode because of the high fixed costs of providing a station, especially in urban areas; the high costs of an extra stop, caused by the relatively high time penalty for stopping a train, the large number of people affected by it (all on board), as well as the relatively high VOT for rail travelers. Furthermore, changes in the number of rail nodes might imply a longer access journey but not necessarily more transfers, given that a journey by rail involves the use of other modes to access or egress the station.

5.3   RAILWAY STATIONS IN AMSTERDAM

In 2003, the Dutch rail network consisted of 2812 km of lines with an average density of 68 m/km^2. This is higher than the EU15 and EU25 average of 50 and 47 m/km^2, respectively (European Commission, 2005). Looking at the spread over the network and the spread of population, the mean distance of residents to the nearest railway station is about 4.5 km, with the mode of the distribution at about 1.3 km only. Just 8.4 percent of the population lives more than 10.0 km away from the nearest railway station (Keijer and Rietveld, 2000).

Within the Amsterdam area,[1] the density of the rail network is higher. This area, shaded in Figure 5.1, is served by no less than 12 stations and has a well-developed local public transport system (including metro, tram and bus), which serves all railway stations except Schiphol airport station. The relative proximity of a rail station to most people living in Amsterdam, the well-developed cycling infrastructure and the cycling culture (Pucher and

Index: 1 – Amsterdam Centraal; 2 – Amsterdam Amstel; 3 – Amsterdam Zuid; 4 –
Amsterdam Sloterdijk; 5 – Duivendrecht; 6 – Amsterdam Lelylaan; 7 – Amsterdam
Muiderpoort; 8 – Amsterdam RAI; 9 – Diemen; 10 – Diemen Zuid; 11 – Schiphol; 12 –
Amsterdam Bijlmer. Stations are numbered according to their rank in Table 5.3.

Note: The large dots and numbers refer to stations. The small dots represent six-digit
postcodes with one or more rail passenger using one of the 12 railway stations – in this
case Amsterdam Central. Schiphol Station (11), located at the international airport, is not
within the Amsterdam area but is relatively important for many passengers living in the
Amsterdam area, especially in Amstelveen. Amsterdam de Vlugtlaan station (located on
the line between stations 4 and 6) was hardly used in the period and was later closed, it is
excluded from the analysis.

Figure 5.1   The Amsterdam area and railway stations analyzed

Buehler, 2008) causes cycling (28 percent) and also walking (17 percent)
to be important means of getting to railway stations, in addition to public
transport (49 percent). Due to parking capacity limitations, only 3 percent
of passengers use their car to access a railway station in Amsterdam.

Table 5.2   Choice of station within Amsterdam postcodes (4 digit)

Station choice	Average share	Average distance (m)*
1st	71%	3448
2nd	18%	2937
3rd	9%	4478

Note: * From postcode centroid.

Source: based on data from NS.

A case like this, where the population has a large choice set of departure stations with good access links by different modes offers a situation where there may be a case for closing stations.

We start with an examination of the choice of a particular departure station viewed from the perspective of the various residential zones in Amsterdam. At the four-digit postcode area scale there are 94 zones in Amsterdam. The Dutch Railways (NS) measured the distance from the postcode centroid to the three most used stations by residents of that postcode. The results (Table 5.2) show that passengers have a clear preference for a specific station given the area where they live, but this preference is certainly not unanimous. The first choice station attracted on average 71 percent of the rail passengers within a postcode area. The shares of the stations on the second and third position were 18 and 9 percent. The first choice station, on average, was farther away from the respondent's residence than the second choice station. Thus, distance does not appear to be the main factor influencing the choice of station. The choice of station is probably closely related to the choice of access mode to the station. The same data show that in 27 out of 83 postcodes the nearest station is not the first choice for people living in that postcode when they travel by rail and for these 27 postcodes the first choice station is on average 2.3 km farther away than the second choice. For 56 postcodes, the first choice station is the nearest station, and it is 3.2 km closer than the second choice station. The above is indicative as it only considers the postcode centroid, instead of a specific home location.

More refined data is provided by the Dutch Railways (NS) through its customer satisfaction survey, where passengers are asked for their home postcode (at the six-digit level) and their 'usual' departure station (as opposed to their departure station for the trip on which the survey was undertaken). This NS survey, known as the KTO, includes about 70,000 respondents per year across the Dutch railway network and is considered to be representative for the population of passengers traveling on the

Table 5.3   Distribution of surveyed passengers across Amsterdam railway stations (2001–2005) and station's levels of service

Station name	Number of passengers	% of passengers	RSQI*
Amsterdam Centraal	8,721	58	1.381
Amsterdam Amstel	1,543	10	1.126
Amsterdam Zuid WTC	1,047	7	0.948
Amsterdam Sloterdijk	813	5	1.286
Duivendrecht	803	5	1.832
Amsterdam Lelylaan	699	5	1.000
Amsterdam Muiderpoort	466	3	0.870
Amsterdam RAI	345	2	0.784
Diemen	220	1	0.627
Diemen Zuid	146	1	0.890
Schiphol	100	1	1.497
Amsterdam Bijlmer	92	1	0.815
Total	14,995	100	

Note: * RSQI – Rail Service Quality Index (Debrezion, 2006).

Dutch rail network in a particular year. From the NS surveys, covering 2001 to 2005, all passengers, who reported using one of the 12 stations in Figure 5.1 as their usual departure station and who were living in Amsterdam, were extracted.[2] These 14,995 passengers were surveyed in a period in which there were no major changes to the transport system in this area. The distribution of passengers across the 12 stations is shown in Table 5.3, together with information on the level of service at each station. The Amsterdam area covered in the survey includes over 15,000 postcodes at the six-digit level allowing detailed analysis of departure station choice relative to home location.

Considering the geographic spread of the population within the Amsterdam area and the location of railway stations, it is perhaps surprising that the use of the available railway stations is not spread more evenly. Four factors seem to play a major role in the choice of railway stations in Amsterdam by its residents. First, the distribution of the population with respect to station location. For those living in the north of Amsterdam, located across the IJ-river, Amsterdam Centraal is the nearest station. This can partly explain the high share of passengers choosing this station.

Second, the level of service provided at each station is a crucial factor in the choice of a station. This level is captured by the RSQI index. The

Rail Service Quality Index (RSQI) for a departure station (Table 5.3) is a function of the number of trips attracted to all other stations on the network, the generalized travel time from the departure station to all other stations on the network (accounting for service frequency, actual travel time and penalties for having to transfer), and the generalized travel time to distance ratio, which is used to control for the effect of other modes of transport on the attractiveness of rail transport.[3] There is some noticeable correlation between the share of passengers attracted by a station and the level of service provided by the station, but this cannot explain the high share of passengers choosing Centraal station. In this respect, Duivendrecht station attracts less passengers than would be expected given its high RSQI. Although Schiphol airport station offers the highest level of service in the Amsterdam area, its location outside the city explains its relatively low share of passengers.

Third, railway stations in Amsterdam offer different direct services to different destinations. For example, Lelylaan station (No. 6 in Figure 5.1) offers a direct service to Rotterdam, but not to Utrecht. On the other hand, Amstel station (No. 2 in Figure 5.1) has a direct service to Utrecht, but not to Rotterdam. The exception is Centraal station, which offers services on all lines leaving Amsterdam. This could also explain its high share of passengers. However, given that a person only chooses one combination of destination and departure station, there is probably a closer station than Centraal for most passengers in any direction of travel.

The fourth factor that explains the market shares of railway stations – the quality of the access journey – is probably an important one.

Whatever the explanation is for the choice of departure station within Amsterdam, Table 5.3 indicates that perhaps some stations are redundant and that the distance to the nearest railway station is probably not the primary consideration for deciding which station to use as the starting point of a rail journey out of Amsterdam.

5.4 STATION CATCHMENT AREA ANALYSIS

To investigate the use of railway stations in Amsterdam by residents in more detail, the catchment area of each station is mapped using GIS, based on the six-digit postcode home location and the choice of station from the KTO survey. The maps indicate the area and shape of the catchment area. For the purpose of this analysis it was considered unnecessary to actually draw the line of the catchment area. Three catchment area types can be distinguished for railway stations in Amsterdam.

*Figure 5.2   The catchment areas of Amsterdam Centraal (1) and
Amsterdam Muiderpoort (7) stations*

The Circular Catchment Area

The population of Amsterdam is relatively evenly spread. Therefore, the catchment area of each station is expected to roughly have the form of a circle around the station. Furthermore the size of the virtual circle is expected to increase with the size of the station and with the level of service provided by the station.

Indeed, the catchment areas of Amsterdam Centraal and Amsterdam Muiderpoort stations are of this type. The differences in the size of the areas seem to reflect differences in the level of service provided by the stations. Centraal station, being the largest of the Amsterdam stations, attracts passengers from almost the entire Amsterdam area. Muiderpoort station on the other hand is a much smaller station with a much lower level of service, which is reflected in its very localized and small catchment area (Figure 5.2).

The Linear Catchment Area

The catchment areas of Amsterdam Lelylaan and Amsterdam Zuid stations roughly follow a line (Figure 5.3). A relatively small number of passengers is attracted to these stations in addition to those from the east–west axes at Lelylaan and the north–south axes at Zuid station. The explanation for the shape of these catchment areas could be that the tram and/or metro line which serves these stations runs along these axes. In addition, in both cases, major roads run along these axes as well, but, since

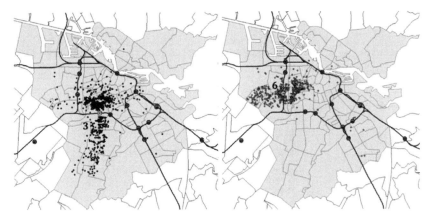

*Figure 5.3   The catchment areas of Amsterdam Zuid (3) and Amsterdam
Lelylaan (6) stations*

car use is relatively low as an access mode to stations in Amsterdam, the
wide and segregated bicycle lanes leading to the railway stations along the
same roads are most probably more important. But, since in Amsterdam
the share of public transport as an access mode to railway stations is
higher than the share of the bicycle, the presence of good public transport
services most probably is the main determinant of the shape of the catchment area. If this is the explanation, it provides evidence for the ability of
good public transport services to a railway station to determine the station
catchment area.

The Sporadic Catchment Area

The catchment area of Duivendrecht station is more difficult to define
and explain (Figure 5.4). It is expected that passengers from areas close
to and south of this station will be attracted to it, but the attraction of
passengers from across the Amsterdam area is less obvious. This can
likely be explained by a mixture of the choice of destination station, or
the direction of travel out of Amsterdam, and the accessibility of the
station largely by public transport. Duivendrecht station is relatively
easy to access by metro and reasonably accessible by bus, but it has very
limited car parking and no tram services. These two factors can explain
to some extent the relatively large spread of the catchment area. At the
same time, Duivendrecht station is unique in the sense that two lines
which offer connections to a distinct set of destinations intersect at the
station. The station is relatively new. It is the natural result of the crossing

Figure 5.4   The catchment area of Duivendrecht (5) station

of the existing north–south line between Amsterdam and Utrecht and the more recent east–west line between Almere and Schiphol, created in the 1990s. The initial idea of the railway company and the municipality of Amsterdam was that Duivendrecht would just serve as a transfer station for railway passengers, and that it would not be served by local public transport, because the municipality was afraid that a full development of the Duivendrecht station would attract real estate developments that would conflict with other planned real estate developments in the city (an important detail is that Duivendrecht was and still is a municipality separate from Amsterdam). At the same time, the railway company was afraid that Duivendrecht would start to compete with other stations at the southeast side of Amsterdam. As a result, the spatial development around the Duivendrecht station has been moderate; however, accessibility by local public transport has improved.

Figure 5.5   *The overlap in the catchment areas of Amsterdam Amstel*
                 (2) and RAI (8) stations (and the junction at Duivendrecht
                 station)

The influence of the direction of travel on the choice of station is shown
in the case of Amsterdam RAI and Amsterdam Amstel stations for those
living in between them (Figure 5.5). In Figure 5.5 the darker dots represent
postcodes with more than one surveyed passenger and where one or more
passengers choose to use RAI station, while others, from the same postcode, choose to use Amstel station. Given that each station offers a different set of destinations served directly, to save a transfer in Duivendrecht
station, it is better to determine the choice of departure station based on
the desired direction of travel.

Considering the spread of postcodes from which passengers access
Duivendrecht station, it still appears that whatever the direction of
travel, a closer departure station would be available. This, again, shows

the influence of the quality of public transport serving a station as a determining factor in the choice of a departure station. Moreover, from those farther away postcodes it might be that the total travel time to the destination city is faster and more convenient if using the urban transport network to access the rail network and beginning the rail journey at Duivendrecht and not before at a different, closer railway station. Starting the journey at other railway stations might mean taking first a slow train with several stops before Duivendrecht.

5.5   CONCLUSIONS

A key factor in railway use is the number and location of stations and their catchment areas. Opening new stations, to reduce access/egress distance to/from the station, is often seen as one of the main ways to increase rail use. This strategy is, however, costly and might be counterproductive as some existing rail travelers could be adversely affected, resulting in them ceasing to use the rail network. There are particular challenges in the decision-making process involved in opening new stations in urban areas that are already well served. A major consideration in deciding whether to build a new station in this situation is the ability of potential users to access the new facility. In other words, a holistic approach that takes into account the entire urban transport network is needed.

In Amsterdam, there are considerable overlaps in the catchment areas of the stations. These overlaps may be an indication of an oversupply of railway stations, which, from a network or a city perspective, can be inefficient when increasing rail use and improving the profitability of rail operations are policy objectives. We have seen that while there is a demand across the system in the Amsterdam area this does not necessarily mean that it is high enough to justify all these stations in operation.

There is a case for looking carefully at the different factors affecting the choices of passengers of departure stations and the weight given to each. The factors that seem important are travel time to each station by different modes and the destinations served by each station, or, more generally, the level of service including scheduling. The balance between the access time to stations and the travel time by rail between stations should be determined when considering the optimal number of stations. To reduce any adverse environmental- or congestion-related impacts of passengers switching mode if a station is closed, policies to improve access to the remaining stations may be needed.

ACKNOWLEDGMENTS

This research was supported by a Marie Curie European Reintegration Grant within the 7th European Community Framework Programme. We thank the Dutch Railways for the data and Shirily Gilad for the geographical information system analysis.

NOTES

1. The Amsterdam area includes the municipalities of Amsterdam, Amstelveen and Diemen, and will be referred to, for simplicity, as Amsterdam, unless specifically stated otherwise.
2. These data are the basis for the modal split on access journey to the stations.
3. For comparison with Table 5.3, the station with the highest RSQI on the network is Utrecht Centraal (RSQI = 2.001) followed by Duivendrecht (1.832) and Leiden Centraal (1.818). The average RSQI for all the stations on the Dutch network is 0.44. The lowest RSQI value for a station on the Dutch network is 0.112.

REFERENCES

Brons, M., Givoni, M. and Rietveld, P. (2009) Access to railway stations and its potential in increasing rail use, *Transportation Research A*, 43, 136–49.

Debrezion, G. (2006) Railway impacts on real estate prices. PhD thesis, Vrije Universiteit, Amsterdam.

European Commission (2005) *European Union Energy and Transport in Figures 2005*. European Commission, Directorate-General for Energy and Transport.

Givoni, M. and Rietveld, P. (2007) The access journey to the railway station and its role in passengers' satisfaction with rail travel, *Transport Policy*, 14, 357–65.

Keijer, M.J.N. and Rietveld, P. (2000) How do people get to the railway station? The Dutch experience, *Transportation Planning and Technology*, 23, 215–35.

Pucher, J. and Buehler, R. (2008) Making cycling irresistible: lessons from the Netherlands, Denmark and Germany, *Transport Reviews*, 28, 495–528.

Rietveld, P. (2006) Urban transport policies: the Dutch struggle with market failures and policy failures, in R.J. Arnott and D.P. McMillen (eds), *A Companion to Urban Economics* (Blackwell Companions to Contemporary Economics). Singapore, Blackwell Publishing.

Van den Heuvel, M.G. (1997) Openbaar vervoer in de Randstad. Dissertatie TUD.

van Nes, R. (2001) Fietsen in het voortransport van stedelijk openbaar vervoer: een ander vervoersconcept nodig?, *Tijdschrift Vervoerswetenschap*, 37, 33–7.

6. Parcel distribution networks for online shopping business

Hyunwoo Lim and Narushige Shiode

6.1 INTRODUCTION

One of the challenges faced by society is the rapid growth of e-commerce trade and its wider implications on transportation and economic develop- ment. Aside from its direct impact on the market economy, the emergence of the online market place has radically altered the notion of accessibility and opportunity in that it enables us to trade and complete transactions online without the need for the trip to a retail store. This, however, does not free us completely from the physical constraints of the real world. We remain dependent on the existing physical transport network as long as the need for delivering the products ordered online persists. This chapter is inspired by the imminent challenge brought forth by the growth of e-commerce; specifically, it explores options to better cope with the volatility as well as the continual growth in the pattern of logistic freight transport for online shopping activities.

E-commerce can be generally defined as commercial activities carried out by the use of intelligent communication technologies (ICT) includ- ing the internet, and it can be divided broadly into three categories: business-to-business (B2B), consumer-to-consumer (C2C) and business- to-consumer (B2C) (Mokhtarian, 2004). In the case of the United States, e-commerce has grown, in recent years, at a much faster rate than the overall economic activity across the four major economic sectors: manufacturing, merchant wholesale trade, retail trade, and selected services. As of 2007, B2B accounted for 93 percent of e-commerce activities, which has predominantly relied on proprietary electronic data interchange (EDI) systems. Although B2C e-commerce only marked 4 percent of the entire sales of the retail sector in 2007, it increased by 19.7 percent from 2006, making it by far the fastest growing retail segment among all of the economic sectors (US Census Bureau, 2009). Despite its relatively modest share at present, B2C e-commerce should not be overlooked, as its potential impact on transportation and land use

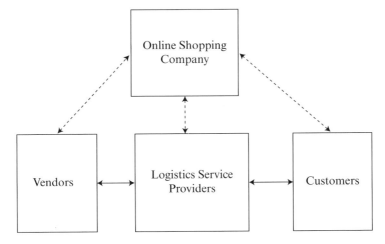

Source: Lim (2009).

Figure 6.1   Four major stakeholders in the online shopping market

patterns can be profound (Mokhtarian, 2004; Visser and Lanzendorf, 2004).

This chapter focuses on the logistics of B2C e-commerce in the retail sector (hereafter referred to as online shopping) and discusses transport planning that considers such retail activities. Online shopping enables consumers to purchase commercial products from practically any location, provided that both the business firms and their customers have access to the internet. On the consumers' side, online shopping saves time and money by saving them the trips to retail stores; while on the suppliers' side, online shopping helps significantly reduce the cost of investing in and maintaining physical stores, which in turn is reflected in the competitive price of online shopping products (Bakos, 1997; Cairncross, 2001; Steinfield and Whitten, 2003).

Chen and Chang (2003) identified three main phases of online shopping: interaction, transaction, and fulfillment. Interaction refers to a customer's action to search for products and compare prices while shopping around websites. Once the customer identifies a product of interest on a certain website, the placement of their order and payment take place; and this constitutes the transaction phase. Finally, fulfillment refers to the activities after the purchase, including delivery, exchange, and return; and it is this final phase of online shopping that demands closer attention in terms of the logistics of shipping and delivery.

As illustrated in Figure 6.1, there are four major stakeholders involved

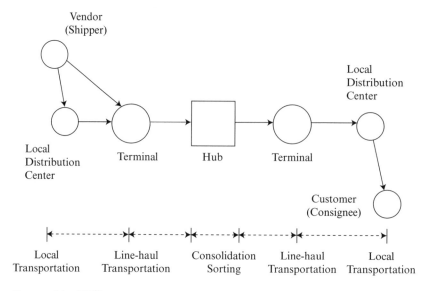

Source: Lim (2009).

Figure 6.2   Overview of parcel flow in a physical distribution network

in the online shopping business: online shopping companies, vendors (suppliers), consumers, and logistics service providers (Strader and Shaw, 2000). The dashed arrows represent flows of information and monetary transactions while the solid arrows represent flows of the actual commodities. Some online shopping products may take the form of information itself or online tickets/vouchers, such as an electronic ticket for an airline trip, but here we will focus on products that have a physical entity and require delivery by a logistic service provider. The online shopping company provides a virtual market place on the internet that enables vendors to sell their products online, or promotes and sells such products on behalf of the vendors. Once the order is placed by the customer and the transaction is completed, a third-party logistics service provider (LSP) takes on the responsibility of shipping and delivering the product from the vendor's warehouse to the individual customer location.

Figure 6.2 shows how online shopping driven products are shipped through a parcel distribution network by a typical logistics service provider. Transporting parcels throughout the distribution network consists of two main parts: local and line-haul transportation. Local transportation includes pick-up and delivery activities near vendors and customers.

Local distribution centers are responsible for collecting products from vendors and delivering packages to customers. If a vendor has a warehouse to hold its inventory, products can be directly transported from the warehouse to the origin terminal. Line-haul transportation refers to transporting parcels between terminals. If the destination of the package is outside of the logistics boundary of the origin terminal, it is transported to a hub terminal for consolidation. Once packages are sorted at the hub terminal, they are sent to the destination terminal, then to a local distribution center, and finally delivered to individual customer locations.

As the volume of online shopping sales grows, so does the demand for small package delivery services (Hesse, 2002). Responding to the increasing volume of small-sized frequent shipments incurred by online retailers can thus pose a great challenge to the logistics service providers responsible for operating and maintaining their parcel distribution network (Huppertz, 1999). E-fulfillment, or the delivery of packages to customers, has thus become more important in e-commerce. Customers purchase their products within minutes through online transactions but must wait for up to several days to have them delivered. Physical distribution is a critical component, yet often considered the weakest link in the chain of process. Delivering products to customers distributed across a large geographic market area in a timely manner depends on the successful operation of the parcel distribution network, including its terminals, distribution centers, and the network paths that connect them. Maintaining cost efficiency and high level of service in the distribution system is crucial for the logistics service providers to stay competitive in the online shopping business (Anderson and Leinbach, 2007).

Many researchers have pointed out the importance of physical distribution for supporting online shopping business and the critical relationship between them (Mokhtarian, 2004). For example, Visser and Lanzendorf (2004) discussed the effect of B2C e-commerce on mobility and accessibility, especially those on the consumer's activity patterns and travel behavior, freight transportation and logistics decisions of the LSP firms, and location decisions of households and firms. However, most of the previous research was conducted at the conceptual level, and few studies have provided empirical evidence or analytical results on the relationship between the growth of online shopping and possible operational and structural changes in physical distribution.

This chapter identifies the implications of online shopping on parcel distribution both from the viewpoint of the industry and the individual firm. In particular, it addresses the following questions:

- How would the growth of an online shopping market affect the pattern and the structure of parcel distribution that serves its customer base?
- How can parcel distribution networks adapt to the increase in online shopping demand and overcome capacity overflow at different planning horizons?

To address these questions, we focus on the online shopping market of South Korea, which is one of the most advanced online societies with a higher share of the B2C sector in its economy. In the following, we first discuss how South Korean online shopping business has experienced a tremendous growth both in terms of sales and geographical expansion of market place. We then present a conceptual model explaining the interdependent relationship between online shopping business and parcel distribution from a system dynamics approach. Next, we suggest possible short-term and long-term adaptive measures taken by an individual logistics firm to respond to capacity overflows caused by the increase in the demand of online shopping. Finally we discuss their implications for urban landscape and regional economic development.

6.2   GROWTH OF THE ONLINE SHOPPING MARKET

As one of the leading countries in ICT, South Korea has experienced a tremendous growth in B2C online shopping sales, from \$2.5 billion in 2001 to \$9.1 billion in 2006. Popular products sold in the online shopping market include books, music CDs, movie DVDs, and electronics. There has also been an increasing trend for products that used to be sold exclusively in conventional retail stores, such as clothes and convenience goods, to be sold in the online shopping market (Korea National Statistical Office, 2007). Such growth of online shopping market can be explained by the increase in sales and market share and the geographical expansion of online shopping market.

Growth of Online Shopping Sales

As shown in equation 6.1, profit in the retail sector can be generally expressed as the product of profitability per unit and sales, where sales can be expressed as a function of various factors such as purchase needs, purchase power, purchase opportunity, and the number of customers (Mason and Burns, 1998).

$$\text{Profit} = \text{Profitability} \times \text{Sales} \qquad (6.1)$$

This suggests that it is critical to maintain steady sales to make profits in any retail business including an online shopping business. As more daily necessity items like diapers and non-perishable foods become available for online shopping, a greater portion of purchase needs for customers are satisfied. The fact that most of the products are offered at a lower price online than the conventional offline retail stores charge gives more purchasing power to the online shopping customers.

Unlike the conventional brick-and-mortar (B&M) retail environment, shopping activities such as searching for items, checking their price, and purchasing them are performed virtually within the online shopping market place. Since providing market information to the customers and performing monetary transactions are both services that may be performed online, e-retailers can save labor costs associated with sales and maintenance in comparison with B&M retail facilities (Borenstein and Saloner, 2001). Furthermore, e-retailers can achieve significantly lower inventory carrying cost than the B&M retailers can, because goods sold online tend to have a higher turnover rate.

The spread of high-speed internet service in South Korea has taken place at a relatively rapid rate even when compared with that of other developed countries. This is primarily due to its relatively small national boundary, high population density and a government-led policy in promoting investments in ICT-related infrastructures nationwide (Hong, 2003). Proliferation of high-speed internet services throughout South Korea has enabled customers to engage in online shopping activities 24 hours a day and 7 days a week, providing nearly unlimited purchasing opportunities.

Another contributory factor to the growth of the online shopping market in South Korea over the past five years is the marketing strategy adopted by the online shopping firms. Many of these firms have introduced to the online shopping market the strategy to trade relatively low-priced products with a high turnover rate at significantly lower shipping prices (Lim et al., 2007).

$$\text{Profitability} = \text{Margin Rate} \times \text{Inventory Turnover Rate} \qquad (6.2)$$

As shown in equation 6.2, profitability of a certain product can be defined as the product of its margin rate and the inventory turnover rate in retail business (Mason and Burns, 1998). Margin can be defined as the sales less the cost incurred, and the margin rate is derived as a proportion of the sales. Inventory turnover rate indicates the frequency of the average inventory of a product being sold during a period of time. It is derived by dividing the cost of goods sold by the average amount of inventory. Luxury goods such as jewelry usually have an extremely high margin rate, yet their turnover rate may be low. On the other hand, daily necessity goods may have a low margin rate, but their turnover rates are usually quite high.

In South Korea, goods that were conventionally sold in offline retail stores have increasingly penetrated the online shopping market as hot commodities. For example, between 2001 and 2006, the sales of clothing goods have increased by 1248 percent, followed by those of cosmetics (772 percent), infants' and kids' items (665 percent), sports and leisure items (472 percent), daily necessities (472 percent), books (242 percent), electronic home appliances (185 percent), and computers (49 percent) (Korea National Statistical Office, 2007). These types of goods are often compact in size, thus allowing them to be tightly packed and easily transported, which in turn helps further promote online shopping.

Competition among logistics service providers and parcel carriers in South Korea has significantly reduced the shipping price in the online shopping market, and this tendency holds even for overnight express deliveries. Having a sufficient demand (i.e. customer base) around destinations is critical for parcel carriers in reducing the cost of the logistics and generating sufficient profit to maintain their businesses; that is, establishing more demand than the threshold through the economies of scale. Given the price elasticity of their products, online shopping companies often attempt to entice more customers by charging little or no delivery fees, as the average shipping cost can be reduced by accomplishing economies of scale.

Once a critical amount of demand for online shopping is secured, the shipping price and the primary carrier who will be in charge of the physical distribution are determined through a competitive bidding process. To outbid their competitors, carriers are willing to lower their bids to reach as low as the marginal shipping cost. The shipping price for online shopping products can be thus determined at a level that is much lower than the average shipping cost charged for individual parcels by a regular carrier. To keep up with the price competition, the carriers should investigate various structural innovations to improve their physical distribution network and make them more cost efficient. This whole process would result in the elimination of the unfit, and only the fittest, most price competitive carriers who have achieved a reliable and efficient distribution network would prevail in the parcel delivery market.

Geographical Expansion of Online Shopping Market

With the growth of sales in online shopping, its market area is expected to expand over space. While the market area of brick-and-mortar retail business is determined by the distance customers are willing to travel to the retail stores, the market area of an online shopping retailer is only bound by the extent of space where the products ordered online can be physically delivered within promised lead time and with reasonable shipping price. The growth in the geographic extent of the customer base of online shopping markets leads to further reduction in shipping prices, which completes the circle by attracting even more customers and bringing in more online shopping trade. A case study conducted by Lim et al. (2007) shows that market areas of online shopping businesses can cover the entire nation of South Korea, even for low-priced daily necessities such as clothes, cosmetics, and diapers. Successfully maintaining such a large market area would not be possible without the solid support of a reliable physical distribution system.

As the market area of online shopping expands, more suppliers and consumers can participate in economic activities through the virtual market place provided by the online shopping firms. This enables small-to medium-sized suppliers and vendors to sell their products to a nationwide market with relatively lower market entry barriers compared to the scenario where they enter the conventional retail business, thereby contributing to the growth of local economies (Steinfield and Whitten, 2003). Likewise, the proliferation of online shopping may also help consumers in the peripheral regions with limited access to discount stores or large shopping malls in their local towns to gain access to a multitude of shopping opportunities with a diverse supply of products over a large price range.

Physical proximity to markets is an important factor of location for both suppliers and customers in brick-and-mortar retail business. However, physical proximity of suppliers to major customer locations becomes less important for both suppliers and customers in online shopping markets – so long as the distance of shipping the parcel does not reflect on the shipping charge – since it is a third-party logistics provider that transports products from suppliers to individual customer locations (Anderson et al., 2003). This would eventually expand the geographic market of the online shopping business. Therefore, location factors other than physical proximity to markets may matter more to suppliers in terms of being successful in online shopping business. For this reason, the distribution of suppliers participating in online shopping market can be also expanded over space and over time.

6.3   DYNAMICS OF ONLINE SHOPPING AND PARCEL DISTRIBUTION

Interdependent Relationship between Online Shopping and Parcel Distribution

Physical distribution plays a critical role in fulfilling orders generated by online shopping. Therefore, building an efficient and reliable physical distribution system is essential to cope with the long-term growth of an online shopping business. Figure 6.3 shows a conceptual diagram that illustrates the interdependent relationship between the growth of online shopping and the competitiveness of logistics service providers at the macro-scale industry level. The diagram comprises two feedback loops: the reinforcing loop on the left and the balancing loop on the right.

Increase in online shopping sales can be explained by various reasons, but one critical factor is the reduction in delivery price caused by the competition among the logistics service providers. Lowering the delivery price is also a marketing strategy on the online retailers' side to attract more customers. Some firms offer a free delivery service when the amount of a customer's purchase exceeds a certain amount. Other factors that promote the increase in online shopping sales, including the characteristics of consumers and online shopping firms, are considered exogenous.

As the online shopping market expands geographically and its share in

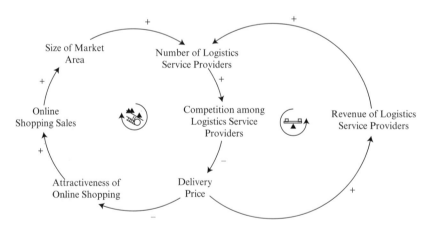

Source: Lim et al. (2007).

Figure 6.3   The dynamics of an online shopping and parcel distribution business

the retail sector continues to increase, more and more logistics service providers will join the market for delivering online shopping products. This intensifies the competition among the logistics service providers. Online shopping firms usually outsource their physical distribution to a third-party logistics service provider on a one- to two-year contract. Logistics service providers are subjected to a competitive bidding process to win the contract and they will try to become more competitive by improving the cost efficiency of their physical distribution network. This streamlining will increase their revenue and provide them with a greater chance of winning larger contracts with online shopping firms, as these online vendors usually give their contracts to the carrier who promises the lowest price for the delivery operations. This may further reduce delivery price, which would promote the attractiveness of online shopping and increase its sales.

However, the excessive competition may also drive some of the less successful carriers out of the parcel delivery market for online vendors. In addition, even if a logistics service provider secured a contract with an online retailer in the first instance, if they cannot keep up with the increase in online shopping demand or fail to remain cost efficient in operating their physical distribution network, their revenue structure will deteriorate and eventually they will be closed out from the market. This means that the right side of the loop is a negative feedback loop that does not guarantee that the online shopping market will grow indefinitely. The competition among the logistics service providers will act as a balancing mechanism where the online shopping market will eventually saturate and no additional firms will join the market.

As the online shopping firms invariably wish to run a profitable yet reliable business, they try to identify a logistics service provider that can carry out the delivery operation with very low distribution cost without compromising the quality of customer service. At the same time, the online shopping firms must attract a sufficient number of orders from their customers so that their logistics service provider can benefit from the scale economy and remain profitable in operating and maintaining their physical distribution network that requires a lump sum investment and fixed maintenance costs.

Despite the steady increase of online shopping sales especially in South Korea over the past few years, it is quite possible that its demand will soon reach a point of saturation and its growth will slow down due to economic and environmental limitations. Online shopping products would be still price competitive in the foreseeable future. Their delivery price, however, may not stay low forever. For example, the recent hike in the price of fuel in early 2008 inevitably increases the overall transportation cost, and

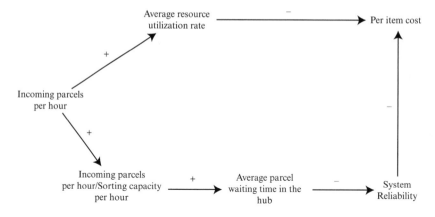

Source: Lim (2009).

Figure 6.4   The dynamics of parcel flow and hub terminal performances

logistics service providers may be forced to increase their delivery price; and, should the delivery price keep increasing, online shopping may lose its relative advantage over the conventional retail market.

Capacity Overflow Problem in the Parcel Distribution Network

Figure 6.4 illustrates the effect of parcel flow reallocation and increase in the hub terminal capacity on the performance of the physical distribution network at the scale of individual logistics service provider. In contrast with Figure 6.3, which shows the interdependent relationship between online shopping businesses and physical distribution at an aggregate, macro-scale, Figure 6.4 shows the immediate impact of increased parcel flow on the individual network performance at the level of disaggregate, micro-scale.

Assuming that the logistic network takes a hub-and-spoke structure, the incoming parcels will concentrate at the hub facility with the amount of flow subject to a further increase as the online shopping demand increases. The level of congestion at the hub can be represented by the ratio between the number of incoming parcels per hour and the hub's sorting capacity per hour. The utility of the hub facility will continue to improve with the increase in the number of incoming parcels as long as the incoming flow does not exceed the limit of its sorting capacity. The increase in the parcel flow would also result in the growth of the overall resource utilization rate such as average truck loading factor. This would lower the per-unit distribution cost, as the whole operation would benefit from the economies of scale. However, as soon as the incoming parcel flow exceeds the hub terminal's sorting capacity, congestion would occur at the main hub. Parcels will be placed in the queue before they go through the sorting process at the hub, and it would take longer for the parcels to be delivered to the individual customer location. This enhances the risk of failing to deliver the parcel to the customers on time. If we define the system's reliability to be proportional to the rate of parcels delivered to the customer on time, the capacity overflow in the main hub can be considered as a source of degradation of the overall system's reliability.

6.4   POSSIBLE ADAPTATIONS TO IMPROVE HUB TERMINAL CAPACITY

As the demand for online shopping increases, individual logistics service providers will eventually face the problem of capacity overflow in their distribution networks. When designing and operating the physical distribution network, decisions can be made at three different levels of planning: operational, tactical, and strategic levels (Crainic, 2000). Thus the adaptive measures to accommodate the increasing online shopping demand should be considered at each of the three levels of decision making.

Adaptations at the Operational Level

Usually made by local managers and dispatchers on a daily basis, operational level decisions include the implementation and adjustment of schedules for services, personnel, and maintenance activities (Crainic, 2000). This includes efficient planning and management of routing and dispatching vehicles and crews to and from local distribution centers and terminals. As the whole operation takes place in a highly dynamic environment, modeling operational planning requires a detailed and careful coordination of vehicles, facilities, and activities with the volume and timing of the parcel flow.

One of the problems in operational planning is the pickup and delivery problem (PDP), which pertains to the identification of the optimal set of routes for a fleet of vehicles to satisfy the transportation requests (Savelsbergh and Sol, 1995). Each transportation request includes pickup/delivery locations and the load at each location. Studies in PDP have been extended further to consider time windows, where there is a time interval between pickup and/or delivery locations (Jian et al., 2004). Practitioners in South Korea have pointed out that adapting to the increase in the parcel flow can be more easily achieved by controlling the local transportation including pickup and delivery operations rather than by managing the line-transportation, especially in the hub terminals.

If the number of incoming parcels at the hub terminal is expected to exceed the regular load, the hours of operation can be extended by starting the operation earlier than is regularly scheduled. However, delaying the end of operation would also increase the sorting capacity but may be of little help in terms of ensuring on-time delivery of the parcels to their destination. Incentives may need to be paid out to early arriving trucks from the local distribution center to cover their loss for early cut-off time at the respective local center. Secondly, the sequence or the order of parcel sorting at the main hub can be adjusted by the destinations of parcels. Assigning higher priority to the parcels headed for farther destinations may prevent those parcels from arriving late for on-time delivery at their destinations.

Adaptations at the Tactical Level

Mid-term tactical level decisions are made through the efficient allocation of existing resources to improve the system performance. Tactical level decisions include the assignment of local delivery centers to the terminals, an act that can be achieved in a relatively short period of time. If the increase in the parcel flow cannot be absorbed at the operational level, tactical level decisions can be made to modify the configuration of the distribution network. For instance, one or more of the existing terminals can be promoted to so-called 'sub-hubs' or secondary hubs, and these locations may be tasked to perform a sorting operation, if perhaps with a limited capacity, to relieve the main hub from the burden of capacity overflow. By reducing the number of end-of-line terminals that are directly linked to the main hub, the load of incoming parcel flow and congestion at the main hub will be reduced. Although introducing such secondary hubs in the logistic network would mitigate capacity overflow in the main hub, it requires an additional sorting process at the secondary hub terminals as well as additional transportation links between end-of-line terminals and sub-hubs.

We define the average frequency of sorting (AFS) to denote the number of sorting frequency for an average parcel throughout its shipment on the distribution network. Figure 6.5a illustrates a pure hub-and-spoke (H&S) network consisting of a single hub and ten terminals with OD (origin-destination) flow of 100. In this hypothetical scenario, the AFS converges to one, since all parcels are being sorted only once at a single hub terminal. Suppose that the OD flow is increased by 30 percent (130 parcels) and one of the terminals in the system is promoted to a sub-hub to correspond to

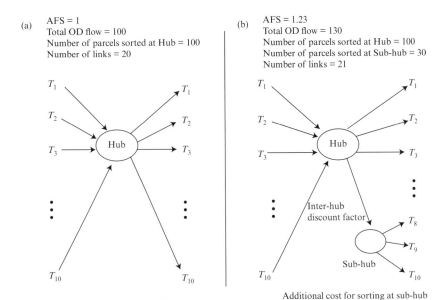

Source: Lim (2009).

Figure 6.5   Promotion of an existing terminal to a sub-hub

the increase in the parcel flow. Let us also suppose that seven terminals are directly connected to the main hub, while the other three terminals are delegated to the sub-hub and have only indirect connection to the main hub (Figure 6.5b). If 30 out of 130 parcels are sorted at the sub-hub, then the AFS becomes 1.23. Reducing the number of direct links to the main hub and, thereby reducing its incoming parcel flow, may reduce the sorting load in the main hub. However, it may also raise the cost, because of the extra sorting process delegated to the sub-hub, which is expected to be less efficient in sorting the parcels than the main hub can manage and hence incurring an additional cost per parcel.

Adaptations at the Strategic Level

In contrast with the operational and tactical level adjustments, decision making at the strategic level would involve reviewing and redesigning the structure of a physical distribution network over the long term. Where necessary, such changes would require a large amount of capital investment. Constructing the overall physical structure of the distribution network is performed mostly at the initial stage of network construction. Once the physical distribution network is established, modifying the existing structure often takes an enormous amount of time and resource. Decisions made at the strategic level include consideration of the following:

- number, size/capacity, and location of terminals
- type of network: point-to-point vs. hub-and-spoke system
- hierarchy of nodes
- assignment of spokes to hubs.

Problems of deciding the number and location of terminals have been extensively studied with various facility location models. One of the examples is the p-median problem where p number of facilities are located in a network such that the weighted sum of distance (or cost) between the nodes of the network and their nearest facility is minimized (Goldman, 1972).

Regarding the distribution of freight from origin node to destination node, the physical distribution network can assume three different types of structures: point-to-point (P2P), hub-and-spoke (H&S), or a hybrid H&S network which is a combination of the P2P and H&S. A P2P network is designed to directly transport commodities from origin node to destination node, which requires $_nC_2 = n(n - 1)/2$ number of links with n nodes; that is, the network forms a complete graph (Taaffe et al., 1996). A direct P2P shipment ensures a relatively fast delivery by saving the travel time that would be required to transport the parcels by way of other nodes, and it also requires no investment on and maintenance of a large trans-shipment hub terminal. A P2P network system is cost effective when a sufficient amount of shipments are ensured between the origin and destination nodes (Liu et al., 2003). However, as the number of nodes in the network increases, the number of links that connect the nodes within the network would increase geometrically and hence rapidly push up the overall line-haul transportation cost in the network.

The H&S network structure has been widely used in servicing the transportation of passengers, freights, and information between multiple origins and destinations. Serving as the central trans-shipment facilities, hubs can effectively replace the numerous direct links between origins and destinations and reduce the whole network by connecting the nodes through fewer indirect links through the hubs. For instance, if there are n nodes including a single hub in the network, $(n - 1)$ links are required to connect all nodes (Taaffe et al., 1996). This configuration of network has been applied to many different types of transportation systems including air passenger carriers, package delivery services, and rail-road transportation. In comparison with the direct point-to-point (P2P) connection system, H&S networks

Table 6.1   The costs and benefits of hub-and-spoke operations

Benefits of H&S networks:
- Fewer links are required to connect the nodes, and the network configuration can be simplified.
- The process of handling and sorting the freight can be centralized at hubs.
- Since the transportation flow is concentrated to a fewer number of links, a higher load factor or carrier filling rate can be achieved.
- Carriers can take advantage of scale economy through consolidation of flows.

Drawbacks of H&S networks:
- The average distance between each pair of nodes is longer than in a P2P network, especially if the end nodes are spatially close to one another but are not directly linked.
- Average lead time is increased.

have a number of benefits and drawbacks as shown in Table 6.1 (Lumsden, 1999; Zapfel and Wasner, 2002).

To overcome limitations of H&S networks, hybrid H&S networks have been suggested. It allows direct connection if there are enough truck-loads of flow between the origin-destination pair and/or if the distance between the node pair is close enough (Chong et al., 2006). Unlike the distribution network for a supply chain or the business-to-business (B2B) sector with fewer OD pairs and predictable OD flows, parcel distribution networks supporting B2C online shopping have to accommodate the logistics of transporting a large number of packages that come in different shapes and sizes and are widespread across different combinations of origins and destinations. Therefore, H&S networks have been widely used in parcel distribution to save the overall cost by accomplishing economies of scale through consolidation at hub terminals (Lappierre et al., 2004). However, the risk of capacity overflow and its impact on the entire network operation would be substantial, especially in the pure H&S network system where the sorting operation is centralized to a single hub terminal.

If the network flow is expected to increase by a significant margin in the long term, a large capital investment plan needs to be considered so as to improve the sorting capacity of the existing main hub terminal. This strategic plan can be achieved by either introducing a more efficient sorting facility or constructing a parallel sorting facility equivalent to the existing one to double the sorting capacity.

Figure 6.6 illustrates the relationship between hub terminal capacity and the average distribution cost in terms of the average cost function. Suppose F_1 and F_2 respectively denote the cost function for two firms

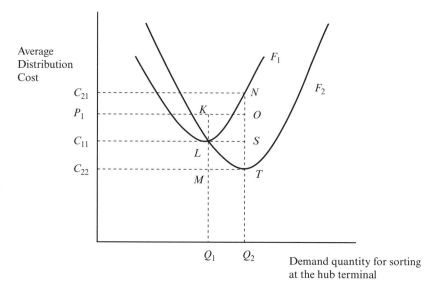

Source: Lim (2009).

Figure 6.6   Average distribution cost curves at two different hub terminal capacities

operating hub terminals 1 and 2 with different sorting capacity. With the economies of scale, hub 1 can reduce its average cost to as low as C_{11} with demand level Q_1. If the incoming flow exceeds Q_1, then hub 1 will start to experience increase in the average cost. In contrast, hub 2 can reduce its average cost even lower to C_{22} and accommodate a larger demand Q_2 because of its greater sorting capacity. Let us assume that the unit price for distribution is determined at P_1 in the market. If the demand is Q_1, both firms 1 and 2 will make a profit of $P_1C_{11}KL$. When the demand increases to Q_2, firm 1 will suffer the loss of $C_{21}P_1NO$ while firm 2 will continue to enjoy a profit of $P_1C_{22}OT$. This hypothetical example illustrates that, under the scenario where an increase in the overall demand is expected over a long period of time, a firm that possesses a greater sorting capacity can prevail over its competitor.

Results

Based on a case of South Korean logistics service provider, Lim (2009) developed a discrete-event simulation model to study how the overall cost efficiency and the network performance measures would change with the change in the parcel flow. In this model, cost efficiency refers to the average distribution cost for transporting and sorting individual parcels, and reliability is measured as the percentage of parcels transported to the destination terminals by the cut-off time. As the parcel flow exceeds the hub terminal capacity, the simulation model shows how the congestion at the hub can cause delays in parcel deliveries, and how that is reflected in the reliability of each local terminal location as well as that of the entire system. If financial penalties are applied to delayed parcels, the hub terminal congestion problem will also reduce the overall cost efficiency, in particular by increasing the per-item distribution cost. As a means of overcoming the congestion problem at the main hub, adaptive measures corresponding to the increase in parcel flows are tested at three different levels of logistics decision making: the operational level that corresponds to a short-term peak, the tactical level that copes with mid-term increases, and the strategic level that offers solutions to the long-term increase.

Operational level adaptation includes extending the operation hours at the hub terminal and rescheduling the timing of truck dispatching which may require early arrivals of trucks from local terminals. It is shown that congestion at the main hub can be lowered simply by assigning higher priorities to parcels heading for terminals that are farther from the hub, and this would help improve the reliability of the system under all scenarios of increasing demand levels. However, even with the application of priority assignment, the entire system still suffers from parcel delays under the scenarios with excessively large amounts of parcel flow. Operational level adaptations such as priority assignment in the main hub are therefore unsuitable as long-term solutions for increasing demand.

If an increase in the network flow cannot be accommodated by operational level adaptations, tactical level adaptation can be considered, such as promoting an existing terminal to a secondary hub. In the simulation model, existing terminals were gradually promoted to sub-hubs one after another as the parcel flow was increased. The results from the simulation suggest that introducing a secondary hub into the network can solve the problems of delayed parcels for all of the demand levels tested. However, it also incurs additional costs, mainly due to the extra parcel sorting at secondary hubs and maintaining the additional links between the secondary hubs and their respective local terminals. This results in reduced efficiency in operating the overall network.

Finally, there is a strategic level adaptation, which may require a significant amount of investment to deal with the long-term increase in the B2C online shopping demand for small packages. The simulation result showed that increasing the per hour sorting capacity in the main hub guarantees the system to maintain 100 percent reliability up to an extremely high demand level with the least amount of per-item cost. Therefore, it can be concluded that increasing the hub terminal capacity would be the best option among the three adaptation scenarios, if the return-on-investment is expected to be great enough. The findings from the simulation model suggest that the structure and configuration of the existing physical distribution network would evolve into a more centralized one with an increased capacity for trans-shipment.

6.5 CONCLUSIONS

As stated at the beginning, this chapter was inspired by the rapid growth of e-commerce and its wider implications for transportation and economic development. The amount of transaction from e-commerce is likely to continue increasing its share within the whole retail economy, thus taking away more business from the conventional retail sector. This means that while the amount of logistic flow between the online economy and the conventional offline retail market may not change by a significant margin, their proportion will likely change in favor of e-commerce. And, within the e-commerce sector, the online shopping activities by private custom-ers (i.e. B2C: business-to-consumer trade) in particular, appears to be following a trajectory of an acute and constant rise. In many respects, the B2B (business-to-business) portion of *e*-commerce can be considered as an extension of the regular off-line business and its logistics can also be treated in much the same way as conventional freight transport.

However, recent growth in the B2C portion of e-commerce makes it more difficult to predict and schedule the logistics, as it is a collection of individual orders from private customers, and the pattern of parcel flow can be thus highly volatile. The best strategy for the logistic service providers would be to study the general trends that can be deduced from empirical evidence. For instance, B2C transactions have a strong tendency to concentrate at certain times, for example: around the holiday seasons or before a significant festivity when people would exchange gifts; during a sale season when online shopping firms offer discounts on a wide range of items; on a particular day of the week (e.g. Friday) when people have a better chance of receiving items at their home location; and when a new product comes out on the market and becomes very popular. This means that the flow of parcels that passes through the main hub as well as the logistic network will change from day to day and that a large number of parcels may be observed only on a limited number of days. In other words, investing in the construction of a super-hub with very high sorting capac-ity may result in overinvestment and would not necessarily make financial sense; but during one of the peak seasons, they would need to temporarily increase the sorting capacity to process the extra amount of parcel flow. Promoting some of the existing end-of-line terminals to sub-hubs can be considered as one of the tactical level solutions to deal with a temporary hike in the volume of parcels.

In the long run, however, capital investment on a hub terminal with a higher sorting capacity would be inevitable if the demand is expected to increase steadily. The physical distribution system supporting B2C e-commerce should not only accommodate the short-term fluctuation of parcel flows but should also correspond to the long-term projection of online shopping demand. The result is a natural combination of counter-measures at the operational, tactical, and strategic levels where the abrupt and volatile changes in the parcel flow will be dealt with by operational and tactical adaptations, while the long-term growth in the flow will require a strategic response. As an alternative, public logistics networks can be proposed at an industry level so that multiple companies can share distribution centers and trans-shipment facilities to reduce the cost on unnecessary overinvestment in their private distribution networks, thus alleviating traffic congestion and saving energy and labor as a whole nation.

REFERENCES

Anderson, W.P. and Leinbach, T.R. (2007) E-commerce, logistics and the future of globalized freight, in T.R. Leinbach and C. Capineri (eds), *Globalized Freight Transport: Intermodality, E-Commerce, Logistics and Sustainability*. Cheltenham, UK and Northampton, MA, USA, Edward Elgar.

Anderson, W.P., Chatterjee, L. and Lakshmanan, T.R. (2003) E-commerce, transportation, and economic geography, *Growth and Change*, 34, 415–32.

Bakos, J.Y. (1997) Reducing buyer search costs: implications for electronic marketplaces, *Management Science*, 43, 1672–92.

Borenstein, S. and Saloner, G. (2001) Economics and electronic commerce, *Journal of Economic Perspectives*, 15, 3–12.

Cairncross, F. (2001) *The Death of Distance.* Cambridge MA, Harvard Business School Press.

Chen, S.-J. and Chang, T-Z. (2003) A descriptive model of online shopping process: some empirical results, *International Journal of Service Industry Management*, 14, 556–69.

Chong, L., Kennedy, D. and Chan, W.M. (2006) Direct shipping logistics planning for a hub-and-spoke network with given discrete intershipment times, *International Transactions in Operational Research*, 13, 17–32.

Crainic, T.G. (2000) Service network design in freight transportation, *European Journal of Operations Research*, 122, 272–88.

Goldman, A.J. (1972) Minimax location of a facility in a network, *Transportation Science*, 6, 407–18.

Hesse, M. (2002) Shipping news: the implications of electronic commerce for logistics and freight transport, *Resources, Conservation, and Recycling*, 36, 211–40.

Hong, G. (2003) *Towards a Strategic Transportation Policy in the Knowledge-Based Society: Teleshopping Implication for Personal Travel and Freight Transportation*. Seoul, The Korea Transport Institute.

Huppertz, P. (1999) Market changes require new supply chain thinking, *Transportation and Distribution*, 40, 70–74.

Jian, Y., Jaillet, P. and Mahmassani, H. (2004) Real-time multi-vehicle truckload pick-up and delivery problems, *Transportation Science*, 38, 135–48.

Korea National Statistical Office (2007) Statistics on South Korean cyber shopping malls in 2006, http://www.nso.go.kr (accessed 10 June 2008).

Lappierre, S.D., Ruiz, A.B. and Soriano, P. (2004) Designing distribution networks: formulation and solution heuristics, *Transportation Science*, 38, 174–87.

Lim, H.J. (2009), Geographical implications of online shopping on physical distribution networks, PhD thesis, Department of Geography, University at Buffalo.

Lim, H.J., Lim, J.W. and Lee, H. (2007) Exploratory study on the efficient operation of parcel delivery network with the growth of online shopping industries, *Korean Journal of Marketing*, 9, 97–129.

Liu, J., Li, C-L. and Chan, C-Y. (2003) Mixed truck delivery systems with both hub-and-spoke and direct shipment, *Transportation Research E*, 39, 325–39.

Lumsden, K. (1999) Improving the efficiency of the Hub and Spoke system for the SKF European distribution network, *International Journal of Physical Distribution & Logistics Management*, 29, 50–64.

Mason, J.B. and Burns, D.J. (1998) *Retailing*. Houston, Dame Publications.

Mokhtarian, P.L. (2004) A conceptual analysis of the transportation impacts of B2C e-commerce, *Transportation*, 31, 257–84.

Savelsbergh, M.W.P. and Sol, M. (1995) The general pickup and delivery problem, *Transportation Science*, 29, 17–29.

Steinfield, C.W. and Whitten, P. (2003) Community level socioeconomic impacts of electronic commerce, in C.W. Steinfield (eds), *New Directions in Research on E-commerce*. West Lafayette, IN, Purdue University Press.

Strader, T.J. and Shaw, M.J. (2000) Electronic markets: impact and implications, in M. Shaw, R. Blanning, T. Strader and A. Whinston (eds), *Handbook on Electronic Commerce*. Berlin, Springer.

Taaffe, E.J., Gauthier, H.L. and O'Kelly, M.E. (1996) *Geography of Transportation*. Upper Saddle River, NJ, Prentice Hall.

US Census Bureau (2009) 2007 E-commerce multi-sector E-Stats report, http://www.census.gov/econ/estats/2007/2007reportfinal.pdf (accessed 20 July 2009).

Visser, E-J. and Lanzendorf, M. (2004) Mobility and accessibility effects of B2C E-commerce: a literature review, *Tijdschrift voor Economische en Sociale Geografie*, 95, 189–205.

Zapfel, G. and Wasner, M. (2002) Planning and optimization of hub-and-spoke transportation networks of cooperative third-party logistics providers, *International Journal of Production Economics*, 78, 207–220.

7. Discussion of the necessity of accessibility standards: the German 'Guidelines for Integrated Network Design' (RIN)

Regine Gerike, Andreas Rau and Jürgen Gerlach

7.1 INTRODUCTION

Societies are facing a number of ecological, financial and demographic challenges, which are likely to impact on their future development. The transport sector both causes problems and has the potential to help solve them. Modern transport enables global trade and communication but at the same time is responsible for a significant amount of negative environmental, social and political effects; with issues of energy supply and climate change as examples of the most pressing problems.

Given that financial and natural resources are becoming scarcer, the question of how much and what type of mobility today's societies want gains significantly in importance. The goal is to increase the efficiency of the transport system, while at the same time, maintaining basic mobility for all people. The spatial and the transport system should enable all people to satisfy their basic needs, even with the reduction in natural and financial resources. That is, people must be able to reach the destinations where they can satisfy their basic needs.

In addition to today's needs, we must include the needs of future generations in this discussion if we base our argument on the goal of sustainable development as a politically driven and broadly accepted qualitative vision.

According to the Brundtland Commission, the qualitative vision of sustainable development can be defined as a development 'that meets the needs of the present without compromising the ability of future generations to meet their own needs' (World Commission on Environment and Development, 1987). Hence, the goal is not only to ensure the satisfaction of basic needs for the current population, but also for future generations.

Meeting people's needs is, however, an ambitious goal because human needs are variable and they are dependent on the individual and the context. They are unstable and contradictory and administrative planning is not flexible enough to promptly determine and satisfy human needs. There is always a lag between determining human needs (e.g. from surveys, observations, elections) and satisfying human needs (e.g. through transport policy measures).

The market mechanism embedded in an appropriate transportation policy is the only instrument that is able to simultaneously determine and satisfy human needs. With its ability to satisfy human needs in an efficient way, the market is an important component for achieving sustainable transport development. A vital prerequisite for enabling the market mechanism to successfully satisfy needs is the right framework. Prices must send the correct signals, so that the market participants are able to correctly weigh costs and benefits.

However, even with an optimal allocation of resources, the satisfaction of certain needs in certain groups of people might not be achieved because the market mechanism does not take distributional issues into consideration. It is conceivable that despite good market results (e.g. measured in terms of GDP), basic needs of certain groups of people are insufficiently satisfied due to imbalances in the distribution of market results. Efficient and profitable public transport that only serves profitable lines and does not provide an all-encompassing supply is an example of this. In this case, there might be people who are unable to reach destinations where they can satisfy their basic needs even though the market functions properly.

From this line of reasoning comes the need to set administrative boundaries for the distribution of certain goods: basic mobility should not fall below a certain level and consumption of natural resources should not exceed a certain level. The goal should be to provide basic mobility for all people while at the same time meeting ambitious environmental targets. This basic mobility should be defined by measurable standards to accurately document the degree to which goals have been achieved.

Hence, it can be stated that quantified goals that secure basic mobility for all people and thus enable all people to satisfy their basic needs represent a fundamental component of the concept of sustainable development. However, precisely defining basic needs is not any easier than defining people's needs in general. Which of the needs in Maslow's hierarchy can be regarded as basic needs? Human beings cannot survive only with food. They need contact with other people, a sense of belonging and esteem. Even if we focus on some very basic needs such as food, whose basic status seems to be beyond dispute, the question remains: What does this mean for the discussion on basic mobility? Should everybody have a supermarket within walking distance? What type of supermarket should this be? Should we set better standards for the availability of restaurants or of delivery services?

The definition of basic needs and basic mobility is a highly normative task that can only be done with the help of societal discussion. It is most likely that the level of mobility people claim in industrialized countries goes far beyond satisfying basic needs such as food or education. Each society has to decide on its own which 'basic' mobility to provide.

Hence, concrete basic mobility might differ between countries and points in time; we could also call it society-driven mobility. We will nevertheless use the concept of basic mobility throughout this paper with respect to the claim and assumption that this basic mobility should at the very least guarantee the satisfaction of needs whose basic status is beyond dispute.

The focus of this paper is the question of how to define the qualitative goals of such basic mobility, that is, how to make this concept manageable in terms of concrete planning. Thus, the goal is to develop requirements and possible criteria for describing this basic mobility and to illustrate them with the help of the German 'Guidelines for Integrated Network Design' (RIN) as an example of transport components in a system of accessibility standards.

7.2   CRITERIA FOR DESCRIBING BASIC MOBILITY

Requirements for Basic Mobility

Based on its Latin origin, 'mobility' is defined in this paper as the ability to move and to reach certain destinations. Thus, mobility refers more to opportunities than to realized activities. The opportunities people have are determined by the accessibility that the transport and spatial system provides:

- Quality and quantity of available destinations (spatial system)
- Quality and quantity of opportunities to reach those destinations (transport system)
- People's ability to make use of the available opportunities (individual characteristics such as car availability or reduced mobility).

Therefore, mobility refers in this paper to particular individuals, goods, or information, and focuses on a subject or object and its ability to move. Mobility does not necessarily require a destination; it is more a general measure of the ability to move. For example, people who are able to climb stairs have higher mobility than people who are unable to do so.

However, accessibility in this paper refers to certain locations or areas and their connection to other locations or areas. Thus, accessibility mainly takes the 'system perspective', whereas mobility primarily takes the 'individual perspective'.

Accessibility has been chosen for this paper as a suitable concept to describe the spatial and transport components of people's mobility because accessibility effectively describes the two external system components of people's mobility: the type and number of destinations available and the opportunities to reach these destinations. Hence, the goal of this paper is to develop options for a system of accessibility standards that guarantees basic mobility as initially discussed.

The benefit of measurable standards or reference values is a matter of debate in the literature. Fixed standards are rigid and therefore become outdated easily. Furthermore, it is difficult to find consensus regarding the selection of indicators, especially where quantitative target values are concerned. Criticism of standards can result if values are set too high, and are not achieved despite great effort. In other situations, unrealistic goals might simply be ignored because there is no chance of reaching them. The danger of neglecting the standards also occurs if the standards are set too low and can be met without concerted effort.

Among the advantages of standards is the possibility to compare different areas and to determine degrees of goal achievement. If goals are vaguely formatted then it is not always clear what measures need to be put in place to achieve them.

These are the critical arguments for a system of measurable standards, which describe the basic accessibility that the spatial and the transport system should provide. This goal remains an empty promise if it is not made concrete. Guaranteeing accessibility to satisfy basic needs is always related to cost and effort, and society must decide the scale of this cost and effort. 'How much' basic accessibility should each individual be entitled to? This question can only be answered through quantitative standards.

Several of the aforementioned points of criticism concerning standards can be addressed through a flexible design of the standard system. However, it is always a challenge to find the optimal balance between flexibility and thoroughness.

Development of Possible Criteria for a System of Accessibility Standards

A good basis for the spatial planning component of minimum standards is the German system of central locations, which is used at all levels of spatial planning. Under this system, inhabited areas are assessed on their spatial significance and classified as either central locations (with different levels) or as areas which do not provide any central location functions. Central locations include those areas that provide service functions to both their own residents as well as to others within their catchment area, or those areas which fulfil a specific service function. They are favoured locations for public and private service facilities as well as centres of business, employment and education. Areas without a central location function are dependent on the central function areas for the provision of services.

In accordance with German federal spatial planning, the following levels of centrality are usually defined:[1]

- Agglomerations (A): international or very large area of influence
- Upper-level centres (UC): administrative, service, cultural and business centres and which provide more specialized services
- Mid-level centres (MC): cover special needs and are focal points for business, industry and services
- Basic centres (BC): provide basic services covering everyday needs to people within their own local area including sub-centres and small centres that must be specified in spatial planning at the regional level.

All other settlements are classified as communities (C) without any central location function. Higher level central locations always provide services to centres at the lower levels. Locations which provide some of the functions of a higher level centre are treated as higher level centres.

The facilities available in central locations are a vital aspect of guaranteeing basic mobility and should reflect the importance of the centre. Lists of facilities that should be available in central locations according to their level are given in the spatial planning documents of some German states.[2] From the viewpoint of basic mobility, such facility catalogues are necessary for central locations because only the combination of their position, their facilities and their connection to each other (and to communities) can guarantee that the required destinations are available and accessible.

Previous work regarding basic needs is helpful in the discussion of which facilities should be available in central locations to guarantee a basic spatial supply.[3] In German spatial planning, the term 'basic existence functions' (Grunddaseinsfunktionen) is used to specify the concept of basic needs (Akademie für Raumforschung und Landesplanung, 2005). The basic existence functions commonly used are: shelter, work, access to provisions, access to education, access to recreation, access to transport and communication.[4] To guarantee these functions and thus to guarantee a local supply of goods and services such as food and health care, we need a very detailed system for central locations.

Such a system can be designed not only by assigning levels of centrality to municipalities and large populated areas such as cities and towns, but also to areas within municipalities. There is no legal framework in Germany for this intra-municipal structuring as it is primarily for land-use planning in central locations.

The intra-municipal functional structure should be developed based on the significance of the land-use and the available facilities. Intra-municipal areas of concentration can be classified as main centres, city districts or city centres, district centres, and groups of shops (small centres). Main centres should be categorized one level below the central location itself with subsequent intra-municipal levels following in decreasing order starting from this level.

Using this procedure, a system of intra-municipal central locations can be established that fits well into the system of inter-municipal central locations and that is able to ensure local supply to residential areas.

In addition to the advantages of the central locations system in guaranteeing the spatial components of basic accessibility, the following problems are discussed in the literature (Akademie für Raumforschung und Landesplanung, 2005; Gerike, 2007): the locations, the levels and the facilities of central locations are determined at the state and the regional level, which leads to differences in the number, description and facilities of central locations. A further critical point is the sense of normative structuring of regions in general, as in many cases transport flow does not correspond with the system of the normatively-fixed central locations. Nevertheless, a central locations system is an effective way of establishing the spatial components of basic accessibility: their location ensures that the transport system can make them accessible. Their facilities ensure that the necessary quality and quantity of destinations are available.

The core element of making central locally-distributed facilities accessible to inhabitants is the connection of central areas to each other as well as to residential areas. Here, the transport components of accessibility standards are addressed.

Target values for journey times between central locations are derived from spatial planning and have been used in transport planning for many years.[5] Tables 7.1 and 7.2 show target values as found in the 'Guidelines for Integrated Network Design' (RIN).[6] Journey time includes getting to transport from home, waiting and travel time, and getting from transport to final destination. The listed target values are not quality criterion for transport planning on their own. However, they form the basis for

Table 7.1   *Target values for accessibility to central locations from*
                residential areas

Central location	Journey time (min)	
	Car	Public transport
Basic centres (BC)	≤ 20	≤ 20
Mid-level centres (MC)	≤ 30	≤ 45
Upper-level centres (UC)	≤ 60	≤ 90

Source: Forschungsgesellschaft für Straßen- und Verkehrswesen (2009).

Table 7.2   *Target values for accessibility to central locations from*
                neighbouring central location with the same level of centrality

Central location	Journey time to nearest neighbour (min)	
	Car	Public transport
Basic centres (BC)	≤ 25	≤ 40
Mid-level centres (MC)	≤ 45	≤ 65
Upper-level centres (UC)	≤ 120	≤ 150
Agglomerations (A)	≤ 180	≤ 180

Source: Forschungsgesellschaft für Straßen- und Verkehrswesen (2009).

assessing the quality of infrastructure supply with the help of speed-based target values for specific network elements and for assessing the quality of complete transport routes between central locations.

A focus on public transport is recommended when designing the links between central locations as a component of basic accessibility. This is because travel times with private transport are generally quite low and bicycle and pedestrian traffic are not relevant to linking central areas with higher levels of centrality. Eighty-eight per cent of the German population need less than 45 minutes to reach the nearest upper-level centre and less than 15 minutes to reach the nearest mid-level centre by car (Bundesamt für Bauwesen und Raumordnung, 2005). Moreover, standards for private transport are only useful for part of the population and thus, are unsuitable for providing basic transportation supply to all people.

Linking central locations to each other, and to residential areas, is often done in cost terms such as journey times, which take into consideration travel times, access times to and from transport, and operating frequencies.[7] In addition to travel times between centres, the quality of public transport services are included (density of stops, operating times and amount of seating provided).

An important domain of basic accessibility is the neighbourhood because many basic needs are satisfied within this area; thus functions are addressed that are assigned to the intra-municipal centres. In this context, minimum standards for pedestrian and bike traffic are important as they represent the most favourable options for short distances, both from an ecological and economic viewpoint. Already 59 per cent of all trips are shorter than five kilometres and in private transport this share is 43 per cent.[8] The proportion of short distance trips can be further increased by good accessibility to nearby destinations. Distance measures are conceivable as minimum standards for the neighbourhood, but further criteria such as the quality of town planning should be included. Thus, the following are possible transport components of basic accessibility:

- Distance measures of pedestrian and bike traffic in the neighbourhood, for instance, maximum distance of x metres to a shop (e.g. general store) for y per cent of the population
- Measures of cost and effort such as time, money, comfort or combined measures for linking housing to central locations as well as central locations to each other
- Density of stops for public transport, for instance, maximum distance to stop of x metres for y per cent of the population
- Operating frequency of public transport, for instance, frequencies differentiated by different traffic times.

7.3   THE GERMAN 'GUIDELINES FOR INTEGRATED NETWORK DESIGN' (RIN)

There are several approaches to implementing elements of the accessibility standards system as described above. These are found not only in spatial and transport planning, but also in other political areas such as welfare policy.[9]

The 'Guidelines for Integrated Network Design' formulate standards for all transport modes and for all spatial levels reaching from the macro level of connecting agglomerations to the micro level of securing a local supply of infrastructure for pedestrian, bicycle, public and car transport. The RIN focus mainly on passenger transport. They include car, public passenger transport (railways, underground rail, tram and bus), bicycle and pedestrian transport modes as well as the design of linkage points for intermodal transport (Park+Ride, Rail+Fly and Bike+Ride). The RIN orientate these standards directly towards the system of central locations identified as suitable bases for the spatial components of a basic accessibility. Additionally, the RIN are an attempt to integrate scientific knowledge of transport planning into a highly binding planning guideline.

The RIN are not explicitly orientated to guaranteeing basic accessibility, but also provide target values that build on the goals of land use and regional planning and derive standards for transport planning out of these goals. Based on the argument that these standards can be interpreted as standards of a socially desirable, and therefore basic, accessibility. The system is designed as a flexible system that allows for exemptions in both directions.

The RIN suggest targets for connecting central locations to each other and to residential areas. The following are goals of the RIN:

- To guarantee the supply function for people living within the catchment areas of central locations
- To guarantee the exchange function between central locations
- To support the development of population structures that are concentrated on the system of central locations
- To support the special importance of the interconnection between national and international agglomerations.

The RIN are assigned the highest category in the publications of the German Research Society on Roads and Transport (Forschungsgesellschaft für Straßen- und Verkehrswesen) and are thus strongly binding for German authorities and transport planners. They were announced by the German Federal Transport Ministry with the request that they be applied to trunk roads. The RIN are the first part of a highly complex set of guidelines that sets standards for all steps of infrastructure design; from network design to the alignment and assessment of specific street sections.

Figure 7.1 offers an overview of the three main parts of the RIN:

1. *Functional structure and hierarchy of the transport network:* A category is assigned to each section of a transport route. A transport route is defined here as the connection between two central locations or between a central location and residential areas. The category that is assigned to a specific segment is based on the significance of the connections that use this section of the network and the level of demand from adjoining areas. The aim is to classify the sections of a transport route as appropriate to their functions.

2. *Quality requirements for the development of transport networks, network segments and linkage points:* General quality requirements are established for the transport routes of all included transport systems (beyond only single network sections) based on the general

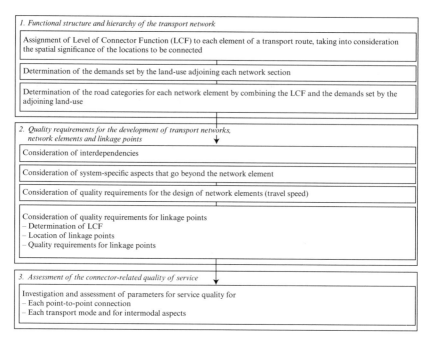

Figure 7.1   Structure of the RIN

requirements from spatial planning and the functional structuring of the transport network. From these network requirements, quality requirements for single network segments are developed depending on the classification of the section that was made in the first step.

3. *Assessment of the connector-related quality of service:* Characteristic values for the quality of service are developed for each relevant transport route within one individual transport system or for a combination of transport systems. A comparison of these characteristic values with target levels of quality allows the transport routes to be assessed as 'good' or 'bad' from the user's point of view.

Functional Structure of the Transport Networks

The starting point for the RIN is the system of central locations. The combination of this system and the target values for journey times between central locations and residential areas builds the basis for the functional structuring of the transport network. In addition, it is the basis for the development of quality requirements for the transport networks and linkage points in the RIN. Each network section is classified according to:

- its importance: level of connector function (LCF)
- its function (road category).

The LCF is derived from the level of central locations to be connected. Six levels of connector function are defined to describe the significance of connection routes. These levels are valid for all modes of transport as long as they are relevant for the respective mode. The importance of a connection results from the importance of the locations to be connected. The RIN distinguish between connections related to the service functions for residential locations in catchment areas and connections that enable exchange between central locations. Table 7.3 gives an overview of the LCF used in the RIN from level 0 to level V.

For each level of connector function, the connections between the central locations is described in a first step by point-to-point speed matrices. The transfer of the LCFs from the point-to-point speed connections to the transport networks is made separately for each transport system and for each relevant combination of transport systems. Preferably, this transfer is made using the existing transport networks. Those elements of the network should be selected that are suitable for taking on the LCF or that could be developed as such. Where necessary, network elements that have yet to be constructed may be included in this process. The criteria for the transfer of the LCFs to the transport network, should include, in addition to the directness of the connection and the journey speed, traffic safety, the relief of built-up areas or other areas worthy of protection, and the bundling of traffic streams.

In the second step a road category is assigned to each network segment in addition to the LCF. Roads may have combinations of functions imposed on them in terms of the expectations set by the adjoining land-uses. A road category is assigned to each road section in accordance with the following criteria:

- Road type (motorways, country roads, urban roads)
- Location (outside built-up areas, bordering built-up areas, within built-up areas)
- Type of adjoining land-use (non-built-up, built-up)
- Main road or access road.

Figure 7.2 provides an overview of the five road categories that are used in the RIN and their combinations with the LCF.

Table 7.4 shows those combinations that can be expected to lead to satisfactory solutions from both a constructional and operational point of view. Further road categories do exist in practice, but in these cases there

Table 7.3   Level of connector functions in the RIN

Level of Connector Function		Ranking Criteria		Description
Level	Designation	Service Function	Exchange Function	
0	Continental	NA	A – A	Connection between agglomerations
I	Wide-area	UC – A	UC – UC	Connection between upper centres and agglomerations and between upper centres
II	Inter-regional	MC – UC	MC – MC	Connection between mid-level centres and upper centres and between mid-level centres
III	Regional	BC – MC	BC – BC	Connection between basic centres and mid-level centres and between basic centres
IV	Local	C – BC	C – C	Connection between communities without central location significance and basic centres and among communities with no central location significance
V	Small area	D – C	NA	Connection between premises and communities with no central location significance and basic centres

Notes: A = Agglomeration, UC = Upper Centre, MC = Mid-Level Centre, BC = Basic Centre, C = Communities without central location significance, D = Premises and NA = Not applicable.

are often significant conflicts between the transport and non-transport uses, which can only (if at all) be resolved with considerable difficulty by using design-related measures. In this case, an effort should be made to separate the three types of connection functions, access functions and place functions. In general, high LCF should be combined with higher level road categories to minimize conflicts in their usage. Level I central locations are connected by motorways and secondary roads. Level II central locations can be connected by the road categories AS, LS or VS. Level III central locations can only be connected by the road categories LS, VS or HS. Lower LCF should be combined by road category LS, HS or ES.

Road category / Level of Connector Function		Motorways	Country roads	Main roads (non-built-up)	Main roads (built-up)	Access roads
		AS	LS	VS	HS	ES
Continental	0	AS 0	▓	–	–	–
Wide-area	I	AS I	LS I	▓	–	–
Inter-regional	II	AS II	LS II	VS II	▓	–
Regional	III	–	LS III	VS III	HS III	▓
Local	IV	–	LS IV	–	HS IV	ES IV
Small area	V	–	LS V	–	–	ES V

AS I	Existing category designation
▓	Problematic
–	Does not exist or is not tenable

Source: Forschungsgesellschaft für Straßen- und Verkehrswesen (2009).

Figure 7.2 Connection matrix showing the assignment of road categories in the RIN

The RIN develop similar systems for public transport, bicycle and pedestrian traffic. Tables 7.6 and 7.7 show the categories for public transport and bicycle transport. For pedestrian traffic, two categories are introduced without any distinction between different LCF: the category AR includes pedestrian infrastructure outside built-up areas (mainly paths for leisure purposes). The category IR includes pedestrian infrastructure inside built-up areas that are mainly used for everyday purposes.

Quality Requirements for the Development of Transport Networks, Network Elements and Linkage Points

Central locations are connected by a series of network elements that together form a transport route. The quality of the transport route can

Table 7.4   Road categories for motor vehicle traffic in the RIN

Level of Connector Function (LCF)		Category	Description
Level	Designation		
0, I	Continental	AS 0/I	Long distance motorway
	Wide-area	LS I	Trunk road
II	Inter-regional	AS II	Inter-regional motorway, urban motorway
		LS II	Inter-regional road
		VS II	Cross-city road, non-built-up arterial road
III	Regional	LS III	Regional road
		VS III	Cross-city road, non-built-up arterial road
		HS III	Cross-city road, inner-municipal arterial road
IV	Local	LS IV	Local access road
		HS IV	Cross-city road, inner-municipal arterial road
		ES IV	Collector road
V	Small area	LS V	Link road
		ES V	Residential street

Source: Forschungsgesellschaft für Straßen- und Verkehrswesen (2009).

only be improved by upgrading the compositing elements of the route. Quality requirements for specific network elements can be derived from target values for the transport routes. The RIN operationalize these quality requirements by standard distance ranges and target values for car travel speed on the network elements. These requirements are formulated at a micro level of specific network elements. Nevertheless, they help to guarantee the exchange function and the provision function of central locations as they are derived from spatial planning.

Table 7.5 shows the classification of network sections for motor vehicle traffic including range and targeted car speed.

The RIN also include quality requirements for public transport and bicycle transport, which are shown in Tables 7.6 and 7.7. These requirements are described by criteria for travel speed and for the quality of pedestrian infrastructure.

Assessing the Service Quality of Connections

The combination of the functional structuring of the transport network and the development of quality requirements for network elements

Table 7.5   Road categories for motor vehicle traffic and target values for median car speed

Level of Connector Function (LCF)		Road category	Standard range (km)	Target car travel speed (km/h)
Level	Designation			
0, I	Continental	AS 0/I	40–500	100–120
	Wide-area	LS I	40–160	80–90
II	Inter-regional	AS II	10–70	70–90
		LS II	10–70	70–90
		VS II	–	40–60
III	Regional	LS III	5–35	60–70
		VS III	–	30–50
		HS III	–	20–30
IV	Local	AL IV	Up to 15	50–60
		HS IV	–	15–25
		ES IV	–	–
V	Small area	ES V	–	–

Source: Forschungsgesellschaft für Straßen- und Verkehrswesen (2009).

enables a comprehensive description of the quality of connections between central locations and from central locations to residential areas. This is because the functional structure and the quality requirements are derived in a top-down-approach from specifications of spatial planning and are broken down into specific network sections.

In addition to the criteria that are related to specific network sections, the RIN introduce criteria for assessing the service quality of complete transport routes between central locations and between central locations and residential areas. The goal of these criteria is to obtain a picture of the overall quality of the network for different transport modes.

Relevant criteria for connection quality at this macro level are journey time, costs, directness, temporal and spatial availability of transport services, reliability, and safety and comfort. Table 7.8 shows the criteria that are used in the RIN.

Two indicators are used for the criterion of time. The point-to-point speed is calculated by dividing point-to-point distance[10] by journey time. Thus, point-to-point speed relates to the distance covered and therefore facilitates the comparison of connections over different distances. The ratio of individual to public transport journey time describes the relative quality of public compared to private transport.

The detour factor is defined as the ratio of travel distance to

Table 7.6   Categories for public transport and target travel speed

Category		Sub Category		Standard range (km)	Target speed (km/h)
FB	Long distance rail transport	FB 0	Continental long distance rail transport	200–500	160–250
		FB I	Wide-area long distance rail transport	60–300	120–160
NB	Regional rail transport outside built-up areas	NB I	Wide-area regional rail transport	40–200	50–110
		NB II	Interregional rail transport	10–70	40–100
		NB III	Regional rail transport	5–35	35–100
UB	Independent rail transport	UB II	Regional rail transport, metro, tram as main connection	–	30–45
		UB III	Regional rail transport, metro, tram as side connection	–	25–35
SB	Light rail	SB II	Light rail and tram as main connection	–	20–30
		SB III	Light rail and tram as side connection	–	15–25
		SB IV	Light rail and tram for accessing an area	–	10–20
TB	Tram/bus	TB II	Tram and bus as main connection	–	10–25
		TB III	Tram and bus as side connection	–	5–20
		TB IV	Tram and bus for accessing an area	–	–
RB	Regional bus transport outside built-up areas	RB II	Interregional bus transport	10–70	30–50
		RB III	Regional bus transport	5–35	25–40
		RB IV	Local bus transport	Up to 20	20–35

Source: Forschungsgesellschaft für Straßen- und Verkehrswesen (2009).

point-to-point distance. The frequency of change is defined as the average number of changes that are necessary on a specific transport route. Changes may occur within one transport mode but also include transfers between private cars and public transport. The two indicators for the criterion of directness should only be used if the criterion of time is poorly

Table 7.7   Categories for bicycle infrastructure and target values for travel speed for daily traffic

Category			Sub Category	Standard range (km)	Target speed (km/h)
AR	Outside built-up areas	AR II	Interregional bicycle connection	10–70	20–30
		AR III	Regional bicycle connection	5–35	20–30
		AR IV	Local bicycle connection	Up to 15	20–30
IR	Inside built-up areas	IR II	Inner-municipal express bicycle connection	–	15–25
		IR III	Inner-municipal standard bicycle connection	–	15–20
		IR IV	Inner-municipal bicycle connections	–	15–20
		IR V	Inner-municipal bicycle connections	–	–

Source: Forschungsgesellschaft für Straßen- und Verkehrswesen (2009).

Table 7.8   Criteria and indicators for describing the quality of transport routes

Criterion	Indicator
Time	● Point-to-point speed
	● Ratio of individual to public transport journey time
Directness	● Detour factor
	● Frequency of change

assessed. In this case, the reasons for low point-to-point speeds and/or bad journey time ratios of individual to public transport can be explained by the indicators found in the criterion of directness.

The RIN do not set target values for any of the indicators but rather work with the six levels of service quality, which are shown in Table 7.9. These LSQs are used in the diagrams in addition to the well-known LOS system for single infrastructure elements for assessing connector-related service quality as a function of point-to-point speed and point-to-point distance. These diagrams were developed on the basis of analyses of

Table 7.9   Levels of service quality

LSQ	Description
A	Very good quality
B	Good quality
C	Satisfactory quality
D	Acceptable quality
E	Poor quality
F	Unacceptable quality

numerous connections. The concept of LSQ is applied to all transport modes consistently and enables an easy and traceable weighing and decision finding by the political decision makers.

Figure 7.3 shows the levels of service quality for a comparative assessment of point-to-point speed of cars versus public transport. With those levels of service quality, it is possible to rate the quality of transport routes. The analyses show that differentiation between LCD is not necessary because point-to-point speed adequately describes the connection quality.

Service quality levels for separately assessing private traffic are more ambitious than those used for separately assessing public transport or those used for the comparative analysis, as shown in Figure 7.3. In addition, service quality levels are given for the ratio between journey times of private and public transport (Figure 7.4) and for the assessment of detour factors (Figure 7.5).

7.4   CONCLUSIONS

Transport policy should not concentrate primarily on improving traffic, but rather on the underlying purpose, that is, on the activities that can be carried out with the help of transport and on the needs that can be satisfied by those activities. The definition of the concepts of basic needs and basic mobility is a normative task and changes over time and between regions. However, this definition is required to formulate concrete standards that guarantee the satisfaction of certain needs, the basic necessity of which is beyond dispute.

These standards should describe opportunities provided by the transport and the spatial system as well as specific needs of certain groups of people. Accessibility standards are a suitable means of describing these components of basic mobility. The system of central locations is an appropriate basis for designing the spatial components of the standards system.

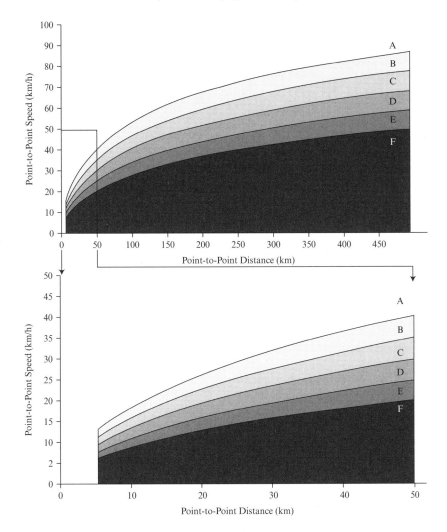

Source: Forschungsgesellschaft für Straßen- und Verkehrswesen (2009).

Figure 7.3   *Service quality level for point-to-point speed for a comparative assessment of private and public transport*

It must be broken down into spatially low levels of centrality to guarantee the local supply of daily goods and services. Standards are necessary for the system's structure and the facilities of central locations.

The transport components of the system should describe the quality of the connections between central locations, and from central locations to

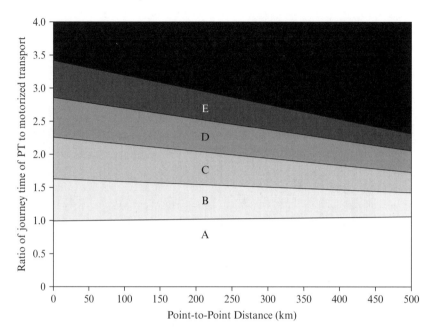

Source: Forschungsgesellschaft für Straßen- und Verkehrswesen (2009).

*Figure 7.4   Benchmarks for the ratio of journey-time of public versus
             private transport*

residential areas. The focus of these transport system standards should
be on public transport and on the 'slow modes' (pedestrian and bicycle)
to enable all people to make use of the standards and to reduce the
environmental impacts of transportation.

   The 'Guidelines for Integrated Network Design' (RIN) are a successful
example of designing the transport components of such a system of accessibility standards. The RIN deal with the design of transport networks
for public, private motorized, bicycle and pedestrian modes of transport.
Firstly, the RIN establish the functional structure and hierarchy of the
transport network. Secondly, the RIN develop quality requirements for
the development of specific network elements. These are derived from the
general requirements, which result from spatial planning and functional
structuring of the transport network. Standard distance ranges and car
speeds are used as criteria to describe these quality requirements. Thirdly,
the RIN develop indicators for assessing the service quality of complete
transport routes (connections between central locations and to residential areas). Service quality levels are determined for point-to-point speed

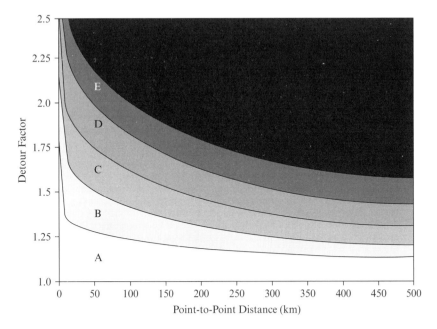

Source: Forschungsgesellschaft für Straßen- und Verkehrswesen (2009).

Figure 7.5 Orientation values for the assessment of detour factors

and the ratio of private to public travel time. This approach allows the transport routes to be assessed as 'good' or 'bad' from the user's point of view.

Hence, the RIN shows that it is possible to develop a comprehensive system of standards that is not only clear and pragmatic, but that also includes all transport modes and all spatial levels from a detailed micro level to the macro accessibility of agglomerations. As such, the RIN are an important component of basic mobility and thus form an important component of sustainable transport development. This component must be supplemented with criteria for the spatial elements of basic mobility and by criteria for the environmental and economic aspects of sustainable transportation development.

ACKNOWLEDGMENTS

The authors would like to thank the members of the Forschungsgesellschaft für Straßen- und Verkehrswesen committee 'Network Design' for developing the RIN method and for their comments and advice concerning this paper.

NOTES

1. In Germany the states ('Länder') are responsible for determining the central locations so that the number and designation of the central locations differs slightly among the states. Here we use the classification that the RIN is based on.
2. See Hessian Ministry for Economy, Transport and Spatial Development (2000).
3. See Gerike (2007) for an overview.
4. 'Access to provision' is sometimes complemented by 'mobility'. Self-defence has also been suggested as the 8th basic function. These basic existence functions correspond to the origin-destinations-groups used in transport planning (Cerwenka et al., 2007). Gerike (2007) argues that access to transport is not a basic function in its own right but is necessary to make such functions possible. This is because basic existence functions are described as basic needs and transport is not regarded as a need in and of itself, but rather as a means to satisfy needs. Transport is referred to as a secondary need because of this.
5. See Gerike (2007) for an overview.
6. The target values for cars were used in the predecessor of the RIN but no target values were given for public transport (Forschungsgesellschaft für Straßen- und Verkehrswesen, 1988).
7. These can be considered as average waiting times.
8. See http://www.mobilitaet-in-deutschland.de/engl/index.htm (accessed 2 December 2009).
9. The most advanced example is the accessibility planning in the UK (Keller, 2008).
10. The distance is measured as a straight line between point A and point B.

REFERENCES

Akademie für Raumforschung und Landesplanung (2005) *Concise Dictionary of Spatial Planning*, Hannover, ARL. (In German.)

Bundesamt für Bauwesen und Raumordnung (2005) *Regional Planning Report, 21*, Bonn, BRR. http://www.bbr.bund.de/BBSR/DE/Veroeffentlichungen/Berichte/2000__2005/Bd21Raumordnungsbericht2005.html, 11/12/2009. (In German.)

Cerwenka, P., Hauger, G., Hörl, B. and Klamer, M. (2007) *Handbook of Transport System Planning*. Vienna, Österreichischer Kunst- und Kulturverlag. (In German.)

Forschungsgesellschaft für Straßen- und Verkehrswesen (1988) *Guidelines for the Design of Roads (RAS): Manual for the Functional Form of the Road Network (RAS-N)*. Cologne, FGSV. (In German.)

Forschungsgesellschaft für Straßen- und Verkehrswesen (2009) *Guidelines for Integrated Network Design (RIN)*. Cologne, FGSV. (In German.)

Gerike, R. (2007) *How to Make Sustainable Transportation a Reality – The Development of Three Constitutive Task Fields for Transportation*. München, Oekom.

Hessian Ministry for Economy, Transport and Spatial Development (Hessisches

Ministerium für Wirtschaft, Verkehr und Landesentwicklung) (2000) Regional development plan for the state, Wiesbaden. (In German.)

Keller, J. (2008) Accessibility planning in UK and Germany, diploma thesis, Technical University Dresden, Chair for Transport Ecology. (In German.)

World Commission on Environment and Development (1987) *Our Common Future: The World Commission on Environment and Development.* Oxford, Oxford University Press.

8. Transportation planning of the future: mitigating GHGs in the US through green litigation

Deb Niemeier, Erica Jones and Roger Cheng

8.1 INTRODUCTION

The US Intermodal Surface Transportation Efficiency Act of 1991 (ISTEA) signaled a paradigm shift in transportation planning, moving the process from a federal–state partnership to one in which the role of regional planning agencies became central to the selection and prioritization of transportation infrastructure (Taylor and Schweitzer, 2005). This devolution of responsibility has been reinforced with the subsequent passages of transportation enabling legislation, including the Transportation Equity Act for the 21st Century (TEA-21) and the Safe, Accountable, Flexible, Efficient Transportation Equity Act: A Legacy for Users (SAFETEA-LU). The broad perspective underlying these legislative actions was, and has been, that regional governance bodies are better suited for selecting and prioritizing transportation projects than are the state transportation agencies. The new, now well trodden path is clear: metropolitan planning organizations are responsible for prioritizing billions of dollars each year to implement long-term, 20-year regional transportation plans.

We now mark more than 15 years since the passage of ISTEA and while it is fairly clear that under this legislation the emphasis shifted from a single mode to consideration of a multi-modal system (McNabb, 1998), it is less obvious that the devolution of responsibility has enabled any greater ability – by being closer to where projects are really needed – in formulating regional responses to significant policy challenges. In this paper, we review two important recent case studies that highlight the difficulties of responding to shifting state and national priorities within the current institutional context of regional transportation planning.

8.2 CALIFORNIA AND CLIMATE CHANGE

California's efforts at mitigating greenhouse gas emissions are establishing a critical roadmap for others to follow. In 2006, California passed the California Global Warming Solutions Act (commonly known as AB 32), which mandates that the California Air Resources Board (ARB) set a greenhouse gas emissions cap for 2020 based on 1990 levels, implement and enforce regulations to meet the 2020 limit, and identify and design greenhouse gas emissions reduction measures. The medium-term 2020 target is coupled with a long-term reduction target of 80 percent of 1990 greenhouse gas (GHG) emissions by 2050.

With a 2020 transportation target reduction of about 25 percent (California Air Resources Board, 2007), even with the implementation of other regulatory mechanisms, there will still likely be an overall shortfall of between 14 and 25 million metric tonnes (MMTs). In part, this gap motivated passage of Senate Bill, SB 375, which is aimed at tightening the relationship between land use and transportation policies and AB 32 climate change goals. Specifically, SB 375 requires that the ARB set a regional GHG emissions target and that metropolitan planning organizations develop sustainable community strategy plans designed to meet the regional targets. These plans are supposed to be oriented toward reducing sprawl and encouraging higher density development. To incentivize this re-direction of planning, under the new law transit and mixed use residential projects will be eligible for a streamlined environmental review if they meet certain criteria (e.g. no wetlands or riparian areas, inclusion of open space and affordable housing, etc.).

While the jury is still out on whether metropolitan areas will be able to adequately respond to the mandates of SB 375 (Bishop, 2009), there are harbingers that suggest the shifting emphases in long-term regional planning towards reducing vehicle miles of travel will not be easy. For example, the process by which GHG emissions are considered in plan updates has been the focus of a number of recent lawsuits, including several by the state attorney general.

Here we look at two case studies of recent high occupancy vehicle (HOV) lane projects that illustrate the ability of regional government to shift priorities towards infrastructure and land use strategies that reduce GHG emissions. We argue through these studies that historical capital has accumulated around what were innovative transportation solutions in the early 1990s, post-ISTEA, and that attachment to these projects and plans are not easily shaken. Moreover, the way in which regional governments have organized themselves may actually prevent the kinds of shifts that are needed to address climate change. We begin with the history of US

Route 50 HOV project, near Sacramento, which was recently settled out of court; we then turn to an historical account of The Narrows, another HOV project, in Marin County, near San Francisco; this case has not yet been decided.

8.3   US ROUTE 50

US Route 50 (US-50) runs for about 3050 miles from Ocean City, Maryland to West Sacramento, California. The segment running through Sacramento begins in West Sacramento where it joins Business Loop 80; US-50 breaks away from I-80 near the Sacramento downtown, traveling eastward to Placerville and serving as the main travel corridor for suburbs east of Sacramento. The region comprises six counties and 22 cities, all under the umbrella of one metropolitan planning organization, the Sacramento Area Council of Governments (SACOG).[1]

By 2050, the Sacramento region is expected to have 1.7 million more people, 1 million more jobs, and around 800,000 new homes (Sacramento Area Council of Governments, 2005). Since 1970, the region's population has grown by more than 110 percent, with much of the historical growth, as well as the projected growth, occurring along the US-50 corridor (Sacramento Area Council of Governments, 2008). SACOG has studied the US-50 corridor since the 1980s in an effort to accommodate this growth (Sacramento Area Council of Governments, 1996)

In 1989, SACOG released what contains perhaps the first mention of the US 50 project, 'Metro Study', which recommended examining the expansion of the Sacramento Light Rail system, widening freeways, and building a regional network of HOV lanes as possible solutions to the pressure that growth was placing on the regional transportation system (Sacramento Area Council of Governments, 1996). This effort resulted in the High Occupancy Vehicle System Planning Study, released by SACOG in 1990, which explored implementation of HOV lanes in the Sacramento region. The study recommended that HOV lanes be added to US-50 between downtown Sacramento and Shingle Springs (Sacramento Area Council of Governments, 1996) (Figure 8.1, between point A and the eastern end of the black line). This recommendation was then included in Sacramento's 1993 Metropolitan Transportation Plan (Sac-MTP) and SACOG began to consider possible phasing configurations of the 33 miles of HOV lanes (Sacramento Area Council of Governments, 1996).

Between 1994 and 1997, SACOG continued to study the best phasing strategy for both building HOV lanes and expanding the regional transit system along US-50 (Sacramento Area Council of Governments, 1996).

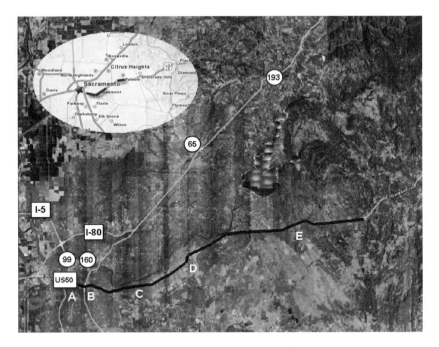

Figure 8.1   The 1990 HOV System Planning Study proposals

A major investment study (MIS)[2] compiled information from previous analysis that had been conducted along US-50 corridor with the intention of producing an investment plan for the corridor. Among the options considered in the study were various phasing plans for implementing HOV lanes as well as an analysis of the impacts of creating new HOV lanes compared to converting existing mixed flow lanes to HOV.

Four alternative phasing plans were developed for HOV lanes between downtown Sacramento and El Dorado Hills (Figure 8.1, between points A and E), which is approximately 7 miles closer to Sacramento than the original end point of Shingle Springs. The MIS also concluded that it would be more advantageous to widen the existing facility and add new HOV lanes than to convert an existing lane; SACOG reported that conversion of an existing lane resulted in 'higher levels of congestion on other freeway lanes and parallel roads', which leads to 'swift and strong public opposition in places it has been tried' (Sacramento Area Council of Governments, 1996). Although undoubtedly, there has been strong sentiment expressed in some places regarding this type of change, SACOG did not provide any evidence. The SACOG board adopted the MIS in December of 1997 (US Department of Transportation Federal Highway Administration, and

State of California Department of Transportation, 2007). From that point on, the HOV project segments identified in the MIS were also included in succeeding MTPs with the intent to build portions of the full project as funding became available.

Once the HOV project was adopted by SACOG and included in the MTPs, Caltrans (the California Department of Transportation) initiated a public outreach process beginning with the community consensus building in 2000. For the next two years, presentations were also made to the Project Steering Committee, the Sacramento Transportation Authority and the Sacramento City Council, and a Corridor Advisory Committee was created to evaluate the pros and cons of alternative plans as well as to recommend potential community enhancements (US Department of Transportation Federal Highway Administration, and State of California Department of Transportation, 2007). The public outreach process culminated in a Notice of Preparation (NOP) distributed in June 2005; this notice signaled to the public that a Draft Environmental Impact Report (DEIR) was being prepared for the addition of HOV lanes on US-50 between Sunrise Blvd and either Watt Avenue or the Highway 99 interchange (Figure 8.1, between point D and either C or B).[3] Within the EIR, three of the four original alternatives were eliminated based upon 'community concerns and cost considerations' and a variation of the fourth alternative was developed. These two variations only slightly differed in terms of their western end point and were the only alternatives considered in the EIR.

A 'Notice To Proceed' Can Mean a Lot of Things

Not long after the NOP was released the Neighbors Advocating Sustainable Transportation (NAST) and the Environmental Council of Sacramento (ECOS) swung into action (Bizjack, 2009a). ECOS is a Sacramento-based non-governmental organization focusing on the preservation of the region's natural resources, and NAST is a loosely affiliated coalition of community organizations and individual members with a focus on creating sustainable neighborhoods. ECOS and NAST raised a number of issues that ultimately resulted in a legal challenge to the approval and certification of the EIR.

Induced Travel and Sprawl

As far back as 1997, SACOG recognized that the 'development of HOV lanes in the outlying areas [vicinity of point E; Figure 8.1] could encourage development of land to higher intensities than provided for in the

General Plans' (Sacramento Area Council of Governments, 1996). A participant of the Corridor Advisory Committee stated that 'the project would encourage suburban sprawl' (US Department of Transportation Federal Highway Administration, and State of California Department of Transportation, 2007), however, when Caltrans drafted the EIR the agency claimed the addition of an HOV lane would not lead to increased sprawl or induced travel because 'given the levels of development being anticipated in Rancho Cordova, Folsom, and western El Dorado County, the proposed project would not add sufficient freeway capacity to affect growth patterns'. The Sierra Club as well as ECOS and NAST maintained that the growth inducing effects were not adequately analyzed in the EIR, while Caltrans stated that they were simply responding to land use decisions made at the local level and that 'the project cannot be said to remove a barrier to development on the US-50 corridor, since this development is already planned and, in many cases, constructed or being constructed'. The judge charged with hearing the arguments agreed with Caltrans and ruled that the analysis contained within the EIR was adequate as it related to induced travel because the project was not expected to greatly improve the peak period level of service or congestion (Environmental Council of Sacramento v. Caltrans, 2008).

Project Options: Conversion, Expansion, or Transit

While there was certainly some publicity when the community consensus building began in 2000,[4] open public debate did not really begin until the NOP was released in 2005 (US Department of Transportation Federal Highway Administration, and State of California Department of Transportation, 2007). The Sacramento City Council, which had been opposed to the HOV lanes since they were first presented to them in July 2001, directed their staff to find possible alternatives that could be considered in the EIR and passed a resolution reaffirming their opposition to the project in April 2006. Their opposition was founded on the belief that freeway expansion was in direct conflict to the smart growth policies that were contained within the Sacramento General Plan. Sacramento County had a similar opinion regarding the project, with the caveat that the county was supportive of HOV lanes provided they were converted from existing mixed flow lanes (Sacramento County, 1993).

In contrast, both the MIS and the long-range transportation plan, the MTP 2035, supported HOV lanes only if they were an expansion of the existing roadway, with the MTP 2035 saying 'carpool lanes are never created by converting existing lanes to carpool-only lanes' (Sacramento Area Council of Governments, 1996, 2006). Despite being members of

SACOG, these views were exactly the opposite of the City and County of Sacramento, which led to continuous conflict throughout the process.

At the end of the day, the published EIR contained only two build options – the only difference between the two was the proposed project's western endpoints. The first alternative added a carpool lane from Sunrise Boulevard to the highway 99 interchange (Figure 8.1, between points D and B) and the second alternative added a carpool lane from Sunrise Boulevard to Watt Avenue (Figure 8.1, between points D and C). Alternatives such as conversion of a mixed-flow lane to a carpool lane or expansion of transit were not considered. Here, the judge ruled in favor of ECOS/NAST on the contested EIR, finding that because the project objectives could have been met with transit, the EIR contained an insufficient number of alternatives (Environmental Council of Sacramento v. Caltrans, 2008).

VMT, CO2, and Air Quality

In terms of air quality, Caltrans determined that the project complied with federal Clean Air Act standards and because of this, no further analysis of actual traffic based emissions was necessary. In part, this derives from the inclusion of the project in the long-range transportation plan, which ensures that any specified future projects – as a group – do not create air quality violations. In addition, Caltrans did not analyze the project's impact on vehicle miles traveled (VMT), simply assuming that VMT would not increase beyond that already planned for. Finally, Caltrans argued that the lack of a 'working framework' for estimating project level GHG impacts precluded any analysis and made any conclusions regarding GHG impacts 'speculative' (Environmental Council of Sacramento v. Caltrans 2008).

On the other side, ECOS/NAST claimed the EIR misconstrued the increase of VMT related to the project, resulting in inadequate analysis of air quality impacts and CO2 emissions, a position with which the court agreed. The court found that Caltrans must '[meaningfully] attempt to quantify the project's potential impact on GHG emissions and determine their significance' (Environmental Council of Sacramento v. Caltrans 2008). This decision was the first time a California court ordered a study of GHG emissions related to a transportation project to make the EIR valid (Bizjack, 2008).

Project Length

The release of the NOP also marked a change in the length of the project. The initial 1989 Metro Study discussed the possibility of establishing a network of HOV lanes throughout the region, which was followed by the

1990 MIS which dealt specifically with building carpool lanes on highway 50 from Shingle Springs to downtown Sacramento (Figure 8.1, between the end of the black line and point A). By the time the NOP was prepared in 2005 this project had become one of many that encompassed the original goal of a network of HOV lanes in the region. The NOP was for a section between Sunrise Boulevard and downtown Sacramento (Figure 8.1, between points D and A), but the Draft EIR lists two alternate plans, one from Sunrise Boulevard to the Highway 99 interchange (Figure 8.1, between points D and B), which is just east of downtown, and the other from Sunrise Boulevard to Watt Avenue (Figure 8.1, between points D and C), which is even farther east. As each subsequent document came out the span became shorter. This is not to say that the other sections were not planned or built.

Based on the project history ECOS/NAST claimed that the project was actually a small part of a larger project that had been divided up to segment the environmental review. The judge disagreed, finding that the project and environmental review were not segmented because the project meets all the criteria of a separate project: it is of substantial length, located between two logical end points, with independent utility, serving state and local needs. He also found that the construction of the project did not commit Caltrans to constructing the entire network of HOV lanes, nor was the construction of a complete network a 'reasonably anticipated future project' at the time the EIR was drafted (Environmental Council of Sacramento v. Caltrans 2008).

Community Impacts

ECOS/NAST both argued that there was an inadequate discussion of local traffic impacts and community enhancement impacts. The finding of the court with respect to the first point was that even though the discussion of local traffic impacts was 'less than perfect' this did not 'preclude informed decision making (Environmental Council of Sacramento v. Caltrans 2008). The second argument, that community enhancements were not sufficiently evaluated in the EIR, the judge viewed more favorably. The EIR specified that Caltrans was to give a percentage of the funds to jurisdictions in which the project transected to mitigate any project impacts. Caltrans had some sense of the types of possible projects that might be funded based on recommendations from the Corridor Advisory Committee and the affected jurisdictions, but no environmental analysis was conducted on the possible improvements. In fact, these projects are largely sound walls along adjacent properties. The court found that portion of the EIR to be inadequate for this reason.

Because the court found that the air pollution analysis, climate change analysis and number of alternatives analyzed were inadequate, the EIR was inadequate. This resulted in the project being halted, at which point Governor Schwarzenegger threatened to exempt the project from having to comply with the California Environmental Quality Act (CEQA) to ensure it could qualify for federal money for shovel-ready projects as a boost to the economy (Bizjack, 2009b; Yamamura, 2008). The project also became embroiled in a budget stalemate, with Republican Party legislative members demanding that the project be exempt from environmental review.

With a conundrum of either a continued budget stalemate or setting a precedent for environmental oversight of transportation projects, Assembly Speaker Karen Bass (D-Los Angeles) and Assembly Member Mike Bass (D-Los Angeles) stepped in to facilitate a settlement. Feuer, in his capacity as Chair of the Assembly Judiciary Committee, was considered particularly instrumental in bridging the gap between the environmental groups and Caltrans.[5] As part of the agreement, ECOS and NAST agreed to not pursue any further legal action in exchange for funding of significant light rail improvements (approximately $7.5m), the construction of a bicycle–pedestrian crossing over US-50 (slightly less than $1m), and a promise from Caltrans to 'enter into discussions with affected communities regarding the allocation of community enhancement funds to maximize access to and use of the [light rail]' (Environmental Council of Sacramento, 2009).

The lawsuit was settled in plenty of time to influence the project in our next case study, the US 101 Narrows projects. But as will become apparent, nearly the same rollout occurred, with the net effect that a lawsuit was brought.

8.4 US 101

Like the Sacramento region, there has been a longstanding debate over how to limit congestion, particularly along US 101 in Marin and Sonoma Counties (Barton-Aschman Associates, 1987; Community Advisory Group, 1987). The corridor connects a string of cities and towns that lie along the highway with the largest gap between population centers occurring at the county line between Marin and Sonoma Counties. This segment of the highway, called the Marin Sonoma Narrows, is approximately eight miles long with Petaluma in Sonoma County at the north end and Novato in Marin County at the south end; it's a rural highway with uncontrolled access points. Area transportation planning agencies have generally agreed that there needs to be a multi-modal approach to easing congestion along the entire 101 corridor, including adding HOV lanes in each direction. Adding lanes to the Narrows has proven to be the most contentious and expensive, as well as arguably the lowest priority, of the US 101 improvements

Planning in the region is complicated by the presence of a multitude of overlapping regulatory and policy institutions. The northern end of the Narrows is in Sonoma County and the southern end is in Marin County. This means that project planning oversight includes the regional planning entity, the county planning entities for each county, and the state transportation agency, Caltrans. At the regional level both Sonoma and Marin Counties are within the Metropolitan Transportation Commission (MTC); the MTC serves as both the Metropolitan Planning Organization (MPO), which is the entity charged with drafting the Regional Transportation Plan, and the Regional Transportation Planning Agency (RTPA), which prioritizes transportation projects throughout the entire San Francisco bay area (Metropolitan Transportation Commission, 2010). A 19-member board makes decisions at the MTC. The board includes 14 voting members appointed by mayors, council members, and county supervisors; one from the Association of Bay Area governments; one from the San Francisco Bay Conservation and Development Commission; and three non-voting members from the California Business, Transportation and Housing Agency, the Federal Department of Housing and Urban Development; and the US Department of Transportation.

Each county also has its own county planning agency, or Congestion Management Agency (CMA) that prepares a Congestion Management Plan (CMP) for the county. In Sonoma County the CMA is Sonoma County Transportation Agency (SCTA) and in Marin it is the Transportation Authority of Marin (TAM). Decisions at SCTA are made by the 12-member Board of Directors. The Board of Directors includes one representative chosen from each of the city and town councils and three representatives from the county Board of Supervisors (Sonoma County Transportation Authority, 2010). TAM is similarly organized with a representative from each of the city and town councils and all five members of the Board of Supervisors.

All Knowledge has its Origins in Our Perceptions

There have been multiple attempts to raise funds for expanding and improving the 101 corridor through Marin and Sonoma Counties. In 1990, Sonoma and Marin voters rejected measures to implement a $0.005 sales tax in Sonoma and a $0.01 tax in Marin to fund various transportation improvements, including the widening of 101. The popular sentiment was that the Sonoma measure (Measure B) did not pass because environmentalists in Sonoma County opposed widening 101 and business groups opposed spending on transit (Smith, 1996). In Marin County the problem was slightly revised; Marin environmentalists opposed the measure because they feared the transportation improvements would induce growth while business leaders supported a commuter rail line (Norberg, 1996).

After the defeat of Measure B, congestion didn't abate so the business community and environmentalists decided to join forces to try to find a solution they could both support. Many felt that this was the best way to get enough votes to support the tax increase needed to fund any transportation plan. The group commissioned Calthorpe Associates to do a transportation study of the entire 101 corridor encompassing both Sonoma and Marin Counties and to have the results sent to SCTA and TAM (then called Marin Countywide Planning Agency).

The preferred scenario of the Calthorpe study[6] called for a multi-modal approach to easing congestion along the 101 corridor, recommending the addition of HOV lanes from Windsor to Cotati and within Petaluma and San Rafael, improving other highways and arterial roads in the region, and constructing a rail line from Healdsburg to Larkspur with compact, mixed use transit stops (Calthorpe Associates Consulting Team, 1997). While HOV lanes were recommended along much of US 101, they were not recommended through the Narrows. The analysis showed that the level of service during the peak period would not be significantly improved and that the costs for just that section would be in the order of $120–125m, which, according to Calthorpe, was as much as the cost of an entire rail line (Chorneau, 1997).

In spring of 1997, environmental groups and the business community reached an agreement to support the preferred alternative and worked together to produce a 1998 ballot measure that would fund the plan; local officials from both counties also decided to support the plan (Young, 1997). But this progress was shaken after The Santa Rosa Press Democrat conducted a poll in early summer which found that while 77 percent of Sonoma County voters supported raising taxes to fund the US 101 improvements, only 6 percent favored a plan that did not include widening the Narrows. A subsequent poll commissioned by the Petaluma Area Chamber of Commerce found that Petaluma voters would not support a new sales tax to fund transportation unless it included the Narrows by a margin of more than two to one (Kovner, 1997). City Councils for both Petaluma and Novato met in January of 1998 and decided to pressure Caltrans to widen and improve the Narrows while the Petaluma Chamber of Commerce continued their efforts to have the Narrows included in the ballot measures (Young, 1998).

In preparation for a Board of Supervisors public hearing on the transportation tax measure, the Sonoma County Transportation Agency endorsed the Calthorpe plan with minor revisions (Chorneau, 1998b). The following week over 200 people, including the owner and employees of a large excavation and paving company, came to the Board of Supervisors meeting to support expanding the Narrows (Chorneau, 1998c). The jostling was intense. Calthorpe warned elected officials not to be swayed by public opinion into making bad policy decisions (Chorneau, 1997). On the other hand, Mike Cale, a County Supervisor, framed the discussion as pitting consultants and special interests groups against the will of the people. In the end the Board of Supervisors unanimously approved a list of projects to be placed on the ballot, which included adding a third lane through the Narrows, to the county line (Chorneau, 1998d).

A two-measure approach was used. One asked voters if they wanted to fund the listed transportation improvement projects and the second asked if they approved of a 0.5 cent sales tax to actually fund the improvements (*Santa Rosa Press Democrat*, 1998). The Marin County Board of Supervisors voted to place similar measures on their ballot, however, the Narrows widening was not included in the list of transportation projects (Smart Voter, 1998). Marin County supported the Narrows widening, but wanted to pursue state money to fund the expansion.

In both counties, the measure asking voters if they supported funding specific transportation projects won and the measure asking for a sales tax increase to actually pay for the projects failed (Smart Voter, 1998; Sonoma County Clerk-Recorder, 1998). It is reasonable to assume that many voters supported – in theory – improving the transportation system, but were not willing to prioritize the necessary improvements sufficiently high enough to pay for them. In fact, many voters did not trust the elected officials to actually spend the increased tax revenue on the specific projects (Chorneau, 1998a).

Begin Anew

After the failure of the 1998 tax measures Marin County began a five-year visioning process which resulted in their Transportation Vision Plan and called for HOV lanes to be added through the Narrows. Marin also listed the Narrows as a 2001 Regional Transportation Plan Project (DKS Associates, 2004). Likewise, also during this post-1998 failed tax measure period, Sonoma County produced their own Countywide Transportation Plan and it too included widening the Narrows, although it was listed as the lowest priority among a list of four US 101 widening projects (Sonoma County, 2001). Critically, once the Narrows had been placed on the ballot it automatically became part of future county transportation plans. This is important because County plans are sent to the regional transportation agency (in this case, MTC) so they can be evaluated for inclusion in the regional plan (Klein, 2010). The first official sign of support from the MTC appears in the Phased Implementation Plan adopted in March of 2000, which lists adding HOV lanes to the Narrows as part of the highway investment package (Metropolitan Transportation Commission, 2000).

Around this time, Caltrans was also evaluating how to expand or improve the corridor. As early as 1998, Caltrans had identified the Narrows corridor as being unable to accommodate planned-for growth and was actively pursuing additional analysis on the feasibility of using a multi-modal approach for accommodating future growth. This is likely what prompted Caltrans to investigate various alternative plans for the Narrows in a May 2000 MIS, but the MIS remained in a draft version and was never publicly circulated because with the passage of TEA-21 in 1998 it ceased to be a requirement.

With all the planning agencies now in agreement that HOV lanes should be added to the Narrows, the challenge became one of funding. Sonoma County tried to raise funds through sales taxes again in 2000, without coordinating with Marin County, and the measure failed (Smart Voter, 2000). In 2004 the two counties again coordinated their efforts and both placed transportation measures on the ballot. Measure M in Sonoma was a ¼ cent sales tax to fund transportation improvements, including widening 101, and to 'generate local revenue to become a "self-help"[7] county and leverage state and federal funding for transportation needs' (Smart Voter, 2004b). The Marin Measure A specifically stated that the Narrows project would not be funded, but that passing the measure would increase 'Marin County's ability to receive matching state and federal funds for transportation improvements' (Smart Voter, 2004a). Both the Marin and Sonoma measures passed. Then in 2006, the state passed Proposition 1B, or the Highway Safety, Traffic Reduction, Air Quality, and Port Security Bond Act, which ultimately provided much of the remaining needed funding for the project (US Department of Transportation Federal Highway Administration, and California Department of Transportation, 2009). The Federal Environmental Impact Report (FEIR) cites the support of both counties, including Measure M funds, and MTC's subsequent recommendation for project funding through the Corridor Mobility Improvement Account (CMIA) of Proposition 1B.

A Draft Environmental Impact Report (DEIR) for the Narrows widening was released in October of 2007. In response, a comment letter was formally filed by The Transportation Solutions Defense and Education

Fund, known as TRANSDEF,[8] citing the lack of an MIS, and noting that the closest thing to an MIS was the Calthorpe study, which did not call for the Narrows project. TRANSDEF has filed multiple other lawsuits joining with the Environmental Defense Fund, the Natural Resources Defense Council, and the Sierra Club against the EPA, MTC, Bay Area Air Quality District, and the California Air Resources Board (TRANSDEF, 2010). TRANSDEF's position is that a train system, the SMART train, which had been previously proposed, but was never fully analyzed, should be used to reduce traffic through the Narrows. The train system has also experienced continuous funding problems despite a long push to build it and a cost similar to the Narrows project, leading TRANSDEF to argue that it should be considered a viable project.

TRANSDEF also claimed the DEIR's statements regarding GHG emissions were too simplistic (TRANSDEF, 2007),

> One of the main strategies to reduce GHG emissions is to make California's transportation system more efficient. The [Marin Sonoma Narrows] Project would relieve congestion by enhancing operations and improving travel times in a high congestion travel corridor and, thus, lead to an overall reduction in GHG emissions. Accordingly, the contribution of the Build Alternatives and the Access Options would be less than cumulatively considerable so that the overall cumulative impact would be less than significant. (US Department of Transportation Federal Highway Administration, and California Department of Transportation, 2007)

TRANSDEF also contended there should be an analysis that included VMT as well as induced demand when making GHG assumptions. In the Final EIR Caltrans performs some calculations estimating GHG emissions using the state approved emissions factor model, EMFAC. Despite an increase in VMT that doubles peak hour delay by the project build year, Caltrans concludes,

> . . . both the future with project and future no build show increases in CO_2 emissions over the existing levels. As discussed above, there are limitations with EMFAC and with assessing what a given CO_2 emissions increase means for climate change. Therefore, it is Caltrans [sic] determination that in the absence of further regulatory or scientific information related to greenhouse gas emissions and CEQA significance, it is too speculative to make a determination regarding significance of the project's direct impact and its contribution on the cumulative scale to climate change. (US Department of Transportation Federal Highway Administration, and California Department of Transportation, 2009)

The FEIR was certified in July of 2009. TRANSDEF filed suit in August of 2009 stating the EIR was flawed as a result of not analyzing the significance of the increase in GHG emissions generated by the project (TRANSDEF, 2009). Almost immediately, the North Coast Rivers Alliance, a non-governmental organization, also filed suit against Caltrans for certifying the EIR, claiming that members of NCRA would be adversely affected by the project's impacts on air quality, global warming, water supply, and other environmental resources. There were three major points of contention, as follows.

Induced Travel and Sprawl

TRANSDEF maintained that the project would promote sprawl and create additional VMT. Caltrans claimed that a growth study concluded that added HOV lanes in the Narrows would support planned growth and not result in inducing unplanned growth in either Sonoma or Marin County. Caltrans also claimed that it is 'correct that traffic may well continue to expand into the future and that accommodating it may pose a challenge. However, the additional lanes that this project will construct will still be a valuable transportation asset and the system will function better with them than without them' (US Department of Transportation Federal Highway Administration, and California Department of Transportation, 2009).

Project Alternatives: SMART Instead

TRANSDEF argued that funding used to add HOV lanes on the Narrows project would be better spent on the SMART train. Two SMART train alternatives were suggested: one that provides the same amount of funding as the HOV lanes and a second which provides the capital cost. Caltrans claims that the SMART train would be a 'complementary' transportation service, but the HOV lanes are needed as well. (US Department of Transportation Federal Highway Administration, and California Department of Transportation, 2009).

VMT and CO2

Caltrans has stated that congestion relief was a higher priority than reducing CO_2 emissions, but since CO_2 emissions are higher at lower speeds 'congestion reduction is a close substitute for evaluating GHG-reducing alternatives' (US Department of Transportation Federal Highway Administration, and California Department of Transportation, 2009). But it is also clear that CO_2 emissions increase, substantively (as much as 27 percent), under either scenario. Finally, Caltrans noted that GHG emissions reporting is still evolving, which it is.

8.5 DISCUSSION

There is much that is similar with respect to these two projects: both have long histories and a connectedness to a larger conceptual system; both were publicly vetted, at least in theory; both were HOV lanes to be added to an existing highway segment; both were responding to growth and congestion; and both have landed in lawsuits over sprawl, GHG emissions, and the lack of a robust evaluation of alternatives. What's interesting about these cases and why they bear some consideration, is that both hint at the difficulties associated with changing priorities for transportation improvements in California. They also point to a fundamental misunderstanding of the degree of change – absent any technological revolution – that must be accomplished to reduce California's transportation GHG emissions.

How much VMT Reduction is Needed?

The roadmap for accomplishing the requisite GHG reductions was laid out in the California Air Resources Board Scoping Plan (California Air Resources Board, 2008a), which was adopted in December of 2008. This document outlines the necessary reductions by each sector that are needed to achieve the 2020 target (1990 emissions level), as well as laying out a basic framework for a cap and trade system. The transportation system is expected to achieve approximately 62 MMT in reductions through seven different measures (Figure 8.2), roughly a quarter of which are discretionary. Only the Pavley and Low Carbon Fuel Standards[9] are mandated at this time; these account for about 47 MMT of the expected reduction.

The next largest planned reduction is 5 MMT from land use, to be achieved through smart growth planning. The 5 MMT reduction is equivalent to a roughly 4 percent per capita reduction in VMT by 2020. Although the Scoping Plan only addresses the 2020 target, it does state that an 8 percent per capita VMT reduction below the business as usual case would be required by 2030, achieved through land-use strategies, to stay on track. However, this would also be coupled with a new ambitious Pavley-like regulation that would reduce tailpipe emissions by another 40 percent and a vehicle fleet in which roughly one-third of the passenger cars would be battery-electric, plug-in hybrid, and/or fuel cell vehicles.

If we assume that a new aggressive Pavley-like regulatory strategy and significant fleet changeover may not actually occur by 2020 (a not unreasonable assumption given the long path to implementation of the current Pavley legislation), then decisions about new infrastructure become very critical if the infrastructure is being developed to accommodate – rather

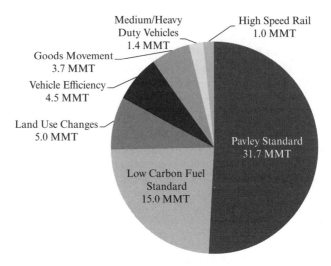

*Figure 8.2   Distribution of GHG reductions outlined in the ARB Scoping
          Plan*

than reduce – projected VMT. That is, after accounting for current regulations (Pavley and LCFS) and for the planned 4 percent per capita VMT
decrease to be achieved through smart planning, with population growth
expected to be more than 12 percent between 2020 and 2030 there is still
a significant gap remaining to achieve the 2050 target (Figure 8.3). To put
things into perspective, closing the gap would be equivalent to attaining
roughly 100 percent fleet sales of zero emission vehicles (ZEVs) by 2050
(California Air Resources Board, 2009).

Institutional Inertia

This is the backdrop against which current regional transportation plans
(RTPs) are being evaluated. Most of the RTPs have not been updated
to reflect new priorities and none formally address reductions in VMT
to achieve GHG emissions. And yet, the feasibility of achieving even a
5 MMT reduction by 2020 rests solely on the MPO's capacity to funda-
mentally re-think infrastructure. With the passage of ISTEA in 1991 the
emphasis shifted from adding single occupancy vehicle (SOV) capacity to
HOV capacity as a means of addressing both air quality as well as congestion (mobility) concerns. There are more than 345 HOV lane facilities in
the United States, and at 25 percent California has the largest proportion
of HOV facilities in the country (Booz Allen Hamilton, 2009).
    Most of California's MPO systemwide HOV plans were designed in

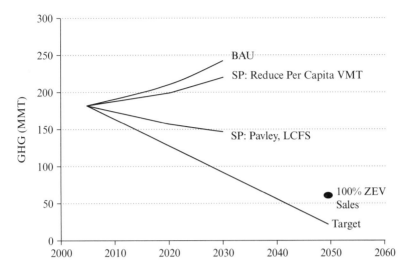

Figure 8.3   Estimated reductions required to achieve the 2050 target

the early 1990s and represent a significant investment in both planning and political capital. For example, in 1992 the Los Angeles County Transportation Commission adopted the 'carpool lane plan' and HOV lane-miles subsequently increased more than seven-fold. Even in SAFETEA-LU, the emphasis is on the use of HOVs (and tolling of HOV lanes) as an important way to reduce congestion, not GHG emissions. Insofar as alleviating congestion also reduces vehicle fuel consumption, the goal of reducing both GHGs and congestion are compatible. However, if the rate of growth in VMT (or the VMT) exceeds fuel savings that accrue as a result of mitigating congestion – which will almost certainly occur in regions that are growing – then HOV lanes represent a (sometimes significant) contributor to GHG emissions. In short, the transport planning paradigm used for the last 20 years no longer applies.

Both the US-50 and the US 101 case studies are about facilities that have deep historical roots; they are part of HOV plans begun in the 1990s, and critically represent significant efforts to address congestion. For example, the US-50 plan represented in the NOP is nearly identical to the initial plan recommended in the 1990 MIS, and there remains a political commitment to building a regional network of HOV lanes on the part of the Governor and Caltrans (California Governor's Office, 2006), stemming from a perception that HOV lanes represent an innovative capacity-enhancing strategy for reducing congestion, and better yet, they also reduce environmental impacts. This historical attachment to meaning, coupled with serious local budget shortfalls and a fairly bureaucratic process make it difficult to redirect energies when policies change dramatically.

Within the SACOG organization, the six member counties and 22 cities represent 31 votes. Each city and county is represented by one director (having one vote) on SACOG's Board of Directors, with the exception of Sacramento. The city of Sacramento is entitled to two directors (representing two votes) and Sacramento County is entitled to three directors (three votes). Sacramento County has 11 votes: six for SACOG member cities with Sacramento County; two for the City of Sacramento, and three for Sacramento County. Regional plans require a two-thirds approval of the Board of Directors. As others have noted (Goldman and Deakin, 2000), MPO boards are mostly geographically-based representation bodies and few include, for example, representatives of transit agencies, land use or environmental agencies. Thus, tension in the US-50 case lay primarily between Sacramento County and its member cities and the outlying counties and their cities, where future development goals may differ.

In the case of US-50, many of the complaints concerning lack of analysis of local traffic impacts were from the City of Sacramento. However, the preferred alternative selected in the EIR specified a terminus that is not in the City of Sacramento, making these complaints irrelevant. There is the possibility that the preferred alternative terminus was chosen to avoid further conflict with the City. This tension is particularly evident when considering the HOV lane addition (Figure 8.4, gray line) with respect to work travel time, population and density – characterized by the size of the bubbles, with each representing a city. The HOV project connects cities of much lower populations and densities. The region itself has been highly acclaimed for its emphasis on compact growth and innovative transportation strategies. However, when viewed in context, there are signals suggesting that the region is not as committed to higher density development as is commonly perceived. In part, the US-50 HOV project suggests that there are organizational behavior aspects to the regional governance structure that impact decision-making differently over time.

In both of our case studies, projected VMT growth for the proposed facility is substantial, enough so that the net result from implementing the facility is that it does little to address either congestion or reducing VMT in the out-years. We contend that, despite initial successes (Goldman and Deakin, 2000), over time the organizational structure of regional governance migrates towards a lowest common denominator: everyone gets something as long as it is not outrageous. We believe this is partially a reflection of more complicated governing behaviors that emerge as the outlying areas, the suburbs, become more influential, as has been seen in other studies (Lubell et al., 2009).

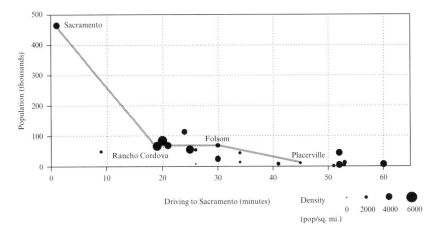

Note: The gray line identifies the primary city to city linkage for US-50 HOV project.

Figure 8.4 Driving duration, density, and population centers in the Sacramento region

The MTC, for example, provides the primary regional governance for the counties in which the US 101 HOV Narrows project resides. Congestion management plans are developed within each county by the Congestion Management Authority (CMA). As noted earlier the Regional Transportation Plan (RTP) is consistent with regional planning goals (Figure 8.5). The CMA for Marin is TAM and the CMA for Sonoma is SCTA. Representation on each CMA is primarily a council member from each city or town within the county as well as members of the County Board of Supervisors.

The MTC then makes the decision as to whether projects are included in the RTP, the only way to have access to federal funds. As a staff member of MTC stated:

> Historically, MTC included in the RTP projects from the county-wide plans if they were consistent with planning goals and could be demonstrated to be fully funded with reasonably expected revenues over the course of the plan. That said, we aim for some consensus about the projects submitted to MTC by the counties in the first plan. We have typically done this through focused studies, in which both MTC and the CMAs participate, such as the HOV Master Plan, Freeway Performance Initiative and corridor investment studies. (Klein, 2010).

But to understand what 'developing consensus' means structurally, it again becomes necessary to examine how voting is undertaken.

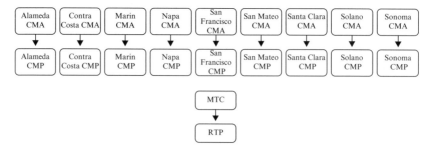

Figure 8.5   Transportation planning in the MTC region

Since the early years of the MTC, policymaking has been guided by a 19-member policy board, 14 of which are appointed by local officials (Klein, 2010). Ten members are appointed from the five most populous counties and four members from the least four populous counties – all have equal votes. In the populous counties, one member represents the county and the other member represents the incorporated cities within the county. In the least populous counties, each county selects one member, who represents both the incorporated and unincorporated areas. Because projects are passed through by consensus if funding seems a reasonable likelihood, projects like the Narrows are never really evaluated within a regional context.

Is Local Control Equivalent to Regional Consistency?

One of the sometimes dramatic changes that are occurring, largely due to the criticalness associated with reducing GHG emissions, is that local communities are going to have to set priorities in ways they have not had to before. It will be difficult to achieve significant reductions in VMT using smart growth in a home rule state without firm priorities. This will require, in the words of one transportation consultant, that general plans be 'internally consistent'.[10] The example that is frequently used is the requirement for greater transit use alongside the requirement of level of service C driving conditions. Transit use is not going to significantly increase when driving is at level of service C.

This, however, is not the only consistency issue that will have to be addressed. Consider the City of Pleasanton, which is located in the MTC region on the east side of San Francisco, and is the subject of a recent lawsuit by the state attorney general. Pleasanton revised its General Plan, adding jobs, but holding in place a cap on housing that had been set in mid-1990s. The Attorney General sued, citing the lack of housing availability and its impact on transit development, further contending that the plan would lead to sprawl and increased GHG emissions. The lawsuit has not yet been decided, but the implication is that, at the minimum, one strategy for reducing future GHG emissions is achieving (or at least planning for) a reasonable jobs–housing balance. In fact, there is a slowly accumulating series of lawsuits that will enforce regional consistency and priority setting (e.g. Stockton, Oakland, etc.).

8.6 CONCLUSIONS

We have examined two recent case studies on roadway infrastructure, planned in the early 1990s and considered innovative at the time, both of which have landed in lawsuits: one settled, that should have informed the second, but did not. The long planning (and approval) processes for regional transportation plans is too cumbersome to manage quick shifts in policy. This is particularly evident when evaluating the types of projects contained within current RTPs. In southern California, the RTPs include significant HOV additions; likewise with the Sacramento region. In short, the current regional governance structure and planning processes make it difficult to re-evaluate the suitability of projects identified more than 20 years ago.

Reducing GHG emissions in the transportation sector, particularly in California, will not be easy. Major shifts in how we think about funding and the ways in which we design our systems require new processes that are more adaptive in nature and flexible in structure. Flexibility and adaptability have not been highly visible priorities in transportation planning in the past, and it is unclear that the regional governance structure as it is practiced produces any more nimbleness than previous state-centered processes. However, it is clear that regional governance results in political compromise that may actually worsen GHG emissions. New ways of organizing and responding to this critical environmental impact are needed.

NOTES

1. In California councils of governments (COGs) are entities that are formed through joint powers of agreement between cities and counties. Legally, the COGs are responsible for identifying each region's share of housing needs and establishing housing goals (Baer, 1988).
2. Major Investment Studies are federally required analyses for projects that were to be included in the long-range transportation plan and are intended to lead to agreement on design scope.

3. The 1990 HOV System Planning Study called for HOV lanes from approximately 9th St in downtown Sacramento (point A) to Ponderosa in Shingle Springs (point G). The 1997 Major Investment Study called for HOV lanes from 9th St to El Dorado Hills (approximately point E). The EIR for the contested project presented two alternatives. The eastern end of both alternatives is Sunrise Blvd (point D) and in one alternative the western end is Highway 99 (point B), in the other the western end is Watt Avenue (point C). There is a HOV lane from Sunrise (point D) to approximately El Dorado (point E). When the contested project is completed the HOV lanes will go from Watt to Greenstone, stopping short of their original intended western terminus in downtown Sacramento, arguably to avoid working within the City of Sacramento, and extending slightly east of the original intended terminus in Shingle Springs to Ponderosa. In effect, the end result will be that the HOV lanes will shift east away from the downtown core of Sacramento and towards lower density outlying communities.

4. Community consensus building began in the spring of 2000 and was completed in the summer of 2000. The public outreach and education process involved: individual meetings with stakeholders and interested parties; briefings for local elected public officials and staff; four public workshops; presentations at neighborhood advisory group meetings, and an interactive website. The final report on these activities was completed in September 2000 (US Department of Transportation Federal Highway Administration and State of California Department of Transportation, 2007)

5. http://democrats.assembly.ca.gov/newsline/releases/20090116ad42pr01.htm

6. The study was formally called the *Sonoma/Marin Multi-Modal Land Use and Transportation Study.*

7. The 'self-help' program allows California counties to issue a local voter approved special sales tax specifically for transportation projects. The tax must be approved by a two-thirds majority.

8. TRANSDEF is a non-profit organization that works to 'bring more sustainable transportation to California and to the San Francisco Bay Area' (TRANSDEF website, http://www.transdef.org).

9. The Pavley standards were established pursuant to AB 1493 signed into law in 2002; the tailpipe standards increase beginning with model 2009, producing a projected 30% reduction by model year 2016 (California Air Resources Board, 2008b). The Low Carbon Fuel Standard was established pursuant Executive Order S-01-07 and provides protocols for measuring the life-cycle intensity for transportation fuels.

10. http://coolconnections.org/2009/07/31/fehr-peers-participates-in-rtp-guidelines-update-for-sb-375/

REFERENCES

Baer, W. (1988) California's housing element: A backdoor approach to metropolitan governance and regional planning, *Town Planning Review*, 59, 263–76.

Barton-Aschman Associates, Inc. (1987) *101 Corridor Study Phase II: Technical Memorandum No. 10.*

Bishop, R. (2009) SB 375's unfinished business. Retrieved February, 2009, from http://www.wrcog.cog.ca.us/downloads/ewrcog/ecomm0901_main2.html

Bizjack, T. (2008) Highway 50 plan may not be green enough for state, *The Sacramento Bee*, August 13.

Bizjack, T. (2009a) Neighbors take action to improve Sacramento transportation system, *The Sacramento Bee*, March 3.

Bizjack, T. (2009b) State budget crisis: Highway 50 project, landmark law collide – Governor seeks environmental act exemption, *The Sacramento Bee*, January 8.

Booz Allen Hamilton (2009) *A Compendium of Existing HOV Lane Facilities in the United States*. Washington DC, US DOT, Federal Highway Adminstration.

California Air Resources Board (2007) *California 1990 Greenhouse Gas Emissions Level and 2020 Emissions Level*. Sacramento, Air Resources Board.

California Air Resources Board (2008a) *Climate Change Scoping Plan: A Framework for Change*. Sacramento, California Air Resources Board.

California Air Resources Board (2008b) *Comparison of Greenhouse Gas Reductions for the United States and Canada Under US CAFE Standards and California Resources Board Greenhouse Gas Regulations*. Sacramento, California Air Resources Board.

California Air Resources Board (2009) *Summary of Staff's Preliminary Assessment of the Need for Revisions to the Zero Emission Vehicle Regulation, White Paper*. Sacramento, California Air Resources Board.

California Governor's Office (2006) Press release: Governor Schwarzenegger highlights additional Sacramento County HOV lanes in Strategic Growth Plan to improve traffic and air quality, Sacramento, California Governor's Office.

Calthorpe Associates Consulting Team (1997) *Sonoma/Marin Multi-Modal Transportation and Land Use Study*. Sacramento, Calthorpe Associates Consulting.

Chorneau, T. (1997) Highway 101: Widening support, *The Santa Rosa Press Democrat*, June 22.

Chorneau, T. (1998a) 101 poll: Officials were not trusted, *The Santa Rosa Press Democrat*, December 15.

Chorneau, T. (1998b) Panel backs extra work in 101 plan, *The Santa Rosa Press Democrat*, March 13.

Chorneau, T. (1998c) Sentiment favors widening all of 101: County mulls plan for November vote, *The Santa Rosa Press Democrat*, March 18.

Chorneau, T. (1998d) Supervisors back highway 101 plan: Tentative OK for full six lanes, *The Santa Rosa Press Democrat*, April 22.

Community Advisory Group (1987) *101 Corridor Transportation Study: Community Advisory Group Workshop #1 Report*. Community Advisory Group.

DKS Associates (2004) *2003 Marin County Congestion Management Program*. DKS Associates.

Environmental Council of Sacramento (2009) Press release: ECOS and NAST settle with Caltrans to enhance transit access and protect our community and the environment, Sacramento, Environmental Council of Sacramento.

Environmental Council of Sacramento v. Caltrans (2008) California Superior Court.

Goldman, T. and Deakin, E. (2000) Regionalism through partnerships? Metropolitan planning since ISTEA, *Berkeley Planning Journal*, 14, 46–75.

Klein, L. (2010) Re: Question about MTC. Email to MTC Senior Transportation Planner.

Kovner, G. (1997). Petaluma Chamber Poll evaluates 101 plan: Widening to Novato key to approval, *The Santa Rosa Press Democrat*, November 25.

Lubell, M., Feiock, R. and Ramirez de la Cruz, E. (2009) Local institutions and the politics of urban growth, *American Journal of Political Science*, 53, 649–65.

McNabb, C. (1998) Viability of a sustainable and feasible national transportation system, *Transportation Law Journal, University of Denver*, 26, 133–40.

Metropolitan Transportation Commission (2000) Bay Area transportation blueprint for the 21st century. Retrieved January 17, 2010, from http://www.mtc.ca.gov/library/PIP/pip_index.htm

Metropolitan Transportation Commission (2010) About MTC. Retrieved February 2, 2010, from http://www.mtc.ca.gov/about_mtc/about.htm

Norberg, B. (1996) Commuter rail at heart of proposal, *The Santa Rosa Press Democrat*, November 10.

Sacramento Area Council of Governments (1996) *US 50 Corridor Major Investment Study Working Paper.* Sacramento, SACOG

Sacramento Area Council of Governments (2005) Factsheet: Blueprint transportation and land use plan. Sacramento, SACOG.

Sacramento Area Council of Governments (2006) *MTP 2035 Issue Brief, Road Expansion.* Sacramento, SACOG.

Sacramento Area Council of Governments (2008) *Appendix D2: MTP2035 Land Use Allocation.* Sacramento, SACOG.

Sacramento City Council (2006) Highway 50 HOV lanes project opposition letter, Sacramento, Sacramento City Council.

Sacramento County (1993) *Sacramento County General Plan Circulation Element.* Retrieved January 10, 2010 from http://www.msa2.saccounty.net/planning/Documents/General-Plan/Circulation-Element.pdf

Santa Rosa Press Democrat (1998) Together at last? Marin–Sonoma cooperation produces tangible transportation results, *The Santa Rosa Press Democrat*, June 18.

Smart Voter (1998) Directory of Marin County, CA Measures: November 3, 1998. Retrieved February 3, 2010, from http://www.smartvoter.org/1998nov/ca/mrn/meas/

Smart Voter (2000) Directory of Sonoma County, CA Measures: March 7, 2000, General. Retrieved February 3, 2010, from http://www.smartvoter.org/2000/03/07/ca/sn/meas/

Smart Voter (2004a) Directory of Marin County, CA Measures: November 2, 2004. Retrieved February 3, 2010, from http://www.smartvoter.org/2004/11/02/ca/mrn/meas/

Smart Voter (2004b) Directory of Sonoma County, CA Measures: November 2, 2004, General. Retrieved February 3, 2010, from http://www.smartvoter.org/2004/11/02/ca/sn/meas/

Smith, C. (1996) 101: It's not getting better, *The Santa Rosa Press Democrat*, April 21.

Sonoma County (2001) *2001 Countywide Transportation Plan for Sonoma County.*

Sonoma County Clerk-Recorder (1998) 11/03/98 Consolidated general election results. Retrieved February 3, 2010, from http://www.sonoma-county.org/regvoter/Elections/pdf/1998/19981103summary.pdf

Sonoma County Transportation Authority (2010) Homepage. Retrieved February 2, 2010, from http://www.sctainfo.org/

Taylor, B. and Schweitzer, L. (2005) Assessing the experience of mandated collaborative inter-jurisdictional transport planning in the United States, *Transport Policy*, 12, 500–11.

TRANSDEF (2007) Comments on Marin–Sonoma Narrows HOV widening project DEIR/S.

TRANSDEF (2009) Press release: Challenge to Marin–Sonoma Narrows environmental report.

TRANSDEF (2010) Litigation report. Retrieved January 20, 2010, from http://www.transdef.org/index_assets/Litigation percent20Report.pdf

US Department of Transportation Federal Highway Administration, and

California Department of Transportation (2007) *Marin–Sonoma Narrows (MSN) HOV Widening Project* (Draft Environmental Impact Report/ Statement).

US Department of Transportation Federal Highway Administration, and California Department of Transportation (2009) *Marin–Sonoma Narrows (MSN) HOV Widening Project: Final Environmental Impact Report/Statement.*

US Department of Transportation Federal Highway Administration, and State of California Department of Transportation (2007) *Sac 50 Bus/Carpool Lanes and Community Enhancements Project: Final Environmental Impact Report/ Environmental Assessment.* Sacramento.

Yamamura, K. (2008) State budget crisis: Governor keeps the pressure on – he seeks concessions that anger unions, environmentalists, *The Sacramento Bee*, December 24.

Young, T. (1997) Marin, Sonoma back 101 plan: Leaders support 70/30 funding split for highway/rail, *The Santa Rosa Press Democrat*, April 24.

Young, T. (1998) Cities establish Hwy. 101 goals: Petaluma Novato push for state, federal funds, *The Santa Rosa Press Democrat*, January 14.

9. Matching words and deeds? How transit-oriented are the Bloomberg-era rezonings in New York City?

Simon McDonnell, Josiah Madar and Vicki Been

9.1 INTRODUCTION

New York City's long-term strategic plan, PlaNYC 2030, envisions a city of over nine million residents by 2030, an increase of about one million over 2000 (City of New York, 2007). Until the 2007 recession hit, the City was well on the way to achieving this with a net increase of 355,000 residents between 2000 and 2008 (US Census Bureau, 2009). To accommodate new residents while simultaneously encouraging economic development opportunities, improving residents' quality of life and improving the City's environmental performance, the City has launched an ambitious transportation, land use and planning agenda, much of which is articulated by PlaNYC 2030.

A centerpiece of this agenda is focusing development in neighborhoods well served by public transit to reduce dependency on the automobile (Holtzclaw et al., 2002). This, in turn, can reduce automobile-related externalities, such as congestion and air pollution, and help mitigate their negative health, economic and quality of life impacts (Sterner, 2003). Achieving this pattern of development requires not only the availability of transit, but also land use regulations that encourage, or at least permit, relatively dense development near transit stations.

Between 2002 and 2009, New York City's government proposed and enacted 100 significant changes to its zoning code, covering more than 20 per cent of the City's land area. This unprecedented period of rezoning activity, all under the mayoral administration of Mayor Michael Bloomberg, constitutes the most significant change to the City's land use regulations since the original version of the current zoning code was adopted in 1961. But while many of these individual rezoning actions have been analyzed by neighborhood groups, advocacy groups and the press, little academic attention has focused on their cumulative impact on the City's residential development capacity, or on how the rezonings match the City's stated development, environmental and transportation goals.

9.2   BACKGROUND

New York City's zoning code (known as the 'Zoning Resolution') is its primary tool for regulating building size, form and use. The Zoning Resolution consists of the zoning map, which divides the City into dozens of different zoning districts, and the zoning text, which sets out the regulations applicable to each zoning district. Since its enactment in 1961, planners have proposed several amendments and additions to the Zoning Resolution to address perceived shortcomings, particularly the indifference of many zoning districts to neighborhood context as a determinant for permitted building form (Cooper, 1975). The City has incorporated many of these proposals into its zoning code, adding neighborhood-specific 'special districts' to the zoning map and zoning text, allowing new flexibility through alternative rules in certain types of zoning districts, and creating new 'contextual' categories of zoning districts that more broadly address the perceived indifference of the original districts to existing neighborhood building patterns. A more comprehensive amendment to the Zoning Resolution proposed in 1999, the Unified Bulk Program, was defeated by real estate developer opposition (Dunlap, 2000).

Since Mayor Bloomberg took office in 2002, the City has embraced a neighborhood-by-neighborhood approach to amending the zoning code. Each of the 100 rezonings enacted by the City between 2003 and 2009 focused on a neighborhood-sized geographic area ranging from a handful of lots to dozens of adjacent blocks. Most rezoning actions included a combination of different types of zoning map changes, adding or subtracting development capacity to some lots, while adding new contextual form requirements to other lots without explicitly changing the amount of permitted development.

These rezonings begin when the City's Department of City Planning (DCP) identifies an area of initial investigation either in response to neighborhood pressure or on its own initiative. After local consultations, the DCP proposes changes to the zoning designations of the land within a study area and commences the city's environmental review process. If the City Planning Commission finds no significant adverse environmental impact or following completion of a Draft Environmental Impact Statement, the DCP certifies the proposal for formal entry into the City's Uniform Land Use Review Procedure (ULURP). ULURP first requires the community board representing the affected part of the City to hold public hearings on the proposed rezoning. The rezoning is then sent to the president of the borough in which the area falls, who may, but is not required to, hold any additional public hearings. The community board and borough president may support, oppose, or recommend modifications to the proposed change, but their recommendations are advisory only. The City Planning Commission then determines whether to recommend the proposal as is to the City Council for final approval, to withdraw the proposal, or to modify the proposal to take account of the reaction of the community board or borough president.[1] Between 2003 and 2009, each of the City-initiated rezonings presented to the City Council ultimately was approved, though some with modifications.

In proposing each of the individual rezoning initiatives, the DCP cited specific planning goals, including protecting existing residential neighborhoods from out-of-context development, changing the permitted uses of areas to encourage economic and residential development, and focusing higher density development in transit-rich areas (Department of City Planning, 2009a, 2009b). These individual zoning changes, accordingly, serve highly localized goals, but also constitute the building blocks of the City's overall development strategies and goals.

The City has expressed broader, citywide planning goals in PlaNYC 2030 as well as in the DCP's strategic plan. PlaNYC 2030, produced by the City's Office of Long-Term Planning and Sustainability, lays out an ambitious agenda for the City's land use and housing development, air and water quality, transportation infrastructure, energy use and production, and preparedness for climate change. Specifically, PlaNYC 2030 sets a goal of adding 265,000–500,000 units to the City's housing supply by 2030, particularly in areas well served by public transit (City of New York, 2007). The DCP's strategic plan articulates the City's more immediate planning goals, including strengthening regional business districts, facilitating housing production (again focused near transit), and fostering mixed use developments, while also protecting 'neighborhood character' (Department of City Planning, 2009c).

Our period of analysis, 2003 to 2007, coincides with a widespread real estate boom: on average across the City, residential properties appreciated by 41 percent between 2003 and 2006 (Been et al., 2009); redevelopment of undeveloped or underdeveloped sites increased significantly; and the number of residential building permits issued annually doubled between 2001 and 2006 (Furman Center, 2010). With that growth came controversy and pushback, ensuring that policymakers engaged in rezoning efforts faced diverse pressures from different stakeholders. One of the paramount pressures came from existing residents concerned about local 'out of context' developments. Though such concerns are long-standing (Oser, 1986), fears of 'overdevelopment' reached new highs in recent years (Department of City Planning, 2004). The period was also characterized by heightened competition for land between existing manufacturing uses and new residential or services uses (Wolf-Powers, 2005).

There is a great deal of work that explores the impacts that particular forms of zoning and other land use and environmental regulations have on land use patterns and on the costs of development. For instance, the effect land use regulations in the United States have had on house prices and rents is particularly well explored. It is too early, especially given the recent turmoil in real estate markets, to estimate the impact the rezoning initiatives we are studying have on land values, housing prices, or actual housing supply. Instead, we analyze the effect these regulatory changes have had on the relationship between permitted residential development capacity and existing transit infrastructure; specifically, we assess whether the rezonings added residential capacity in transit-rich neighborhoods.

There is relatively little work regarding how the City's land use regulations relate to the availability of transit opportunities, despite connections between land use and transportation remaining a contentious issue (Woudsma and Jensen, 2003). For instance, Iacono and Levinson (2009) explore land use patterns in Minneapolis-St Paul and find that presence or absence of a highway influences land use changes between 1990 and 2000. Regulatory interventions such as publically-initiated rezonings, however, are beyond the scope of their study. At a broader level, Ewing and Cervero (2001) conduct a meta-analysis of the relationship between changes in the built environment and travel demand. They find that trip frequencies are more closely related to socio-economic characteristics, but trip lengths are primarily a function of the built environment. They do not, however, investigate how regulatory interventions such as zoning dictate the form of the built environment and, as a result, influence travel behavior.

Recent analysis has explored the possibility that better integrated land use and transport planning, often encapsulated in the concept of transit-oriented development (TOD), may produce more sustainable development patterns (Gómez-Ibáñez et al., 2009). A large number of studies investigate various aspects of TOD. Cervero et al. (2003) explore the political economy of TOD and the practical barriers to its implementation among stakeholders and policymakers. Hess and Lombardi (2004) and Dunphy and Porter (2006) both point out the paradox that the urban sites that are most suitable to TOD because of their transit accessibility are typically more difficult to develop (e.g. more expensive and complicated). Suburban locations that are easier to develop might be less suited to TOD, because of the lower density of surrounding development. Researchers and policymakers often overlook more traditional city center development patterns and strategies that could be labeled as *de facto* TOD. Been et al. (2009) begin to fill this hole by exploring (under)development patterns in proximity to transit stations during the recent construction boom. They find that as of the beginning of this decade, underdevelopment rates in New York City were higher near transit.

A small number of authors have analyzed aspects of the current New York City rezoning agenda. For instance, Wolf-Powers (2005) uses a largely qualitative case-study approach to explore the planner's role in rezoning for economic development in two neighborhoods – Greenpoint-Williamsburg in Brooklyn and Long Island City in Queens. Our citywide quantitative analysis does not attempt to assess the political economy of the rezonings by investigating how these interventions relate to the political activities of the impacted neighborhoods. Instead, we analyze, as a descriptive matter, what effect the rezonings will have on the City's capacity to absorb more population in areas well served by transit. Our analysis complements the political economy literature, however, and should encourage additional work in that vein, by highlighting which neighborhoods have received additional residential capacity and which have been protected from (or precluded from, depending upon one's orientation) additional development.

A number of studies have examined the City's capacity for additional residential development. Alex Garvin & Associates (2006) use aerial photos and other sources to identify rail yards and other conspicuously underused areas that appear to be viable locations for new residential development. Armstrong and Lund (2005) use a case study approach, examining one neighborhood in each of the City's five boroughs to assess whether the City should rezone manufacturing land for housing. They estimate that existing residentially-zoned land does not have the capacity for projected population increases; however, they only look at estimates of vacant land, even though a large share of development in New York involves demolition of existing buildings. Neither study focuses on transit access. In a more comprehensive cross-sectional study, Been et al. (2009) identify lots not built out to their permitted capacity in addition to vacant lots, as of 2003, throughout the entire City. Here we build upon those efforts by adding a longitudinal element, estimating the changes in residential development capacity that have directly resulted from City-initiated rezonings, and exploring the relationship between those changes and access to the City's rail transit. To our knowledge, our project is the first statistical analysis of the cumulative impact of New York City's rezoning program or of any similar series of changes enacted by any American city.

9.3   DATA AND METHODOLOGY

Our analysis identifies lots that were subject to zoning changes during our study period and estimates, for each of those lots, the change in residential development capacity over that period. This lot-level analysis allows us to aggregate groups of lots by borough, neighborhood and proximity to transit. Our study period is from 2003 to 2007, the earliest and most recent years for which reliable data was available at the time we performed the analysis. That period allows us to include approximately three-quarters of the 100 zoning changes proposed by the Bloomberg administration and enacted through 2009.

We created a database of every physical parcel of land in New York City in 2003 and 2007 based upon GIS base maps from LotInfo for 2003 and Primary Land Use Tax Lot Output (PLUTO) for 2007.[2] We joined the databases to the 2003 and 2007 versions of the New York City Real Property Assessment Database (RPAD), a proprietary data set maintained by the New York City Department of Finance for property tax assessment purposes. This annually updated database contains information about each parcel of owned real property recognized by the City of New York ('tax lots'). The data includes information about each lot's land area, the floor area of buildings on the lots, the zoning district the lot is in, and several other characteristics about the lot and any buildings on the lot. Each tax lot is identified in the RPAD and in the GIS base maps with a unique identification number (known as a 'BBL number') based on the property's borough, block and position within the block. The lot database was further augmented with information derived from a GIS analysis performed for each lot in 2003 and 2007.

Been et al. (2009) previously estimated the applicable maximum allowable residential floor area ratio (FAR) for every residentially zoned lot in the 2003 and 2007 database; a lot's FAR representing the ratio of the gross building square footage built on a lot to the lot's land area. A maximum FAR specified in the Zoning Resolution effectively caps the amount of building area that can be built on a lot to a multiple of its land area (for example, a 10,000 square foot lot with a maximum FAR of 2 can only be developed with a building up to 20,000 square feet). To estimate a lot's maximum FAR, we begin with the default maximum FAR specified by the Zoning Resolution for the zoning district in which the lot is located (indicated by the RPAD). We then adjust the default maximum FAR using other lot characteristics that, pursuant to the Zoning Resolution, affect the maximum FAR, such as whether the lot fronts on a wide street, whether it is in certain special districts, or whether it is a waterfront lot.[3]

Because the Zoning Resolution permits residential development in many commercial and mixed use zoning districts, we include all lots in the City in our analysis instead of limiting it to lots in districts that permit only residential uses.[4] This is particularly important because several lots that in 2003 were in zoning categories that prohibit residential development were rezoned during our study period into categories that permit it. For lots in commercial or mixed use zoning districts that permit residential development, we estimate the maximum residential FAR using the 'residential equivalent' zoning category that the Zoning Resolution assigns. For lots in zoning categories that do not permit residential uses, we assign a maximum residential FAR of zero.

We calculate the maximum amount of residential building area (which we refer to as residential development capacity) that can be built on each lot by multiplying our estimate of its maximum residential FAR by its land area (contained in the RPAD). We perform this calculation for each lot in both our 2003 data set and our 2007 data set. Although other regulations, including parking requirements, height limits and open space requirements, may indirectly limit the amount of building area that can be developed on a lot, for simplicity we assume that the building area calculated from the maximum FAR is attainable. Our estimates therefore are likely to overstate the residential development capacity of some lots.

To identify which of the 2003 lots were subject to City-initiated rezonings, we overlay on our 2003 lot base map a GIS shape file of rezoning 'study areas' provided by the DCP. We further expand the boundaries of the initial study areas to incorporate adjacent lots that were rezoned contemporaneously with those inside the initial area, to account for changes to the proposal that occurred during the ULURP process. Of the almost 817,000 identifiable lots in New York City in 2003, we estimate that approximately 244,000 were in a rezoning study area.

Because a lot may undergo a merger with adjacent lots, be subdivided into multiple lots, change identification numbers or undergo any combination of these changes, identification numbers and lot characteristics may change between 2003 and 2007, making tracking them over our study period difficult. To address this, we use a GIS spatial overlay process to compare the 2003 lot to the same parcel of land in 2007. This matching process is described more fully in Been et al. (2009).

Finally, we compare the 2003 zoning district information in the RPAD for each lot within the DCP study areas to its 2007 zoning district information, to identify which lots were actually placed into different zoning districts by the City-initiated rezonings. We then classify all of the rezoned lots as one of the following:

- *Downzoned:* if the 2007 residential development capacity is less than 90 per cent of the 2003 residential development capacity
- *Upzoned:* if the 2007 residential development capacity is more than 110 per cent of the 2003 residential development capacity
- *Contextual-only rezoned:* if there is a change in the lot's zoning designation but the 2007 residential development capacity is within $+/-10$ percent of the 2003 residential development capacity.

We include the 'contextual-only' category because many zoning changes do not explicitly change a lot's residential development capacity at all, or change it by such a very small amount. In these instances, the capacity change (if any) is unlikely to have been the principal intent of the zoning change.

To interpret our results, we aggregated lots affected by City-initiated rezonings at the citywide and borough levels. To investigate the relationship between the rezonings and rail transit access, we use GIS maps of all the City's transit rail station entrances to construct half-mile walking buffers around each. New York City Transit (NYCT), a subsidiary of the Metropolitan Transit Authority (MTA), operates all of the City's subway lines, including the Staten Island Railway. Long Island Rail Road (LIRR) and Metro North, also subsidiaries of the MTA, operate commuter rail services to Long Island and the northern suburb counties, but have stations within the City's boundaries. Future analysis will also include data on express bus stop locations in the City, allowing analysis of transit accessibility will be expanded beyond rail. Figure 9.1 shows the rezoning study areas together with the transit station half-mile catchment areas.

Before presenting the results, we note that this analysis does not explore the wisdom, efficiency or desirability of the rezonings. We rely exclusively on maximum allowable FAR to identify regulatory development capacity as of 2003, and changes in this capacity over the next five years, and remain agnostic as to the desirability or feasibility of actually using the capacity on any specific site. The desirability of using the capacity would depend upon such factors as the existing neighborhood development patterns, the real estate market, existing development on specific sites, among many other factors, all of which are outside the scope of this chapter.

9.4 RESULTS

Table 9.1 shows, for each borough and the City as a whole, the number of lots that were subject to each type of zoning change as a result of City-initiated rezonings enacted between 2003 and 2007. The table also shows

Figure 9.1   City-initiated rezoning study areas (between 2003 and 2007) and rail transit catchment areas

the percentage of lots in each category that were located within a half-mile walking distance of a rail transit station entrance. For context, the first lines of the table show the number of lots in each borough (whether rezoned or not) as of 2003 and the percentage of those that were within a half-mile walking distance of a rail transit station.

As Table 9.1 shows, there were approximately 817,000 lots in New York City in 2003, of which we identified about 187,000 lots that were in a rezoning study area. Of these, the City contextually-only rezoned about 118,000 lots, downzoned about 43,000, and upzoned about 27,000 by the end of 2007. Looking at lot count alone, the City's rezoning efforts appear to have been primarily focused on protecting neighborhoods from relatively large or 'out of context' development rather than on increasing

Table 9.1   Lots subject to city-initiated rezonings and rail transit accessibility between 2003 and 2007

	Bronx	Brooklyn	Manhattan	Queens	Staten Island	New York City
Lots in Borough/City	84,790	270,688	42,227	312,194	106,625	816,524
% w/in half mile of transit	59.1%	68.6%	94.5%	34.3%	20.2%	49.5%
Rezoned lots	25,386	47,957	3,683	73,760	37,080	187,866
% w/in half mile of transit	39.1%	83.2%	91.1%	25.3%	19.8%	42.2%
Upzoned lots	3,621	11,737	2,083	9,082	134	26,662
% w/in half mile of transit	66.5%	78.0%	93.8%	65.9%	53.7%	73.4%
Downzoned lots	6,777	17,737	856	13,408	4,221	42,999
% w/in half mile of transit	51.7%	91.1%	86.5%	31.3%	16.8%	58.9%
Contextual-only lots	14,988	18,478	744	51,270	32,725	118,205
% w/in half mile of transit	26.8%	78.8%	88.8%	16.6%	20.1%	29.0%

capacity. The conspicuous exception was Manhattan, where a majority of the lots rezoned by the City were upzoned.

The table also shows that, overall, upzoned lots were more likely to be located near transit stations than other types of lots. Citywide, almost three-quarters of upzoned lots were near transit, compared to less than half of all lots in New York City. This indicates that where the City did add residential development capacity, by and large it did so in accordance with its sustainable development goals.

Almost 60 percent of all downzoned lots, however, were also were located near rail transit stations. In these cases, neighborhood political pressures, constraints on other infrastructure, or other factors yielded changes at odds with the City's goal of directing growth to areas near transit. In Brooklyn, more than 90 percent of downzoned lots were near rail transit stations compared to fewer than 80 percent of upzoned lots. These results suggest that the City's rezonings, which were motivated by multiple different goals, are not entirely consistent with its professed desires to channel growth to areas with good access to transit.

Because of the varying size of lots and differences in the magnitude of capacity changes, a simple lot count only gives a partial picture of the changes arising from these rezoning actions. To investigate the impact

Table 9.2   Changes in regulatory residential development capacity between 2003 and 2007 from upzoned lots and downzoned lots

	Bronx	Brooklyn	Manhattan	Queens	Staten Island	New York City
Capacity added to upzoned lots (sf)	15.3m	83.3m	38.6m	61.8m	11.0m	210.0m
% w/in half mile of transit	74.5	91.6	82.0	83.0	98.7	86.4
Capacity subtracted from downzoned lots	−15.0m	−56.1m	−4.5m	−21.9m	−5.0m	−102.5m
% w/in half mile of transit	72.5	93.7	96.2	52.0	23.1	78.4

of these changes in more depth, Table 9.2 shows, for the City as a whole and for each borough, the increase in residential development capacity resulting from upzoned lots and the decrease in residential development capacity resulting from downzonings. Table 9.2 also shows the percentage of the gained or lost capacity that was located within a half-mile walking distance of a rail transit station.

As Table 9.2 shows, the increase in residential development capacity from upzoned lots citywide (210.0 million square feet) was much larger than the decrease from downzoned lots (102.5 million square feet). Contextual-only rezonings resulted in an additional net decrease of about 9.3 million square feet of residential development capacity (not shown). As a result, despite the fact that the City downzoned about twice as many lots as it upzoned, the cumulative effect of its zoning changes between 2003 and 2007 was a net increase in capacity of almost 100 million square feet. This net increase represents an approximately 1.69 percent increase in residential development capacity for the City. The rezonings resulted in a net increase in capacity in each borough individually as well, though this increase ranged widely, from less than half a million square feet in the Bronx, a 0.03 percent increase in capacity, to almost 38 million square feet in Queens, a 2.82 percent increase.

By focusing on capacity changes rather than lot counts, Table 9.2 also provides additional information about the relationship between the rezonings and transit access. In the city as a whole, 86 percent of all capacity added to upzoned lots (equal to about 181 million square feet) was added to lots within a half-mile walk of a rail transit station entrance. As of 2003, only about 68 percent of the City's residential development capacity was

Table 9.3 *Changes in residential development capacity between 2003 and 2007 from upzoned and downzoned lots due to City-initiated rezoning – proximity to transit*

	The Bronx	Brooklyn	Manhattan	Queens	Staten Island	New York City
Change in residential capacity within half mile of rail transit stations						
Net change in residential development capacity (sf)	0.5m	17.0m	27.4m	37.9m	9.7m	92.4m
% Increase/ Decrease	0.1	1.4	2.0	6.1	12.0%	2.3
Change in residential capacity beyond half mile of rail transit stations						
Net change in residential development capacity (sf)	−0.2m	3.0m	6.8m	0.0m	−3.7m	5.8m
% Increase/ Decrease	−0.1	0.8	5.5	0.0	−1.04%	0.3

located within a half-mile walk of a rail transit station. Accordingly, the added capacity is likely to encourage a higher percentage of new residential development to be transit-accessible than was possible prior to the rezonings. The City's upzoning efforts, therefore, were highly consistent with its long-range transportation and environmental goals.

The City's downzonings, however, were more severe near transit than they were further from transit. Downzoned lots near transit accounted for about 59 percent of all downzoned lots, but 78 percent of the lost residential development capacity on downzoned lots. The downzonings, then, effectively canceled out a large portion of the gains in capacity near transit that resulted from the upzonings, and appear to be at odds with the City's transportation and sustainable growth goals.

In Table 9.3, we report the net absolute and percentage change in residential development capacity of rezoned lots within and outside a half-mile walking radius around rail transit station entrances. These data indicate exactly to what extent the downzonings of lots near transit canceled out the new capacity added to upzoned lots near transit. These data also reveal whether the City's zoning changes are likely to encourage new development in neighborhoods further away from transit in addition to those well served by transit.

As Table 9.3 shows, City-initiated rezonings yielded a net increase of over 92 million square feet in areas near rail transit between 2003 and 2007, an increase in capacity of 2.3 percent for such areas. Lots further away from transit, in contrast, experienced a net gain in capacity of less than six million square feet, an increase of only about 0.3 percent. In every borough the capacity added to lots near rail stations exceeded the capacity added to lots further away from transit. The borough in which City-initiated rezonings added the most capacity to lots farther from transit was Manhattan, where almost seven million square feet was added to such areas. This increase was far less than the 27 million added to Manhattan lots near transit, however. Furthermore, much of the capacity added to Manhattan beyond a half-mile walk of existing rail transit stations was in the proposed Hudson Yard project area, where an extension of the subway is underway. Even here, then, the additional capacity will be near rail transit in the foreseeable future.

9.5   CONCLUSION

Mayor Bloomberg's administration publicly advocated that new residential development should be targeted to neighborhoods well served by public transit. The administration argues that such a pattern of development offers the City the best hope of accommodating growth while minimizing the impact that growth will have on traffic congestion, energy use and pollution. Implementation of New York City's land use goals, however, is a complicated balancing act often involving conflicting influences. Because of the realities of coordinating transit and other infrastructure and the political pressures of local communities wanting to protect their neighborhoods from what they perceive as excessive growth, among other factors, the administration's stated land use goals might not be reflected in its actual decisions.

This study helps to shed light on the land use consequences of this tension between citywide goals and the political and administrative realities often emanating from neighborhood concerns about development by analyzing the cumulative impact the rezonings the City enacted between 2003 and 2007 had on residential development capacity. By identifying lots that were affected by these zoning changes and estimating the resulting change in residential development capacity, we find that the net impact has been a modest overall increase in the City's residential capacity. Consistent with the City's desired development patterns, this modest increase has overwhelmingly been concentrated in neighborhoods near rail transit stations.

We also find, however, that about half of the capacity added near rail stations from upzonings was effectively canceled out by downzonings of lots near transit. While these downzonings may be important to protect neighborhoods from new development that existing infrastructure cannot support or that is inappropriate for other reasons, they may limit the City's ability to grow, or force growth into other neighborhoods, including, perhaps, those that are even less well served by rail transit (or otherwise even less suitable for development). We take no stand on whether the downzonings were appropriate. However, our finding that the downzonings reduced residential capacity in neighborhoods within the catchment areas of existing rail transit requires, at the very least, that decision makers considering future rezonings take a hard look at the effect the proposal will have on the City's goals of promoting development in areas that give residents better transit options.

This study provides only a first look at the net impact of the unprecedented rezoning activity initiated by New York City's Department of City Planning since 2003. Several crucial questions about the residential development capacity that has been added remain. Much of the new capacity has been added in zoning districts that permit other uses, raising the possibility that residential uses will be at least partly crowded out by commercial or even industrial development. Furthermore, our model for measuring capacity does not acknowledge the many land use regulations in the Zoning Resolution, other than maximum FAR, that likely limit development. A better understanding of these other regulations, such as minimum parking requirements, height limits and open space requirements, may allow us to more accurately estimate the usable capacity that zoning changes add or remove. Finally, several non-zoning factors likely help determine whether residential capacity will yield new residential units in areas near transit. In future work, we will investigate the relationship between added capacity and such factors, including market demand, available subsidies, infrastructure other than transit, and the capacity of existing transit.

NOTES

1. Under the New York City Charter, the City Planning Commission is responsible for 'the conduct of planning relating to the orderly growth, improvement and future development of the city. . .'. The commission is comprised of 13 members: the Mayor appoints a Chair, who also is Director of DCP, and six other members. Each of the five Borough Presidents and the Public Advocate also make one appointment. All appointments are subject to advice and consent of City Council. All except the chair serve for staggered five-year terms, subject to removal for cause. The DCP is a city agency composed

of professional planning staff that supports the City Planning Commission, mayor, borough presidents and other parts of the city's government with regards to urban development issues. For more information about the City Planning Commission and DCP, see http://www.nyc.gov/html/dcp/html/subcats/about.shtml.

2. The methodology is an extension of a project investigating lots that were built out at substantially less than their zoning capacity as of 2003 and their subsequent rate of redevelopment to 2007 (Been et al., 2009).

3. This estimate also makes several assumptions regarding discretionary and bonus programs in the Zoning Resolution that permit developers to either exceed the base maximum FAR if they include certain amenities (affordable housing, for example), or exclude the square footage of certain building elements (enclosed garages, for example). For a full description of this model, including the assumptions it relies on, see Been et al. (2009).

4. This is an expansion of the methodology used in Been et al. (2009) that was focused on underdevelopment rates in residentially zoned lots as of 2003.

REFERENCES

Alex Garvin & Associates (2006) *Visions for New York City: Housing and the Public Realm*. Prepared for The Economic Development Corporation, The City of New York.

Armstrong, R. and Lund, T. (2005) *Up from the Ruins: Why Rezoning New York City's Manufacturing Areas for Housing Makes Sense. Rethinking Development Report No. 2*, Center for Rethinking Development and the Manhattan Institute.

Been, V., Madar, J. and McDonnell, S. (2009) *Underused Lots in New York City*. Lincoln Institute of Land Policy Working Paper.

Cervero, R., Murphy, S., Ferrell, C., Goguts, N., Yu-Hsin, T., Arrington, G., Boroski, J., Smith-Heimer, J., Golem, R., Peninger, P., Nakajima, E., Dunphy, R., Myers, M., McKay, S. and Witenstein, W. (2003) *Transit-Oriented Development in the United States: Experience, Challenges, and Prospects*. TCRP Report 102, Transit Cooperative Research Program Report 102, Transportation Research Board, Washington, DC.

City of New York (2007) *PlaNYC: A Greener, Greater, New York*. Mayor Michael R. Bloomberg, The City of New York.

Cooper, A. (1975) New York's Housing Quality Program, *Design Quarterly*, 94/95, 23–4.

Department of City Planning (2004) Mayor Michael R. Bloomberg and Queens Borough President Helen Marshall announce the rezoning of Queens neighborhoods to help curb over-development. Press release #150-04, New York City Department of City Planning.

Department of City Planning (2009a) Kew Gardens and Richmond Hill: Overview, New York City Department of City Planning.

Department of City Planning (2009b) Bensonhurst: Overview, New York City Department of City Planning.

Department of City Planning (2009c) Greetings from the Chair, Amanda M. Burden, New York City Department of City Planning.

Dunlap, D.W. (2000) Battle lines drawn on new zoning plan, *New York Times*, June 4.

Dunphy, R.T. and Porter, D.R. (2006) Manifestations of development goals in transit-oriented projects, *Transportation Research Record*, 1977, 172–8.

Ewing, R. and Cervero, R.B. (2001) Travel and the built environment: A synthesis, *Transportation Research Record*, 1780, 87–114.

Furman Center (2010) *State of New York City's Housing and Neighborhoods 2009*, Furman Center for Real Estate and Urban Policy, New York University, New York.

Gómez-Ibáñez, J.A., Boarnet, M.G., Brake, D.R., Cervero, R.B., Cotugno, A., Downs, A., Hanson, S., Kockelman, K.M., Mokhtarian, P.L., Pendall, R.J., Santini, D.J. and Southworth, F. (2009) *Driving and the Built Environment: Effects of Compact Development on Motorized Travel, Energy Use, and CO2 Emissions, TRB Special Report 298.* Washington, DC, The National Academies Press.

Hess, D.B. and Lombardi, P.A. (2004) Policy support for and barriers to transit-oriented development in the inner city: Literature review, *Transportation Research Record*, 1887, 26–33.

Holtzclaw, J., Clear, R., Dittmar, H., Goldstein, D. and Hass, P. (2002) Location efficiency: Neighborhood and socio-economic characteristics determine auto ownership and use – studies in Chicago, Los Angeles and San Francisco, *Transportation Planning and Technology*, 25, 1–27.

Iacono, M. and Levinson, D. (2009) Predicting land use change: how much does transportation matter?, *Transportation Research Record*, 2119, 130–36.

Oser, A.S. (1986) Perspectives: High-rise housing; the stakes in 'contextual zoning', *New York Times*, March 2, 1986. Available at: http://www.nytimes.com/1986/03/02/realestate/perspectives-high-rise-housing-the-stakes-in-context ual-zoning.html?&pagewanted=all (retrieved July 12, 2009).

Sterner, T. (2003) *Policy Instruments for Environmental and Natural Resource Management.* Washington, DC, Resources for the Future.

US Census Bureau (2009) *Population Estimates for the Largest US Cities based on July 1, 2008 Population Estimates: April 1, 2000 to July 1, 2008*, Table 3, US Census Bureau News, US Census Bureau, Washington, DC. Available at: http://www.census.gov/Press-Release/www/releases/xls/CB09-99Table3.xls (retrieved July 3, 2009).

Wolf-Powers, L. (2005) Up-zoning New York City's mixed-use neighborhoods: Property-led economic development and the anatomy of a planning dilemma, *Journal of Planning Education and Research*, 24, 379–93.

Woudsma, C. and Jensen, J.F. (2003) Transportation's influence on land use development: Historical spatial–temporal approach, *Transportation Research Record: Journal of the Transportation Research Board*, 1831, 166–74.

10. Policymaking on waterside industrial sites: an empirical study for Flanders

Tom Pauwels, Eddy Van de Voorde, Thierry Vanelslander and Ann Verhetsel

10.1 INTRODUCTION

Given the scarcity of land and expected growth in inland navigation in Flanders (Belgium),[1] there is a strong case for government accurately forecasting demand for waterside industrial sites where cargo transfers are made to inland waterways. Some of the forecast growth in inland navigation can be accommodated by existing facilities, but a need for additional land seems inevitable. For allocation purposes, it is also important that a priority list of possible locations be drawn up.

At the request of the Flemish Government's Agency for the Economy (Agentschap Economie), Arcadis and the University of Antwerp (Department of Transport and Regional Economics) are conducting a study into policy-making on the supply of waterside industrial land and water-based trans-shipment locations. Part of the study aims at a quantitative and qualitative assessment, on the basis of the most likely scenarios, of future developments in industrial and trans-shipment activity along Flanders' navigable waterways (Horizon: 2020). The focus here is on the quantitative analysis, which was performed by the University of Antwerp.

10.2 THE ISSUES

This study focuses on a particular set of questions:[2]

(a) What is the pattern of water-related land-use in Flanders? Which stakeholders are involved? What are the policy and societal developments?

(b)   What are the critical success factors and which elements are crucial for matching the demand for and supply of waterside industrial land?

(c)   Can we develop indicative scenarios for future evolutions in the inland navigation market?

(d)   How can we select priority regions for investment in waterside industrial land on the basis of a quantitative analysis?

Arcadis and University of Antwerp (2008) analysed water-related land-use in Flanders, its suppliers and users, and relevant policy and societal developments. Micro as well as macro trends were taken into account. The various players in the transport chain, and particularly in inland navigation, were analysed. Implemented or planned policy actions were assessed. A strengths, weaknesses, opportunities, and threats (SWOT) analysis was performed on the market for waterside industrial land. The resulting strengths, weaknesses, opportunities and threats provide insight into the success of policy actions with respect to waterside industrial sites, allowing the identification of important success factors, with a view to assisting government in outlining an optimal reservation and allocation policy.

The quantitative analysis involves the following:

● Simulation of inland navigation flows on the basis of scenarios
● Survey-based determination of regional demand for waterside industrial sites
● Prioritization of regions for further investment in the availability of such sites.

The methodology applied is demand-oriented. The analysis starts from the existing pattern of demand, and assumptions are made regarding future trends. The horizon is 2020 and the analysis is carried out at the Flemish NUTS-3 level (*arrondissementen*, or districts) of spatial aggregation.

10.3   DETERMINING FUTURE DEMAND FOR INLAND NAVIGATION

At the request of the public authorities (Kenniscentrum Verkeer en Vervoer, afdeling Verkeerscentrum), a new 'Freight Model Flanders' has been developed by K&P Transport Consultants, Tritel and Mint.

On the basis of this freight model, it is possible to simulate future freight flows in the road, rail and inland waterways and NST freight categories. A classic four-step model is applied:

- *Flow generation:* This determines the freight flows arriving at or departing from a particular zone within a given timeframe. In the case of freight transport, this relates to the tonnage of freight category k, departing from or arriving in zone i (j) within a given period.
- *Distribution of flows:* The generation of flows serves as an input for the determination of the tonnage that moves between zones i and j.
- *Modal choice:* This determines which mode is used to transport goods from zone i to j.
- *Assignment:* This step relates to route choice of the vehicles that move the goods.

Transport logistic nodes, distribution centers for road transport, and inland terminals, for inland navigation, are also included in the model.

The Freight Model Flanders is used to illustrate the implications of a number of scenarios on future freight transport flows. In the model, ongoing infrastructure projects ('lopende programma') of the Flemish government are taken into account.[3] More specifically, the infrastructure investments are assumed to have been completed by 2020:

- the Oosterweel connection completed[4]
- AX connection between N49 and N31
- Liefkenshoek rail tunnel completed
- Seine–Scheldt connection completed
- Albert Canal capacity increased.

10.4   SCENARIO BUILDING

Each scenario is a combination of three types of assumptions relating to: economic conditions, policy initiatives, and inland navigation.

Economic growth will lead to an increase in transport but their exact link is not clear. Hence, a number of different assumptions regarding the rate of economic growth are explored.

In *European Energy and Transport Trends to 2030 – Update 2005* (European Commission, 2006) a 2 percent annual economic growth is forecast up to 2020 for Belgium. This is taken as the basis for three economic growth scenarios:

- *Economic assumption 1:* 'Low growth' or growth GDP – 0.5 percent, i.e. 1.5 percent
- *Economic assumption 2:* 'Normal growth' of GDP, i.e. 2 percent

- *Economic assumption 3:* 'High growth': growth GDP + 0.5 percent, i.e. 2.5 percent.

Insofar as the model requires input in relation to foreign countries, the assumptions in European Commission (2006) are used.

Economic growth is not used directly in the Freight Model Flanders to determine incoming and outgoing flows for the Belgian regions, but rather the model uses employment per region. It is possible to examine the relationship between economic growth and employment.[5] Walterskirchen (1999) reports an elasticity of 0.41 for the European Union, suggesting that an increase in economic activity of 1 percent leads to employment growth of 0.41 per cent.

On the basis of available Belgian employment figures and GDP in 2000 prices, we estimate:

$$\ln(employment) = \alpha + \beta.\ln(GDP) \qquad (10.1)$$

The estimated β is 0.478, with a t-value of 3.62 and $R^2 = 0.972$.[6] This estimated value may be read as follows: if GDP increases by 1 per cent, employment will rise by 0.478 percent. This result is also in line with Walterskirchen. A yearly economic growth of 2 percent in Belgium may also be expressed in a yearly growth of employment by 0.956 percent.

On this basis we make the following assumptions for the Belgian regions and apply them in the freight model:

- *Low growth:* Growth employment – 0.239 percent = 0.717 percent
- *Normal growth:* Growth employment = 0.956 percent
- *High growth:* Growth employment + 0.239 percent = 1.195 percent

A distinction is made between a 'continuation of current policy' and the 'implementation of a dynamic policy'.

In the assumption of 'continuation of current policy', a yearly increase of 0.1 per cent is assumed in the costs of road and rail transport. An increase in the costs of road transport is considered probable given the advanced deregulation of the road haulage sector. For rail freight, it is assumed that the dominance of national railway companies shall persist. Deregulation will lead to a reduction in national subsidies and will drive prices up (NEA Transport Research and Training & the University of Antwerp, 2007).

These growth rates should be interpreted as relative figures, with road haulage and rail freight experiencing a slightly higher cost increase than inland navigation.

Under the assumption of dynamic policy, we opt for a one-off increase

Table 10.1   Overview scenarios

	Economic assumptions	Policy assumptions	Assumptions for inland navigation
Reference scenario	Normal growth	Continuation of current policy	Continuation of current policy
Scenario 1	Normal growth	Continuation of current policy	2% annual cost reduction
Scenario 2	Normal growth	Dynamic policy	Continuation of current policy
Scenario 3	Normal growth	Dynamic policy	2% annual cost reduction
Scenario 4	High growth	Dynamic policy	Continuation of current policy
Scenario 5	High growth	Dynamic policy	2% annual cost reduction
Scenario 6	Low growth	Continuation of current policy	Continuation of current policy
Scenario 7	Low growth	Continuation of current policy	2% annual cost reduction

in vehicle cost of 20 percent, followed by annual increases of 0.1 percent. The reasoning for this is that we assume the externalities of road transport are fully internalized, implying that vehicle costs could rise by as much as 60 percent. This increase is regarded as a maximum to be incorporated in the base model. We also assume an increase of 20 percent which is taken as more politically feasible.

To simulate cost advantages for inland waterways transport, specific assumptions are introduced – continuation of current policy and additional inland navigation measure: 2 percent annual reduction in the cost of inland navigation, for example as a result of more efficient use of inland waterways.

It is not necessary to consider every possible combination of the foregoing assumptions. Low economic growth combined with a dynamic policy, or high economic growth combined with a continuation of current policy are, for example, rather nonsensical. Table 10.1 provides an overview of the scenarios that are taken into consideration.

10.5   DETERMINING THE FUTURE DEMAND FOR WATERSIDE INDUSTRIAL LAND

To determine the need for additional waterside industrial space, we initially predict the tonnage that will be transported by inland navigation in 2020.

For each district and goods category, an indicator is created expressing the need for land in 2004 and 2020. Some of the growth will be accommodated through land already available, with the rest requiring newly created space.

The indicator is set on the basis of regional transfer coefficients that represent the annual tonnage per m^2 to be transported to and from a given region. They are determined using internet surveys and personal interviews, with the latter just providing information about waterside industrial sites, the sum of transfer and storage areas, and production. The data used is provided by W&Z and De Scheepvaart.

The area indicator for 2004 is calculated per district and per NST-R freight category as:

$$area_{ri(2004)} = tonne_{ri(2004)} / k'_{ri(2004)} \qquad (10.2)$$

where: $area_{ri}$ is m^2 needed to handle $tonne_{ri}$; $tonne_{ri}$ is the tonnage per district r per freight category i (incoming + outgoing flows); and k'_{ri} is the real relationship between $tonne_{ri}$ and $area_{ri}$, per freight category i, expressed in $tonne$ per m^2. Important in the analysis is the determination of k'_{ri}. We use an average value for the relationship between tonnage and area estimated on the basis of internet surveys and personal interviews.

Next an indicator for 2020 based on simulated tonnages generated through the freight model is estimated. Suppose that the surface area used in 2020 is identical to that in 2004, then we can calculate:

$$k^*_{ri\,(2020)} = tonne_{ri(2020)} / area_{ri(2004)} \qquad (10.3)$$

We can also define the theoretical, optimal relationship between tonnage and area as k_{ci}: where k_{ci} is the theoretically optimal relationship between $tonne_{ri}$ and $area_{ri}$ at full capacity per freight category i. If, for example, k^*_{ri} equals six tonnes per m^2 and k_{ci} equals 11.5 tonnes per m^2, then there is a surplus of available space and capacity is wasted.

If $k^*_{ri\,(2020)} > k_{ci}$ then a capacity problem will present itself in 2020 in district r regarding freight category i. If $k^*_{ri\,(2020)} < k_{ci}$ then no capacity problem will present itself in r insofar as freight category i is concerned.

Future demand for a given area is:

$$(tonne_{ri(2020)} / k'_{ri\,(2020)}) - area_{ri(2004)} \qquad (10.4)$$

Three values for $k'_{ri\,(2020)}$ may be considered, based respectively on the current regional transfer coefficient ($k'_{ri(2004)}$), on the economically optimal regional transfer coefficient, and on the maximum regional transfer coefficient (which is not necessarily the economically most efficient one).

If one starts from the current regional transfer coefficient, it is assumed that the company cannot handle more than the present situation. This may be due to the fact that the technology presently applied cannot cope with an increase (for example cranes at maximum capacity), or to the fact that the company has reached its production limits. If one starts from values that are higher than the current coefficient, then the underlying assumption is that the handling facilities or the available storage area are not being used to full capacity.

Surveys were conducted of companies physically located in the proximity of water and to find which uses were for the transfer of goods, we employed two approaches:

- *Extensive surveys:* Students from the University of Antwerp conducted interviews with a number of companies in waterside locations. Eighteen companies were contacted, 17 of which were retained.
- *Short surveys:* On the basis of an internet survey, a number of questions were presented to these companies. Databases of the waterways administrators were used (Waterwegen en Zeekanaal: 235 companies contacted, 29 of which were retained; De Scheepvaart: 125 companies contacted, 22 of which were retained).

The survey data were used to determine values of the regional transfer coefficients. An alternative would have been to use information from the public–private partnership program of the Flemish government whereby the government co-finances infrastructure for inland-waterways-related transfer. For each company participating in this program, information is available regarding incoming and outgoing goods flows by water. Information about company sites is collected by the waterways administration. The information, however, is incomplete because the administration possesses only the part of it that relates to the size of these company sites.

10.6   RESULTS

To determine future demand for waterside industrial land, regional transfer coefficients are calculated.

Determination of Regional Transfer Coefficients

Table 10.2 shows the values of the regional transfer coefficients. We differentiate between the various freight categories. On the basis of information

Table 10.2   *Regional transfer coefficients in tonne per m² per year per freight category (NST-R) for waterside companies*

NST-R	Regional transfer coefficient	Number of observations	Minimum	Maximum	Average
0. Agricultural products and animals 1. Food	2.99	7	0.05	14.45	4.10
2. Solid fuel	5.00	*	–	–	–
3. Petroleum products	7.38	7	0.38	45.65	14.01
4. Iron ore and scraps 5. Metallurgical products 6. Minerals and building materials	7.33	23	0.03	444.44	36.84
7. Fertilizers 8. Chemical products	1.58	4	0.14	8.35	2.91
9. Diverse products	5.00	*	–	–	–
All observations	5.00	47	0.03	444.44	21.72

Note: * The median value is based on all observations.

about site areas and inland-waterways-related tonnage, the regional transfer coefficient is determined.

Determination of Capacity

We address the question of the extent to which these coefficients may increase before a company needs additional land. From the surveys, information was obtained in relation to the capacity use of the companies' sites (Table 10.3). The capacity data emerged as unrealistically high but closer analysis of the results shows that the companies registered capacity use at company level rather than at site level. For example, if an inland vessel arrives three times each month, the company may have reported a capacity utilization of 100 percent rather than 15 percent (3 vessels/20 working days). This may be due to companies producing at

Table 10.3   Use of capacity per type of land

Type of land	Use of capacity (median)	Number of observations
Transfer area (from water to land or vice versa)	90.00%	47
Area for other transfer	75.00%	29
Area for storing the inland-waterways-related goods	100.00%	46
Area for storing other goods	90.00%	34
Production	97.50%	36

maximum capacity: the arrival of an additional vessel would, in other words, be useless if production cannot keep up. For more freight to be handled, either productivity must be increased (e.g. through technological innovation) or the companies' sites must be expanded for additional storage or production.

It is hard to determine on the basis of the survey the extent to which capacity is utilized. A further complication is that modal shifts may occur from road to inland navigation transport (i.e. a larger proportion of the inland tonnage may be transported by inland waterways). Such a situation does not lead to a need for additional land and thus insight as to what happens with additional flows that were not previously in the production process.

For the purpose of further calculations, the original regional transfer coefficient is multiplied by 1.5 and the original regional transfer coefficients are doubled. Using these values, we calculate the crucial turning points in demand for additional land. The values 1.5 and 2 express the potential increases in transfer given the available capacity and technological improvements. They are, however, not real values but are based on expert information and available foreign data regarding the relationship between site surface area and transfer. More efficient production or storage could, for example, result in a higher coefficient.

Future Demand

The third column of Table 10.4 shows the overall results assuming a constant regional transfer coefficient per freight category. Each increase in the tonnage shipped by inland waterways leads to an increase in demand for space. The results shown in the fourth column are based on the assumption that reserve capacity is available, expressed as 1.5 times the original

*Table 10.4   Additional demand associated with the various reference
           scenario*

Groups	Name of district	Additional demand in ha in 2020		
		k′ constant	k′ = 1.5	k′ = 2
Total		3,135	1,063	148
Great need	Antwerpen	2,144	756	119
	Gent	603	203	12
Moderate need	Sint-Niklaas	132	43	7
	Roeselare	71	25	3
	Kortrijk	40	9	2
	Brugge	31	10	1
	Hasselt	22		
	Tielt	18	6	1
Limited need	Turnhout	14		
	Mechelen	14	2	0.44
	Oostende	12	4	0.99
	Halle-Vilvoorde	10	1	
	Aalst	9	3	0.48
	Dendermonde	5	0.47	
	Oudenaarde	4	0.39	
	Leuven	2	0.47	0.00
	Tongeren	2		
	Maaseik	1	0.03	
	Eeklo	0.13		
	Veurne	0.00		
	Diksmuide			
	Ieper			

regional transfer coefficient and those in the fifth, if the regional transfer
coefficient doubles.

Table 10.4 shows the additional demand for land in 2020 above that in
2004 based on companies located in the proximity of water. If demand
in 2020 exceeds the available land in 2004, the additional amounts are
included in the table. On this basis, it is also possible to calculate the
theoretically surplus land.

The results are used to prioritize across regions with respect to their
need for additional waterside industrial land. In other words, it may be
used by government to draw up a list of locations where there may be a

case for investment in land availability. These absolute figures should be treated with some caution and should be interpreted as a broad indicator.

From the analysis we can also draw up a priority list of NUTS-3 regions associated with each scenario. The observations are divided into three groups: great, moderate and limited need for additional waterside industrial land. The following groups are distinguished in the reference scenario of an unchanged policy:

- *Great need:* Antwerpen and Gent;
- *Moderate need:* Sint-Niklaas, Roeselare, Kortrijk, Brugge, Hasselt and Tielt;
- *Limited need:* Turnhout, Mechelen, Oostende, Halle-Vilvoorde, Aalst, Dendermonde, Oudenaarde, Leuven, Tongeren, Maaseik, Eeklo, Veurne, Diksmuide and Ieper.

Policy on waterside industrial land may be assumed to be directed primarily at accommodating high-priority regions. It should be noted, in this context, that port-related needs are taken into account. Hence, the figures for Antwerpen and Gent also reflect the needs of neighboring industrial zones. Therefore, the additional space need not necessarily be located in the port itself. It may also be advisable in other instances to seek additional land in neighboring NUTS-3 regions rather than in the NUTS-3 region under study (given a lack of space in the latter).

A dynamic policy (single increase of the vehicle cost by 20 percent, followed by a yearly growth of 0.1 percent) results in a higher demand for inland navigation and thus a higher demand for waterside industrial land. This is also the case if the cost of inland navigation declines. However, we find small differences between the rankings under the different scenarios. This indicates a possible slowness. In other words, it would require quite significant policy changes for the various scenarios to impact on the rankings.

10.7   CONCLUSIONS

Governments often need to assess how demand for waterside land may change in the future. Some of the projected growth in inland navigation in Flanders may be accommodated by existing industrial land, but the rest will require additional space. In this context, it is useful that a priority list for investment in such locations should be drawn up. Our analysis offers one way of doing this and provides some quantitative findings.

NOTES

1. Inland navigation in Flanders (Belgium) refers to the use of vessels up to 12,000 metric tonnes.
2. We primarily consider the last two questions. For discussion of the other questions, see Arcadis and University of Antwerp (2008).
3. The model is being developed in cooperation with the Research Centre on Commodity Flows and the Department of Transport and Regional Economics (validation and sensitivity analysis) with comparisons being made regarding traffic counts and the evolution of modal shares using MIRA-T 2007. Preliminary results point at a good match (Borremans et al., 2008).
4. It is assumed that, with the completion of the Antwerp ring road in 2020, road freight will no longer be allowed to use the Kennedy Tunnel.
5. We refer to Okun's Law, which gives the relationship between the growth of GDP and unemployment.
6. This is a simple time-series estimation, whereby cointegration is ignored.

REFERENCES

Arcadis and University of Antwerp (2008) *Aanbodbeleid voor watergebonden bedrijventerreinen en watergebonden overslaglocaties – Werkrapport fase 1.* Antwerpen.

Borremans, D., Grispen, R., Kienzler, H.-P., Organe, K., Peetermans, E., Van Houwe, P. and Zillhardt, D. (2008) Multimodaal goederenmodel brengt goederenstromen in kaart, *Het Ingenieursblad*, 6–7, 14–18.

European Commission (2006) *European Energy and Transport – Trends to 2030 – update 2005.* Brussels.

NEA Transport Research and Training & the University of Antwerp (2007) *Vervoersprognoses IJzeren Rijn.* Rijswijk.

Walterskirchen (1999) The relationship between growth, employment and unemployment in the EU. Paper presented at the workshop, European Economists for an Alternative Economic Policy (TSER network).

Index